The Philosophical Foundations of Environmental Law
Property, Rights and Nature

SEAN COYLE
KAREN MORROW

·H A R T·
PUBLISHING

OXFORD AND PORTLAND, OREGON
2004

Published in North America (US and Canada) by
Hart Publishing
c/o International Specialized Book Services
5804 NE Hassalo Street
Portland, Oregon
97213–3644
USA

Hart Publishing is a specialist legal publisher based in Oxford, England. To
order further copies of this book or to request a list of other publications
please write to:

Hart Publishing, Salters Boatyard, Folly Bridge, Abingdon Rd, Oxford,
OX1 4LB Telephone: +44 (0)1865 245533 Fax: +44 (0) 1865 794882
email: mail@hartpub.co.uk
WEBSITE: http//:www.hartpub.co.uk

British Library Cataloguing in Publication Data
Data Available
ISBN 1–84113–359–0 (hardback)
1–84113–360–4 (paperback)

Typeset by Hope Services, Abingdon Ltd
Printed and bound in Great Britain by
TJ International Ltd, Padstow, Cornwall

THE PHILOSOPHICAL FOUNDATIONS OF ENVIRONMENTAL LAW

Preface

This book represents an attempt to say something genuinely new, and perhaps unexpected, about environmental law. It is also a sustained deliberation on the evolution of thinking about the environment in the legal and political thought of the last 400 years or so. We have therefore (we hope) covered some familiar ground, in law and philosophy, in an unfamiliar, though hopefully explicable, way. The focus of the argument has deliberately been kept very tight. As a result, we have studiously avoided taking the argument in directions which would no doubt prove fruitful and interesting in their own right. Our ultimate justification for adopting such an approach (aside from constraints of time, and skill) has been to produce a book which is of manageable length and possesses narrative cohesion.

In an effort to keep footnotes to an absolute minimum, we have largely refrained from citing works in which one might encounter a similar, or contradictory, point of view, or where an opinion stated in the text receives a further or stimulating treatment. Equally, we have in general not made reference to other works where our stated position was arrived at independently of our subsequent familiarity with a similar point of view in the works of other writers; in most cases, our more profound intellectual debts are revealed in other of our published works which deal with related themes. Capitalisation and punctuation have been normalised in older sources, for the sake of readability.

This book has benefited from the incisive suggestions of several careful readers. In particular, we would like to express our thanks to George Pavlakos, Fiona Donson and Marjan Peeters for valuable discussion. Holly Cullen read the whole manuscript and provided many excellent suggestions. Early versions of a number of chapters were presented at conferences and seminars. Selections from chapters two and three were presented at Queen's University, Belfast in February 2002 and October 2003 respectively. Aspects of chapters four and five were presented at the Irish Association of Law Teachers Conference in Galway in April 2003 and the British Association of Canadian Studies Legal Conference in London in July 2003. A summary of the main lines of argument formed the basis for a talk at the annual conference of the Society for Public Teachers of Law in Glasgow, September 2001. We heartily thank all who contributed on those occasions for their perceptive and helpful comments.

We would also like to thank Colin Warbrick and Bob Sullivan for their support during the writing of this book, and Richard Hart for his characteristically enthusiastic and excellent editing. The bulk of the research for this book was undertaken during the academic year 2001–02. We would like to express our gratitude to Durham University for granting both authors research leave during the Michaelmas term, and for granting Karen Morrow an additional period of leave in the summer term of that year. We gratefully acknowledge the assistance of the Arts and Humanities Research Board of the British Academy for their award of an additional term of leave for both authors during Epiphany term 2002, without which the book could not have been written.

Last, but by no means least, we would like to thank our spouses Dr Allison Cook and Dr Michael Crilly for their endless forbearance, constant support and even willingness to engage in our, at times, somewhat obsessive discussions of our work.

S.C.
K.L.M.
Durham, August 2003.

Contents

Table of Cases

ECHR Cases

Table of Legislation

UK Legislation

Secondary Legislation

International Agreements etc.

European Law

1

Introduction

THE QUESTION OF the 'philosophical foundations' of environmental
thinking in law may strike the lawyer, as much as the legal philosopher, as
a strange one. For while a search for the philosophical commitments of environmental thinking undoubtedly makes sense in the context of ethics, or political theory, environmental *law* (it might be felt) lacks any such philosophical
underpinning: in the eyes of many professional lawyers, environmental regulation manifests itself almost exclusively through an array of statutory provisions,
severally concerned with curbing certain negative consequences arising from
particular spheres of human action. Although these various measures have the
common purpose of achieving a reduction in the erosion of our quality of life,
there is not (on this view) to be found any deeper rationale or overarching
principle beyond this purely instrumental concern with human wellbeing. Legal
regulation of the environment is, therefore, largely a set of facts to be learned
about the way the law deals with environmental issues. Particular statutory
provisions and judicial decisions will, of course, raise some quite interesting
questions of interpretation or application, but such questions, it is felt, are
resolved within the ordinary standards and criteria which influence legal argument, and do not require deeper philosophical explication.

Much of the intuitive appeal of this view derives from a related, though sometimes implicit, claim about the nature of environmental law. Environmental
law, it is sometimes said, is not in the strictest sense a distinctive area of the law
at all, but merely a convenient umbrella term for the collection of particular
legal provisions which are relevant to environmental protection. There may be
many reasons why it is useful and informative to group a set of legal provisions
in a certain way, but (we might say) the underlying motivation for so doing will
always be pedagogic rather than reflective of some penetrating analytical insight
into the materials so arranged. It can be highly illuminating, both academically
and practically, to discover how the law regulates, or interferes in, a particular
aspect of our social life—our pursuit of sport and leisure, for example; but the
pedagogic advantages gained by studying such subjects are not reflective of any
coherent project that the law self-consciously pursues. 'Sport law' is, in the end,
a particular cross-section of tort law, contract, criminal law and medical issues,
but not an established legal category or free-standing body of law. In the same
way, many lawyers regard environmental law as having more in common with
sport law than, say, with contract or property law.

The distinction between established legal categories and mere amalgamations of rules is often said to consist in the degree of doctrinal coherence possessed by the former, and absent from the latter. The established areas of contract, tort and property are the product of sustained reflection upon the framework of thought inherited from Roman law: the bodies of law which emerged from the system of writs represented the attempt to articulate and explore the different ways in which one can fall under an obligation, or of the differences between various kinds of obligation. The emergence of firm categorical distinctions was thus itself an expression of philosophical ideas about the constitution of the political order and of the relationship between individuals and the state. Particular ways of classifying bodies of legal rules into discrete areas therefore reflect differing conceptions of the philosophical foundations of the legal order:[1] for one who regards law primarily as an instrument of the regulatory state, the distinction between established doctrine and legislated rules will be of little significance, reflective only of differences in the way the rules came about; one who conceives of the law, by contrast, as delineating the boundaries between spheres of individual autonomy and collective choices, will tend to place much emphasis on the boundary between pubic- and private law.

These classifications might be drawn in various ways; but the diverse conceptions which underlie these classifications tend to cluster around a number of related distinctions which have long influenced the way lawyers, as a caste, regard their subject: distinctions (for example) between public law and private law, individual entitlement and collective goals, and between laws which suggest a concern with the intrinsic value of their objects and rules which are connected with their objects only instrumentally. Environmental lawyers, too, move within these conceptions. Environmental law is depicted as essentially a modern response to problems raised by contemporary living. It is characterised as a set of policy-driven, statutory limitations on the exercise of private entitlements, and the law is seen as regarding the natural environment as being worthy of protection only instrumentally, rather than as an end in itself. Looked upon in such terms, environmental law lacks a distinctive doctrinal basis. At most, seemingly, it represents a battery of provisions directed systematically at the resolution (or, at least, the management) of a particular social problem.

Our claim, in this work, is that such a conception of environmental law deserves to be, and can be, rejected. But this claim should not be mistaken for a claim to have uncovered an internally consistent and fully worked-out form of environmental legal doctrine which, inexplicably, environmental lawyers have overlooked. The very powerful intuitions which inform what we might call the 'received conception' of environmental law are, in themselves, reasonable. Instrumental and policy values *do* drive environmental legal scholarship, and one may well fail to discover in those values any thoroughly worked-out moral

---

[1] See NE Simmonds, 'The Changing Face of Private Law: Doctrinal Categories and the Regulatory State' [1982] *Legal Studies* 257–68.

project of the kind which lies at the heart of, say, property law or the law of contract. Our claim is, rather, that it is possible to find, in the common law, a philosophical foundation for environmental law of surprising antiquity and sophistication: that, by exploring certain currents in legal thought relating to property and tort, and the relationship between public and private law, one can find the germs of a distinctive philosophical approach to concerns which we would now regard as environmental.

   The possibility of working these strands of thought into a coherent doctrinal basis for modern environmental law is a fragile, but important, one. It is important because, if the argument of this book is correct, the law is revealed as having a concern with environmental protection which is neither as unsystematic and minimal, nor as starkly instrumental, as the received conception suggests. Further, a historically enlightened approach to environmental regulation offers, we believe, a clearer understanding of the import of current trends in legal thought about the environment. The assumptions which underpin these developments do not sit comfortably within the largely crisis-driven, policy-orientated framework of the received conception. Rather, they seem to exhibit concern with the intrinsic worth of aspects of the natural environment, and not merely an instrumental concern with current social conditions. It is, however, partly because these underpinning assumptions cannot be fully articulated within the confining conceptual structures of public law that the received conception derives its continuing plausibility. Some of these developments, explored fully in chapter four, will be touched on in a moment.

   But why, we might want to ask, should a rejection of the received conception be a *fragile* possibility, one not certain to be perennially available? To see why not, consider how the intrinsic/instrumental value distinction lies alongside another, that between public- and private law. One version of the public/private distinction (examined in chapters three and five) is as follows. Private law is characterised as the domain of individual entitlements, understood as a pattern of horizontal relationships among individuals. Public law is depicted as a set of vertical relationships between individuals and the state. These latter exist, broadly speaking, as a set of limitations on the existence and scope of private rights, and controls upon their exercise. Such controls are deemed essential and desirable on a number of grounds, both in the context of distributive projects and projects aimed at increasing overall welfare. But the public/private distinction does not simply demarcate the realm of public choices from that of the uninterrupted pursuit of private projects; it seems to represent a marked difference in the law's treatment of the *content* of those entitlements. Private rights to property, for example, tend to reflect deeply held assumptions about what property, philosophically speaking, is, and about the ways in which, and the extent to which, human beings can hold rights over certain objects. Through the notions of usufruct and possession, the law articulates ideas about the ways in which property in land can come about, and reveals something about the intrinsic nature and value which the law attaches to land.[2] Public law embodies no such theories; at least, not directly. Property statutes re-shape and refine the contours of private property rights in the light of social needs and goals in ways which may have no regard to the philosophical underpinnings of those rights. Where the encroachment of statute is considerable, the character of individual entitlements may no longer embody any coherent legal conception of their intrinsic value, but instead merely reflect competing instrumental conceptions of the good. This development has led many theorists to argue that one can no longer pinpoint an analytically feasible version of the public/private distinction: the saturation of the private realm by the public has eroded virtually altogether the distinctiveness of the private as a discrete realm of human thought.[3]

Theoretically tenable accounts of traditional legal categories are thus likely to require expression within a framework which transcends trite assumptions about the public/private distinction. Such accounts must, however, guard against the danger of altogether losing sight of the philosophical underpinnings of long-established patterns of doctrinal thought beneath the welter of rules generated and sustained through the influence of instrumental rationality. Tension between legal doctrine and the means-ends nexus of instrumental rationality is particularly evident in the law of property. Kevin Gray has recently argued that the legal conception of property is currently undergoing a shift away from a rights-based notion to one in terms of responsibilities.[4] Redistributive projects such as this reflect a shifting moral consensus about what the proper extent of property *rights* should be, but it cannot entirely escape involvement in a deeper philosophical debate about what property is. Changing conceptions of the extent or character of property rights reflect, or embody, differing ideas about what it means to own property, and what it means for something to count as property: if ownership is essentially unlimited, then particular users of property cannot automatically be taken account of in aggregative projects aimed at increasing or sustaining welfare, or in distributive projects aimed at changing the prevailing pattern of entitlements. If, on the other hand, irresponsible user is incompatible with ownership, property becomes a relative and interpersonal concept which has as much to do with *obligation* as it has with *right*.[5]

Much of environmental law is, of course, a set of restrictions and limitations on the use of property. But although such restrictions are articulated overwhelmingly in terms of instrumental conceptions of social and economic welfare, they (cannot fail to) embody a conception of what property *is*. The very notion of property, after all, presupposes a particular conception of the relationship between human beings and the external world, in terms both of what

---

[2] See chs 2–3.

[3] See ch 5.

[4] K Gray and SF Gray, '*The Idea of Property in Land*' in S Bright and J Dewar (eds), *Land Law: Themes and Perspectives* (Oxford, OUP, 1998) 15. These remarks are discussed at various places in this book, but most sustainedly in ch 5.

[5] See the discussion of natural vs non-natural user in ch 4, below.

can be owned, and of what ownership involves. Many of the assumptions of modern environmental law embody philosophically interesting and sophisticated ideas about the intrinsic nature of property and property rights; but such ideas are not easily, and only imperfectly, expressed in the restricting linguistic apparatus of environmental statutes. This book therefore closes by suggesting the terms in which a deeper, philosophically satisfying, explanation of environmental law might proceed.

In this work we will concentrate on the reciprocal influence between conceptions of property and environmental theories, tracing the transition from intrinsic- to instrumental value perspectives (and vice versa) as expressed in legal and political thought. The argument, which unfolds over four long chapters, might be broken down into the following stages:

1. Property law is concerned with the freedom and ability to control and utilise resources, and with ensuring the general efficacy of a scheme for the distribution of rights and duties in this regard. It is therefore concerned with regulating the use of resources. As a result, environmental ideas, particularly within the law, will inevitably be closely tied to prevailing legal conceptions of property and proprietary rights. At a superficial level it is easy to identify the direction of influence: conceptions of property rights tend to delimit the scope of legitimate *legal* concern with our use of property in ways potentially harmful to the environment. At the same time, the increasing importance of environmental law as a distinct discipline with a developing body of distinctive legal principles will profoundly influence attitudes towards the desirability and the extent of legal entitlements freely to use property.

   We contend that a fully developed understanding of modern environmental legal doctrine—and its potential influence over property rights—cannot be achieved unless a further, and prior, level of connection between environmental concerns and ideas of property is identified. Put simply, legal concerns about the legitimate extent of rights to property fundamentally depend upon philosophical preoccupations with what property is; and the roots of those preoccupations, when traced back to the early-modern world-views from which they emerged, can be seen to stem from concerns which would now be identified as 'environmental.' Chapter two is accordingly devoted to an exploration of conceptions of property in the seventeenth century, and addresses the role of property within political accounts of social order and human flourishing. It will be apparent that the varying conceptions of property that may be identified in the seventeenth century canon are all concerned with the attempt to identify humanity's relationship with the world at large: the evolution of ideas about property is shaped by—and a reflection of—

cultural preoccupations with humanity's place in the rest of nature. Although the threads of these beliefs have largely been lost in modern legal doctrine (see chapter three), they are nevertheless vital to understanding modern attempts to provide a rationale for legal regulation of the use of resources on environmental grounds (see chapter five).

2. The second and third chapters focus in detail on the evolution of the idea of property in modern European legal and philosophical thought. With the waning attractiveness of natural law as a philosophy of law, the concept of property became detached from its theological origins and instead came to be defined in terms of rights and duties. The highly legalistic moral vision of the natural lawyers, coupled with the attempts of philosophers such as Hobbes, Locke and later, Rousseau, to characterise the 'state of nature,' led to a concentration upon establishing networks of interpersonal relationships which would form an adequate basis for the modern state. It was thought that the delineation of proprietary entitlements was central to the establishment of effective and peaceful social order. Thus philosophical questions about the nature of property became concerned almost exclusively with questions about distributions of rights and duties between *persons*, and legal questions tended to centre on issues of distributive justice, and upon necessary legal limits to our ability to control or utilise property in the face of the need to maintain peace and good order.

   In the third chapter, the roots of the modern municipal conception of property are traced through the theories of the later natural lawyers, including Blackstone, and the positivist theories of Bentham and his intellectual heirs. The rise of legal positivism encouraged a concern with *rules* rather than rights, and under the pressure of changing conceptions of the relationship between private rights and public law, property rights became separated from their association with the social good, coming gradually to be regarded as inherently competing with the aggregative and distributive projects of the modern state. Rules determining the existence and extent of property rights hence appeared as related to property instrumentally rather than intrinsically.

3. Notwithstanding the rise of instrumental value conceptions, in chapter four we attempt to show how present attitudes to proprietary rights have shaped, and been shaped by, environmental concerns and their expression in law. In particular we will trace the evolution of common law attempts to reconcile pollution-based conflicts of property rights brought about by the Industrial Revolution (eg in the law of nuisance) and the development of statutory strategies to tackle such problems on a larger scale. The present relationship between established concerns of property law and emerging environmental doctrine can be viewed, in this light, as one in flux. An assessment of the future development of doctrine in both the law of property and environmental law—though we defer it until chapter five—depends upon an understanding of the way in which the present situation came about. It will emerge

that the early common law responses to the problems posed by pollution represent a philosophical achievement of surprising sophistication. Contrary to what might be expected, the doctrinal framework within which those problems were considered embodies an underlying concern, not with the utilitarian reconciliation of clashing interests, but with an exploration of the intrinsic moral value of property rights.

4. We close by considering the present status of environmental law and the direction which environmental doctrine is likely to take in the future. We believe that modern environmental law can be presented as a coherent doctrinal whole, which must be seen as a complex and highly distinctive historical product. Viewed this way, it is possible to address in a more enlightening way the central trends of modern environmental thinking: ideas concerning common heritage, stewardship of resources, future generations and sustainable development are, in a sense, imperfect attempts to address the same sorts of concern as were present in early-modern conceptions of property (ie the relationship between humanity and the world, and the limits of our entitlement to use natural resources). However, these attempts all express themselves in a language that cannot support or comprehend such concerns: they are voiced almost exclusively in terms of the scope of our rights to use resources in a way that affects other *people*. The concepts of sustainable development, and of future generations, for example, might be seen as attempts to get beyond the starkly instrumental perspectives on environmental protection which have dominated recent law and social policy; but such attempts are hampered by the fact that they still conceive of property in terms of patterns of rights and duties and the concept of a just distribution. In fact, given that the modern conception of property is fundamentally conceived in such terms, an account of our rights to property and an expression of our environmental concerns in the early-modern sense is probably no longer a possibility: the intellectual conditions, in terms of the relative states of development of knowledge in the sciences and in philosophy and theology, which must exist for such an account to make sense, are simply no longer available. Despite profound societal change, modern ideology remains largely indicative of the continued dominance of instrumentalist thinking over a belief in intrinsic value. We argue that only a fundamental shift in thinking, re-establishing the central importance of intrinsic value, can fully articulate and justify modern approaches to regulating the environment.

2

Nature and the State of Nature

E ARLY MODERN WORLD-VIEWS regarded property as being wedded to ideas
concerning man's place in the world. In this chapter, and the one following,
we shall examine how property came to be associated with the concept of
individual rights. The views on property that emerged in the writings of the
seventeenth century natural lawyers understood property rights as deriving
from, and as shaped by, man's relationship with the world around him, and
hence as being as much a part of the divine order of Creation as the physical
earth itself. Property rights possessed a distinctive theological significance; they
were thought of as benefiting both human life *and* the natural environment. The
eventual decline of that theological framework in the eighteenth century would
ultimately suggest a quite different view of the political assumptions of the position, according to which property rights define the borderline between private
interests and collective goals. A conception of property would emerge which
would regard property rights as instrumentally valuable, and standing in no
necessary relationship to wider moral (or environmental) values.

PROPERTY, RIGHTS AND NATURE

Modern legal scholarship moves within a conception of law which views
property as a pattern of interpersonal relationships of entitlement. Theoretical
characterisations as well as practical invocations of property rights consciously
articulate a specifically *legal* phenomenon which has no immediate connection
with any wider theories of morality, politics or society. The modern lawyer's
idea of property is both technical and deeply positivist: the lineaments of
property rights are regarded as flowing from refined lawyerly definitions and
distinctions, and from rules and principles laid down in statutes and decided
cases, rather than being shaped by wider social, moral or religious notions. A
conception of property will always generate *some* moral and religious questions, of course, but the lawyer's concern with established principle ensures that
legal practice need not become contaminated with open-ended theoretical speculation: legal philosophers may debate the philosophical significance of legal
concepts, but the legal practitioner can carry on with the business of applying
and expounding the law in complete isolation to those debates.

This professional detachment has, in recent times, increasingly given way to
a view of property rights as in some way connected with political, ethical and

even religious debates. Growing concern with the natural environment and the establishment of legal forms of environmental protection are seen as challenging the lawyer's traditional concern with property *rights*, by placing a focus on *responsibility*. Important as such developments are, they are often depicted as merely a collection of restrictions on the use of property, exhibiting no deep systemic significance other than a concern with protection from harm. Those measures are not seen as altering our overall *notion* of property, but as modifying the extent and scope of property rights. In one sense this is quite true, since the idea of property rights as inherently shaped and limited by fundamental obligations was an essential feature of the political thinking of the seventeenth and eighteenth centuries from which the institution of property in its modern form emerged. In another sense, however, the belief that the powers and rights of an owner to use land in prescribed ways might be *inherently* subject to community-directed obligations to nurture and protect the natural environment is a direct challenge to the assumption that the terminology of rights is the appropriate one to use to describe the complex relationship of property between persons and land.

Such is the extent to which rights-talk is embedded in our legal, moral and political culture, it is tempting to assume that the concept of property depends for its existence on that of right. Yet the form of modern property, both legally and in our moral life, is neither historically nor conceptually inevitable. The general shape and form of property at common law were the outgrowth both of established Roman law classifications and of the system of agrarian capitalism which emerged from the social conditions of the feudal order. The political speculation of the seventeenth century natural lawyers, though central to the modern idea of property, might profitably be understood as a series of attempts to articulate the tacit assumptions on which those contingent forms of social order were based, rather than as an attempt to ground property in necessary truths which transcend the social order. Yet the modern tendency to perceive in those developments, not an explanation of immanent conceptions of property, but a *justification* of the institution of property as such,[1] has had the effect of narrowing the rights-based view of property to a series of questions about the relative extents of interpersonal entitlements, themselves seen as separable from wider moral questions about the impact of ownership: once the possibility of private ownership is established, particular claims of right can be understood as resolvable by reference to considerations internal to the institutional arrangements of a given legal order.

As one might expect, this modern conception of right is a somewhat bloodless phenomenon in comparison to that wielded by the seventeenth century natural lawyers. For the term 'right' as it occurs in the writings of Grotius,

---

[1] See, for example, AJ Simmons, 'Original Acquisition Justifications of Private Property', in EF Paul, FD Miller and J Paul (eds), *Property Rights* (Cambridge, CUP, 1994) 63–84.

Hobbes, Pufendorf and their direct intellectual heirs refers to a concept of considerable philosophical sophistication which itself emerged from the complex interplay between notions of justice, power and obligation. Rights in *this* sense, although clearly definitive of various interpersonal relationships, were intimately connected with philosophical understandings of justice, religious obligation and the place of human beings in the world. The intimate connectedness of property with rights in modern philosophy was the product of sustained reflection on mankind's natural state, and the various attempts made throughout the seventeenth century to describe that state.

Rights in the State of Nature

In one sense, property and rights have always gone together: the Roman jurists had articulated and refined the notion of ownership through the concepts of *dominium* and *ius*, and the reception of this vocabulary into the common law produced a social order, in the form of feudal rights and duties, of considerable and enduring significance. Although the terms in which property is conceived have remained fairly static in Western legal thought, theoretical understandings of terms such as 'right' have varied considerably with shifts in philosophical perspective and the form of our social arrangements. The modern idea of legal rights to property as interpersonal entitlements, the existence and extent of which are determined relative to legal, rather than overtly moral, criteria, can survive only in a society which takes some form of legal positivism for granted: the underlying idea will be one of humanly enacted rules devised for the maintenance and smoothing of social relations. It is a commonplace (though slightly inaccurate) observation that the 'rights' described by political theorists of the seventeenth century have more in common with modern *liberties*, and in this sense exhibit a concern with the moral qualities of the individual rather than with explicitly laid down rules. The seventeenth century commentators were themselves re-interpreters of the Roman concepts of *ius*, *dominium*, and *proprietas*, as a means of comprehending the foundations of the political culture in which they found themselves.

The political thought of the classical and medieval worlds had centred on law's ability to embody a society's shared morality and collective experience. The later medieval writers, such as Augustine and Aquinas, gave to this endeavour a peculiarly theological twist, by conceiving of legal rules as a kind of revealed divine injunction on the form of life human beings should take if they wished to fulfil their duties to the Almighty. The law was seen as articulating and safeguarding a pattern of entitlements and obligations understood as promoting human welfare (and defining human duties) through their conformity with transcendent conceptions of reason or justice, to which universal assent could be inferred through rational reflection upon human nature. By the seventeenth century, the underpinning harmony in moral outlooks which allowed for the possibility of such a view had been eroded by the realities of sustained conflict and a waning belief in the powers of unaided reason to uncover moral truth. Civil society came to be regarded as an arena no longer underpinned by universal consensus about the collective good, but a deeply divided and fragmentary association of individuals who articulate and pursue their own conceptions of the good which vie and compete with the rival conceptions of their neighbours. Though Grotius, Hobbes and Pufendorf were, perhaps, no wiser than their contemporaries, their distinctive responses to the breakdown in shared moral, political and religious values were to provide a framework of thought about human society, and the place of law within it, which endures to this day. Central to that framework is the concept of property, and the notion of individual rights to which it gave rise.

Despite obvious and important differences, the conception of property found in the writings of Grotius, Hobbes and their intellectual heirs possesses a unifying and significant characteristic, in that it is both intimately connected with conceptions of social order *and* viewed as taking its essential features from reflection upon humankind's place in the order of Creation. This 'environmental' aspect of property is most clearly explored in the philosophy of Locke, though its centrality to the Grotian account and significance in Hobbes's political thought are less well understood. Nevertheless, the distinctive approach to property evident in these writings was eventually to give rise to a mode of thinking about property which would treat environmental considerations as both separable from, and in competition with, individual rights to property. The developments which led to this dichotomy are, therefore, worth exploring in some detail.

Grotius and Hobbes conceived of property as simultaneously conventional and rooted in natural rights. Though they differ over the characteristics of natural rights, both Hobbes and Grotius describe rights as essentially connected with property and explanatory of the roots of social order. Rights in modern legal parlance define a realm of private entitlement free from official interference in the name of public welfare. An individual's entitlements are said to define and protect a sphere of individual freedom in one of two ways: either by delimiting a realm of protected *choices*, or by articulating a realm of protected *interests*. According to the former interpretation (the 'Will theory') possession of a right vests in the right-holder a power of choice over the performance of someone else's duty. Since most rights are rights to be free from another person's interference in some project (or occasionally to be assisted in some project), the right-holder is given the power to insist upon being unimpeded in her pursuit of some course of action by the duty-bearer, or to be assisted therein, even where such a course of action may have a general and negative impact upon others. On the latter interpretation (the 'Interest theory') an individual's rights define her protected interests; that is, interests in pursuing particular courses of action which are considered worthy of legal protection at any cost, whatever the impact upon the collective good. Individual rights therefore seem inevitably and directly to collide with the common good.[2] The natural rights tradition which began with Grotius saw rights conversely as playing a constitutive role in determinations of the common good which would find its fullest expression in the philosophy of Locke.

The harmony between personal interests and the collective good is achieved by forging a link between sociability and respect for another's rights; a link that would become the subject of intense dispute during the latter half of the seventeenth century, particularly in the writings of those who, like Hobbes, favoured a form of absolutism. The anti-absolutists tended to regard the drive towards sociability as arising not from prudential calculations of long-term self-interest but from mankind's intensely social nature. Natural law was seen, by Grotius, as firmly rooted in man's social nature, and thus as creating obligations to achieve and maintain a peaceful social order; and the preconditions for social peace and stability are the preservation of, and respect for, property:

> This sociability, . . . or this care of maintaining society in a manner conformable to the light of human understanding, is the foundation of Right, properly so called; to which belongs the abstaining from that which is another's, and the restitution of what we have of another's, or of the profit we have made by it, the obligation of fulfilling promises, the reparation of damage done through our own default, and the merit of punishment among men.[3]

The Grotian conception of property rights makes important assumptions about the characteristics of natural law: absolutist versions of natural law, such as those advanced by the medieval scholars, supplant the need for theoretical explanations of property since its exact contours are the subject of divine stipulation. Accounts of property within such theories will, therefore, tend to be regarded as acts of textual interpretation and exegesis rather than as belonging to a wider political theory. The *theory* of property is therefore 'inextricably linked with conceptions of human nature and society, of psychology and history, of action and obligation.'[4] In *Mare Liberum*, Grotius had argued that, while natural law is of divine origin, it should not be regarded as a species of divine *command*, for such a view would boil down to a rather extreme form of

---

[2] The distinction between the Will and Interest theories may be regarded as having its origins in a debate begun in the fourteenth century, concerning the relationship between the Roman concepts of *dominium* and *ius*, between those who viewed any *ius* as involving notions of moral sovereignty and control (ie *dominium*) and those for whom possession of a *ius* might involve no element of moral choice but consist exclusively in their recognition by other people: see R Tuck, *Natural Rights Theories: Their Origin and Development* (Cambridge, CUP, 1979) 5–8. The emergence of the distinction between so-called 'active' and 'passive' rights, and their specific connection with the notion of liberty, would eventually lead to a characterisation of rights in terms of choices or interests. For an examination of the significance of this later debate, see NE Simmonds, 'Rights at the Cutting Edge' in MH Kramer, NE Simmonds and H Steiner, *A Debate Over Rights* (Oxford, OUP, 1998) 113–232.
[3] H Grotius, *De Iure Belli ac Pacis* (Prolegomena) (Kluwer Law International, 1952) 8–9 (Hereinafter referred to as *DIBP*).
[4] S Buckle, *Natural Law and the Theory of Property: Grotius to Hume* (Oxford, Clarendon Press, 1991) 3.

legal positivism, the precepts of natural law emanating from acts of divine will and thus not ascertainable by reflection on the character of human nature but, instead, dependent upon revelation.[5] The lack of any sharp, imposed verbal form meant that natural precepts can only come into view through sustained rational reflection on the necessary course human societies must take if they are to evolve peacefully and create stable and successful conditions for human flourishing. The rationalism of this view is often depicted as a fundamentally anti-empirical position on natural law; yet the underpinning assumptions of such a position are far removed from the motivations of Grotius and Hobbes.

Grotius understood his theory to be offering an account and appraisal of social relations in the light of society's historical beginnings in an age without positive laws of any kind. For Hobbes (as we shall see) social arrangements are inherently just in virtue of the agreement which instituted them and the lawless conditions which preceded that agreement and which led to its formation. Modern writers have tended to perceive the assumption of a 'state of nature' prior to the emergence of positive law as a hypothetical device for the justification of binding standards in established societies, and thus as proffering a fundamentally ahistoric explanation of how those standards developed in the first place. Yet although this form of explanation was not new (the Roman commentators including Cicero used it in their treatises on law)[6] both the Grotian and the Hobbesian states of nature were conceived by their authors as describing a situation which had basis in historical fact. In his discussion of the various ways in which natural laws are presented to the human mind, Grotius expressed a clear methodological preference for *a posteriori* over *a priori* proofs: natural precepts epitomise the intrinsic sociability of man, and an important source of our knowledge of those precepts are the forms of human association across the world in which that nature is reflected. Some nations, however, 'are so strange that no judgment of human nature can be formed from them, for it would be erroneous.'[7] Grotius clearly took himself to be analysing the nature and historical development of *actual* societies; his main source for the formation of the earliest human societies out of loose familial groupings was the Biblical account

---

[5] Grotius, *Mare Liberum* (1609), trans as *The Freedom of the Seas* (Batoche Books, 2000) 8. In his mature writings, Grotius distinguished between what he called 'divine positive law' and the ordinary law of nature. Whilst both are part of natural law, the former remains open to human knowledge only through revelation in sacred texts or by the prophets, the latter by rational reflection on the human situation and constituting the main body of natural law. See Grotius, *DIBP* I.1.x.21.

[6] The best examples of Cicero's use of the state of nature are to be found in *De Inventione* [trans HM Hubbell (Heinemann, 1949) I–2, and *De Oratore* (trans H Rackham, Heinemann, 1969) I–33. The legal writers of the Renaissance were not unfamiliar with such an analysis: see A Brett, *Liberty, Right and Nature* (Cambridge, CUP, 1997) ch 1–3.

[7] *DIBP* I.1.xii.24. For Hobbes's views see *Leviathan* (ed CB Macpherson, Harmondsworth, Penguin, 1968) I.13.187, discussed by MH Kramer, *Hobbes and the Paradoxes of Political Origins* (London, Macmillan, 1997) 64–69 and S Coyle, 'Thomas Hobbes and the Intellectual Origins of Legal Positivism' XV *Canadian Journal of Law and Jurisprudence* (2003) 21–49.

in Genesis and Exodus, and the meditations of the early Roman poets and jurists.[8]

Unlike the Hobbesian depiction of the state of nature, the *De Iure Belli* sees the world as composed of a set of rights and duties concerning property which pre-exist any conventional stipulations regarding who owns what. Grotius cites Biblical authority for the proposition that the earth was given by God to Adam and his descendents in common, and his subsequent task was to show how private property can arise from these communistic beginnings:

> God gave to mankind in general, dominion over all the creatures of the earth, from the first creation of the world; a grant which was renewed upon the restoration of the world after the deluge. All things, as Justin says, formed a common stock for all mankind, as the inheritors of one general patrimony. From hence it happened, that every man seized to his own use or consumption whatever he met with; a general exercise of right, which supplied the place of private property. So that to deprive anyone of what he had thus seized, became an act of injustice . . . A state of affairs, which could not subsist but in the greatest simplicity of manners, and under the mutual forbearance and goodwill of mankind.[9]

We do not yet have private property here, but something which supplies the place of it in the state of nature; yet several important strands of thought are revealed in this short passage which deserve to be picked apart. The first concerns the significance of the Roman law categories of *dominium* and *ius*. A debate about the relationship between these concepts was at the centre of much late medieval and early Renaissance legal scholarship. The question was whether, if someone had a *ius* in something, they thereby had *dominium* over it. The jurists of the Roman Empire had tended to conceive of *iura* in objective terms, as something objectively and ascertainably right, and thus used the term as an effective synonym for 'law'. Such rights had little to do with property because they said nothing (directly) about an individual's *claims*; only later would possession of *iura* be equated with some form of control over one's moral life, and thus as saying something about a person's *ownership* of their liberty, choices and moral qualities. *Dominium* had been regarded by Imperial jurists as delimiting a separate realm from that of *ius*; a person's *dominium* over his property 'was simply given by the fact, as it seemed to the Romans, of a man's total control over his physical world—his land, his slaves or his money' and, unlike some *iura*, 'was not constituted by an agreement or other transaction between individual and private parties.'[10] In Grotius's writings, these two distinct ideas would come powerfully together in a way which was to influence political

---

[8] *DIBP* II.2.ii.87: Grotius's accounts of the original community in goods and their subsequent distribution 'we derive from sacred history, and they are found to agree with the opinions . . . of philosophers and poets,' See for example I.1.xi.23 for Grotius's use of Plutrach. For an interesting account of sacred history in seventeenth century philosophy see PC Almond, *Adam and Eve in Seventeenth Century Thought* (Cambridge, CUP, 1999).

[9] *DIBP* II.2.ii.86.

[10] Tuck, above n 2 p 10.

discourse for the next 300 years. Man's natural liberty in the state of nature, his unfettered freedom to act in the absence of positive laws or well-defined or established obligations which form part of a community's shared morality, could now be described as a form of *property*:

> For God created man 'free and *sui iuris*,' . . . [and] what is that well-known concept 'natural liberty' other than the power of the individual to act in accordance with his own will? And liberty in regard to actions is equivalent to *dominium* in material things.[11]

The general use-right which Grotius described in the passage above can now be understood as bestowing a form of property right (*dominium*) on mankind in common over the resources of the earth. Rights in Grotius's writings retained their objective moral connotations ('right', said Grotius, 'is nothing more than what is just') but became linked with an individual's *claims*.[12]

The immediate consequence of such a move is to invest property rights with an intrinsic theological significance. For God's bestowal on mankind of a *positive* community in the earth's resources creates a network of rights and duties which precede any conventional stipulations about the way in which human relationships are to be understood. Moral and legal thought are to some degree abstract and formal, in that not all aspects of interpersonal relationships count in moral or legal assessments of the actions of the parties. For a positivist, the juristic concepts which structure those relationships are presumably to be thought of as contingent products of human understanding: rights represent just one way in which morally and legally relevant aspects of human relationships might be articulated and expounded. Property rights within conventionalist theories are thus generally determined by their structuring role in human social life, and their exact contours will in the main be thought of as deriving from political and ethical considerations centring on the relationship between individual wants and the specific needs of a particular society. An important strand of Grotius's thought is conventionalist in this sense: the move from original community in resources to a state of property 'was not [made] by the act of the mind alone . . . For man in that case could never know, what others intended to appropriate to their own use, so as to exclude the claim of every other pretender to the same.' Thus, property

> must have been established either by express agreement, as by division, or by tacit consent, as by occupancy . . . [For] it is natural to suppose it must have been generally agreed, that whatever any one had occupied should be accounted his own.[13]

---

[11] Grotius, GL Williams (tr), *De Iure Praedae Commentarius* (hereinafter *DIPC*) (Oxford, OUP, 1950), 18.

[12] 'Right is that, which is not unjust . . . [that is,] repugnant to the nature of society, established among rational creatures'; equally, 'Right is a moral quality annexed to the person justly entitling him to possess some particular privilege, or to perform some particular act.' *DIBP* I.1.iii–iv.18. Rights thus simultaneously embody an individual's moral power to demand what is due (I.1.vi.20) and determine the extent of entitlement according to justice (I.1.ix.20).

[13] *DIBP* II.2.ii.89.

But Grotius's position cannot amount to a full-blooded commitment to conventionalism, because he depicted the evolution of institutions of private property as in some sense a *natural* development of the fundamental, God-given right of human beings to exploit the earth's natural resources.

Prima facie, strongly conventionalist theories depend upon a natural state characterised in terms of negative liberty, in which rights emerge from, and shape, a formless and anarchic world of competing desires and interests. The form and substance of such rights derive from agreements forged between prudentially rational individuals who perceive that their attempts to impose subjective interpretations of virtue are likely to end in violence or anarchy, and whose long-term self-interests are thus best served by the renunciation of their unconstrained freedom and acceptance of conventional rules and standards. Such theories—as would shortly emerge in the writings of Selden and his followers as a *response* to Grotius—are natural rights theories only in a weak sense: normative interpersonal relationships are 'natural' in the sense that their emergence is a necessary condition for human sociability, and thus required by reason; but the form and content of those norms (for instance, in the form of *rights*) is a more-or-less contingent product of the human intellect and particular historical circumstances. The interpretative background of conventional rights and rules will comprise a set of assumptions about their role and purpose in civil life; it will in general be no part of a reflective understanding of the rules that they confer some benefit (or some harm) upon the natural world. Where such beneficial or harmful consequences exist (an injunction against waste, say) they will be treated either as incidental to the rule's central purpose or as in some way directly connected with human wellbeing. Rules and rights will not, for the conventionalist, be thought of as subject to *intrinsic* limitations arising from such consequences.

Grotian natural rights, by contrast, are conventional only in a weak sense: the agreement which establishes the principle of occupation is both tacit and recognitional (rather than constitutive) of an inherent ability of men to acquire property (*dominium*) in natural resources, and the essential lineaments of those rights are determined by *necessary* features of human evolution. As Richard Tuck has observed,

> There [was] something natural in the development into the institution of private property of the basic and inherent human right to use the material world, and no agreement was ever necessary.[14]

Thus, whereas one strand of Grotius's thought emphasises private property as the distinctive product of a civil society, another explains that development as both sanctioned and shaped by natural law: the contours of ownership and property rights are settled by positive law; but because a variety of positive stipulations might be, as Grotius put it, 'patterned after nature's plan,'[15] quite

---

[14] Tuck, above n 2 p 61.
[15] *DIPC* 229.

diverse forms of property are capable of evolving in differing social and historical contexts which are in harmony with natural law. This diversity is not, of course, boundless: although the natural law does not consist of canonical rules of fixed verbal formulation, its precepts must be understood as reflective of certain characteristics of human nature. The basic pattern of use-rights and obligations which structure the pre-legal world could, Grotius maintained, in principle continue indefinitely; only the frailty of human moral steadfastness in the face of countervailing desires prevents such a system from remaining effective. For, Grotius says, 'those original rights were *permissions* of the law of nature, and not commands that were to be *perpetually* enforced.'[16] Specific rights to private property thus supervene upon original liberties as additional restraints upon what can be acquired. This is a natural move in that the existence of liberties alone will fail to structure competing needs and wants as human beings become more numerous and their social groupings grow in complexity; but the particular property rules of a given society will be the outcome of agreement about the extent of ownership and the desirability of certain distributive arrangements. It is quite clear that the convention Grotius had in mind is unlikely to be the *conscious* outcome of a collective act of will, let alone a verbalised agreement of any kind: the emergence of private rights is conventional simply in that the natural law fails to embody hard-and-fast rules about property in civil society:

> The deviations therefore from the state of nature, which have been established by the civil law, are ordained by every principle of natural justice to be obeyed by mankind. For although the civil law can enjoin nothing which the law of nature prohibits, nor prohibit anything which it enjoins, yet it may circumscribe natural liberty, restraining what was before allowed; although the restraint should extend to the very acquisition of property, to which every man *at first* had a right by the law of nature.[17]

In particular, therefore, the civil laws of a society cannot extend the rights of human beings to acquire property in the material world in ways prohibited by the law of nature. It is therefore worth investigating the assumptions Grotius makes about the character and extent of rights in the state of nature: are there, for example, inherent restrictions on our ability to commit waste or to act in ways which are damaging to our common patrimony?

Grotius's characterisation of the original, God-given use-right as consisting in a collection of *liberties* makes it appear as if the widest possible variety of civic property arrangements are compatible with the natural law. Yet such liberties cannot be straightforward *negative* liberties, in the light of God's bestowal of a positive community in goods upon mankind in general: the injunction to utilise natural resources cannot be considered as wholly unrestrained, since it is given to *all*. One individual's pursuit of her use-right may well conflict with another individual's pursuit of his, but the overlapping pursuit of individual use-rights

---

[16] *DIBP* II.3.iii.104.
[17] *DIBP* II.2.iv.91.

generally does not amount to anything like an anarchy of competing *claims*. Grotius was careful not to couch original rights in the terminology of claims, for (as we shall see) he regarded claims as emerging from a situation alien to that characterised by original community. Equally misleading is Grotius's suggestion that such rights amount to *legal* permissions, because such a use of the word 'right' would jar with his insistence that right simultaneously functions as an effective synonym for justice and embodies 'a moral quality annexed to the person justly entitling him to possess some particular privilege, or to perform some particular act.'[18] The Grotian definition of right includes the notion of the rightholder as the *owner* of her liberties or privileges in a way which does not reduce to a straightforward freedom to act. To the seventeenth century mind, liberty entailed a certain basic unstructuredness or freedom from rules, a notion which would eventually blossom into the Hobbesian demarcation of rights as a realm wholly outside that of law. The objective conception of right with which Grotius was working precluded the characterisation of the state of nature as an anarchic sphere upon which conventional rules supervene; the emergence of property rules is, for Grotius, a gradual and inevitable outgrowth of human evolution, and the linkage between civil laws and the law of nature is much tighter than the mainly prudential connection later emphasised by the followers of Selden.

One of Grotius's aims in *De Iure Praedae* was to demonstrate that some property (including the high seas) is irreducibly common, and thus not open to appropriation.[19] He does this by purporting to exhibit the necessary reliance property rights have on personal subsistence. The earliest humans (he argued) subsisted on 'spontaneous productions of the ground.'[20] While such takings are understandable solely in terms of use rather than as making proprietary claims, the consumption of some resources will naturally entail their annihilation (as with food, for example); thus, Grotius observed, there is a natural link between some exercises of the use-right and the kind of exclusive right which is characteristic of private ownership.[21] General resort to the use-right could of course only persist unproblematically as long as the earth's natural bounty was sufficiently plentiful that widespread disputes would not break out in the face of competing wants. The need for positive rules is a function of the steady rise in the number of humans chasing those resources (which was always God's plan) and the increasing complexity of human social relationships: private property is necessary because widespread reliance on the use-right remains stable only in a social world founded upon an 'extreme simplicity of manners' on the part of

---

[18] *DIBP* I.1.iv.19.

[19] *DIPC* 230–31; *DIBP* II.2.xii.94. One need not, however, go along with Richard Tuck's statement that '[Grotius's] object in depicting the growth of private property gradually, through the increasing allocation of goods to individuals that only they could use, was precisely to deny that the sea could ever be so allocated' (see Tuck, above n 2 p 89).

[20] *DIBP* II.2.ii.87.

[21] *DIPC* 228. Grotius speaks loosely of such exercises creating de facto private property.

individuals whose moral purity consists not in any conscious pursuit of the good so much as ignorance of iniquity.[22] As techniques of agriculture and pasturage develop, however, questions of distribution necessarily begin to arise; the relationship between man and the natural world is no longer characterised by individual brute takings, but involves cultivation by and for the benefit of a social *group*. Because the individual is no longer alone at the centre of her moral world, a set of questions about which products of group interaction belong to oneself and which belong to the group are set in train.

Grotius blurred the nature of the transition from simple brute takings to actual occupation and possession, but it is clear that the possession of lands by groups was, for Grotius, an established feature of the antediluvian world: it was in part the bitter conflicts over possession among the Noachidae, and the need to cleanse the world of rampant ambition, which brought on the Flood.[23] Of greatest significance in the early history of humankind, from the Grotian point of view, was the raising and eventual destruction of the Tower of Babel. For it is at that point that the mass of human life is dispersed across the globe (to '[take] possession of different parts of the earth')[24] and humanity is thereby fragmented into separate tribes with distinct languages and customs. This forces the supposition (effectively repeated in the writings of all the major natural rights theorists) that all communal land was appropriated, all over the world, at roughly the same point in history, so that *all* systems of land-holding derive from a common historical source and near-simultaneous acts of original appropriation. As we have seen, Grotius's assertion that private property emerged by agreement does not imply the existence of an historical *consensus in idem* arising among human groupings separated by language and by vast spaces of land and water. The implausibility of such an idea is precisely what led Grotius to deny that the emergence of private property must be the result of a *conscious* decision:

> It was not by the act of the mind alone that this change took place. For men in that case could never know what others intended to appropriate to their own use, so as to exclude the claim of every other pretender to the same.[25]

Private property is something we slide into gradually; though the divisions we settle upon are the outcome of consensus forged in the fire of collective experience, the emergence of those agreements is in some sense an historically necessary part of human evolution: as humanity expands, the common use of land becomes inconvenient and the move from the commons to a state of private property is inevitable. The original use-right is not directly abandoned but fades into obsolescence in the face of increasingly sophisticated wants (food, clothing and permanent shelter) and the necessary division and specialisation in labour

---

[22] *DIBP* II.2.ii.87.
[23] *DIBP* II.2.ii.88.
[24] *Ibid.*
[25] *Ibid* 89.

required to fulfil them; at the same time, the impossibility of bringing all the fruits of that labour together into a common stock for a human population scattered across the globe forces a revision of the assumptions upon which distributions had thus far been effected. The division of common lands into allotments based around family units within a wider social grouping reflects the fact that when 'the reason no longer subsists why men should hold all things in common, the practice ceases also.'[26] Positive rules introducing private property are thus necessary only insofar as human sociability requires a departure from the original simplicity of the general use-right; but the substance of those rules will naturally vary between societies given the distinct cultural traditions and needs of geographically remote civilisations. But since private rights to property necessarily exclude others from what was formerly common patrimony, the content of civil property laws is not open-ended. Civic arrangements must, at some level, respect our inherent rights to earthly resources *and* their limitations.

The story of the development of private rights to property is to some extent the story of the emergence of a purely subjective conception of right; but it is worth remembering that the interpersonal relationships generated by civic property arrangements remain fundamentally linked, in Grotius's thought, to substantive conceptions of justice and right. Grotius's understandings of justice and right are, in common with those of his contemporaries and medieval legal writers, fundamentally anthropocentric. The original use-right was bestowed by God to provide the sustenance necessary for human life to continue and expand. This assertion is a mixture of modesty and presumption. It presumes upon a maximal interpretation of the Biblical suggestion of man's centrality in Creation, as pursued in the Thomist tradition: inter alia, there is no possibility of animals possessing rights, 'for no beings, except those that can form general maxims, are capable of possessing a right.'[27] In consequence 'we are forced by nature to use law and justice towards men only'; the nature and scope of rights are thus fully determined by the role they play in structuring and sustaining human social relationships and our right to exploit and consume essentially finite material resources is at once fundamental and takes precedence over other forms of life in God's creation whose life and well-being also so depend. The traditionally close relationship, preserved in Grotian thought, between rights and justice entails the conclusion that ethical assessments of human action essentially involve reference to the impact of such actions upon other morally-endowed agents: the consequences of human action to the natural world and its non-human inhabitants lies outside the scope of ethical assessment. The effects of this presumption are, however, considerably mitigated by the inherent

[26] *Ibid* 88–89. Buckle, among others, errs in assuming that such agreements must be, at least in part, explicit (see above n 4 p 42). This would, of course, become a feature of later natural rights theories, including that of Hobbes.

[27] *DIBP* I.1.xi.23. This is, in fact, contrary to the position in Roman law which assigned 'one unchangeable right to brutes in common with man,' the common right being the law of nature in distinction to the law of nations particular to man.

modesty of the use-right. For if fundamental rights are tied to human subsistence, it follows that not just *any* acts of exploitation will count as exercises based on right: only those which are necessary for sustaining an individual's immediate bodily needs (at least in the first stages of human evolution) are permitted by natural law. As those needs become more complex (as a necessary consequence of social development) so will our rights expand in ways not prescribed by the original use-right. But such enlargements in entitlement are *developments* of that original right, not a replacement of it.

It is that which Grotius intended to convey by the statement that conventional rights are 'patterned after nature's plan': because human nature is essentially sociable, part of nature's plan is the development of human social relationships and (ultimately) civic arrangements as *fora* for human flourishing.[28] Such arrangements both reflect *and* entail increasingly sophisticated and complex human needs and desires. The earliest humans sought shelter in caves or under trees but knew no concept of possession. As communities formed, tied to particular lands which they could cultivate in the common interest, the need for *permanent* settlements as a basis for family units arose, and de facto private property, and the idea of exclusive rights, grew with it. The rootedness of private property in natural rights, to some extent slurred over in the *De Iure Belli*, was the subject of much finer analysis in Grotius's earlier work *De Iure Praedae*. In that work, Grotius examined in some detail the exact nature and extent of the supervenience of civic property rights over basic natural rights. The Grotian picture is one in which property rights conferred by positive law *extend* our natural rights of ownership in particular ways but at no point *replace* the latter as the basis of our emergent claims of (subjective) right.

Our natural rights are presented by Grotius as stemming from a fundamental form of self-ownership. Some aspects of our lives are, by their nature, incapable of quite unlimited use by others: 'Things belonging to individuals,' Grotius had observed,

> are by nature inalienable or alienable. Inalienable things are things which belong so essentially to one man that they could not belong to another, as a man's life, body, freedom, honour.[29]

(In fact, Grotius later went on to doubt whether the latter three are wholly inalienable: marriage, for example, is a form of contract concerning one's body.) The natural unsuitability of these aspects of ourselves to consumption and use by others is thus accompanied by a natural power to protect them from abuse; this power is thus a power to act *rightfully*, in roughly the same spirit as Roman commentators deployed the concept of objective *ius* with which Grotius

---

[28] '. . . among the traits characteristic of man is an impelling desire for society, that is, for the social life, not of any and every sort, but peaceful, and organised according to the measure of his intelligence with those who are of his kind.' *DIBP* 6.
[29] Grotius, *Introduction to the Jurisprudence of Holland*, 2 vols, trans RW Lee (1926) reprint of 2nd ed (Aalen, Germany, Scientia Verlag, 1977) 70, paragraph break suppressed.

and his contemporaries were familiar. But the aspects of ourselves which are thus protected also embody a domain over which we have a *claim* that others do not interfere. The Roman lawyers had referred to this domain as the *suum* (one's own), and in Grotius's hands this idea became the bridge between objective conceptions of justice and the juridical realm of interpersonal subjective rights. A 'right,' Grotius said, is a moral faculty 'which every man has to his own,' so that a right 'signifies nothing more than what is just.'[30] The realm constituted by 'one's own' is thus the realm of justice and of right (or, alternatively, of objective *and* subjective right). Justice is thereby distinct from other virtues a man might possess (such as compassion or charity) since these are concerned with *collective* goals and goods rather than with personal *rights*. Though Grotius was hardly the first thinker to arrive at a conception of subjective right, in his writings the association of subjective and objective *ius* is far closer than had been contemplated by many of his predecessors in the natural rights tradition. The quite natural (and objective) power of a man to protect his life, limb and liberty had effectively come to be thought of as protected and defined by his *claim*-rights:

> There is another meaning of law viewed as a body of rights . . . which has reference to the person. In this sense a right becomes a moral quality of a person, making it possible to do something lawfully. [It is therefore] through the exercise of rights that the realm of law is extended. It is also through the possession of rights that the obligations of natural (and thus positive) law are limited.[31]

This uneasy relationship of rights to liberty, in which the individual is at once the *owner* of her liberties but has freedom to act rightfully only insofar as her actions do not impinge upon the rights of others, would eventually lead to the Kantian conception of law as the realm of compossible freedoms defined and protected though rights. For Grotius, the rules of positive law, insofar as they might recognise private property in material objects or land, constitute *extensions* to the *suum*. As such, whatever the distributive goals of a particular society might be, its positive laws cannot expand private property rights in ways which intrude upon or interrupt a person's fundamental right to sustain themselves: all human beings, Grotius argued, retain a basic 'right of necessity' to use and consume resources necessary to their own survival. 'All men,' he stated, 'have absolutely a right to do such acts as are necessary to provide whatever is essential to the existence . . . of life,' and this is 'a right interwoven with the very frame of human society.'[32] Just as some elements of original community remain resolutely common property (such as rivers and seas), so the general use-right bestowed by God so that life may continue survives the advent of civil society and the development of private rights to property.[33] Even within civil society, a

---

[30] *DIBP* I.1.v.19 and I.1.iii.18 respectively.
[31] *DIBP* I.1.iv.
[32] *DIBP* II.2.xvii.99 and II.2.xiii.95 respectively.
[33] *DIBP* II.2.xiii.95; see also II.2.iv.91–92.

person in extreme need can rightfully take from another that which he needs to continue living, subject to the proviso that the need is immediate and restitution is made to the owner if and when possible.[34] This is not a natural law of *charity*, since (as we have seen) the virtues in general are incapable of forming the subject-matter of legal obligations; it is rather a right of *property* because the terms of the original use-right demand on-going access to basic resources necessary to life.

In the *De Iure Belli*, in which Grotius had emphasised much more the role of agreement in the establishment of private property, he explained these necessary limitations on our capacity for appropriation as an essential part of (our interpretations of) the original agreement which institutes civil society:

> For the intention of those who first introduced private property must be taken into the account. And it was but reasonable to suppose that, in making this introduction of property, they would depart as little as possible from the original principles of natural equity.[35]

Yet, as we have seen, the conventional aspect of Grotius's thought is quite weak; for Grotius merely wished to emphasise that the right of necessity, as a natural precept, is not one forced upon reluctant human minds, but is rather a dictate of right reason. The slimmest exercise of reason shows that a rule allowing others to use one's property in times of extreme need is fully in accord with our own long-term self-interest. If I am part of a community which assents to a rule demanding that I allow others access to *my* property in times of need, the rule will also demand that when *I* am needy, others allow me access to *theirs*. The relatively minor inconvenience to me of giving succour to others when I am well-off is offset by the great benefit I reap when I am destitute, and the security such knowledge brings.

Just as I must be prepared to acknowledge the rightful claims of others in situations of need, so must I be willing to share the benefits of property which would be useful to the receiver but which are of no use to myself: to allow someone to light a taper from my flame in no way diminishes my own fire; in the same way, the owner who destroys his remaindered crops after his own consumption is satisfied acts against natural law.[36] Although these rights and obligations structure our interpersonal social relationships, they also embody substantive restrictions upon our ability to consume resources per se: natural law demands (albeit for reasons of sociability) that we do not commit waste. In fact, it is far from clear that the natural injunction against waste *is* a function of sociability, as Grotius perceived it. In both *De Iure Praedae* and *De Iure Belli*, Grotius characterised substantive restrictions on private property as arising out of respect for the *suum*: the right of necessity *and* the injunction to forebear from wasteful practices arise because of the essential right of all individuals to

---

[34] *DIBP* II.2.iv.91.
[35] *DIBP* II.2.iv.92.
[36] *DIBP* II.2.xi.94.

continued existence. In the latter work Grotius even treats these as stemming from the same considerations which demand recognition of the inalienable commons:

> The same reason prevails here as in the cases above named. Because property was introduced with a reservation of that use which might be of general benefit, and not prejudicial to the interest of the owner: an intention evidently entertained by those who first devised the separation of the bounteous gifts of the Creator into private possessions.[37]

Yet it is far from obvious that these substantive limitations on ownership are instances of the same phenomenon. Rights which establish and protect the *suum* are essentially 'passive' rights, in that they are rights that others do not trespass upon one's own. The original, God-given use-right, on the other hand, is an *active* right to consume worldly resources. The former do not entail the latter: one's right over one's continued survival and one's body and freedom do not strictly imply the existence of a duty in others to act in ways which guarantee one's access to resources which secure and sustain those things. The use-right, by contrast, *does* constitute an on-going right to succour but does not (as Grotius later argued) imply the inalienability of one's body or freedom. Private property rights, insofar as they are extensions of the original use-right *and* remain rooted in the *suum* thus have a dual basis in Grotian thought. Both of these aspects of Grotius's thought have, in different ways, fundamentally shaped our conception of legal rights. Recognition of the *suum*, as a distinctive and inevitable form of self-ownership, forces upon political thought the conception of a private realm delineated and policed by individual rights which is free from interference in the name of the common good: an individual is understood as being 'free inasmuch as he is the proprietor of his own person and capacities' and owing nothing to society for them.[38] Society, on this view, comes to be conceived in terms of an interplay between roughly equal individuals, their self-possession demarcating a realm of freedom from the will of others.[39] The rootedness of private property in the original use-right, on the other hand, embodies a substantive constraint upon private ownership which is not merely interpersonal: the right authorises consumption of that which is necessary to sustain life (in the state of nature) or commodious life (in civil society); it is not a quite open-ended right to consume the earth's resources in excess of what is necessary to satisfy those needs. Human needs and desires will, of course, grow

---

[37] *DIBP* II.2.xiii.95.

[38] CB MacPherson, *The Political Theory of Possessive Individualism: Hobbes to Locke* (Oxford, Clarendon Press, 1962) 3.

[39] Nigel Simmonds has argued that the possessive quality of liberalism arises out of particular conceptions of juridical equality: see N Simmonds, *The Decline of Juridical Reason* (Manchester, MUP, 1984) 44. Tuck, by contrast, sees possessive individualism as the outcome of an ambiguity within rights-language since its inception (*Natural Rights Theories* above n 2, 3). In truth, the theory is rooted in political standpoints which go beyond linguistic questions, but which are not, or do not seem to be, specifically or exclusively concerned with equality.

in scope and sophistication as society and technology evolve; but the use-right is not capable of justifying desires *tout court*, merely those which are in some way connected with mankind's rational pursuit of peace and sociability (the desire for community and culture and not, for example, the unlimited desire for war or the desire to act unjustly).

Grotian natural rights thus comprised elements of both objective and subjective *ius*: the self-ownership which underlies recognition of the *suum*, and the extensions to the realm of one's own sanctioned in particular systems of civil law, are readily intelligible as a set of *claims* an individual possesses against outside interference, and thus (in Grotius's terms) as delineating a sphere of individual freedom; yet the capacity to act 'rightfully' is essentially limited to acting *justly*, according to interpretative maxims which go beyond the content of rules of the civil law. The fundamental right to exploit the earth's resources likewise naturally develops into private property as human social life becomes more complex; but the ability of citizens to make claims over land and the fruits thereof is bounded by the need to respect the terms of God's original grant to utilise those resources *to sustain oneself*. This latter aspect of Grotian rights would eventually be taken up in a more thoroughgoing way by Locke; the former would be emphasised, in different ways, by Hobbes and Pufendorf.

Hobbes, Pufendorf and the Development of Rights

Grotius had characterised man's natural state as one of moral innocence and gentility of manners. That the moral purity derived from ignorance of evil rather than any innate desire for virtue was the reason why positive rules regulating behaviour were needed in addition to the fundamental right to utilise material resources. Early man's ambition to harness territory arising from the first distributions of original patrimony made the emergence of civil society and rigid social rules a rational imperative.[40] Yet for all its hardship and inconvenience, the Grotian depiction of mankind's pre-social beginnings falls far short of the anarchy of total war which was to emerge in the writings of Hobbes. In societies of brute animals, devoid of reason, Grotius observed, 'we see a natural bias of self-love. For they hurt others to benefit themselves; because they do not know the evil of doing wilful hurt.'[41] But, he went on, 'it is not so with man, who, possessing the knowledge of good and evil, refrains, even with inconvenience to himself, from doing hurt.' Many modern commentators have challenged the assumptions upon which the Hobbesian state of nature rests precisely because it places uncivilised man on more or less the same intellectual footing as brute beasts; this (it is said) generates a paradox because such men must nevertheless, on Hobbes's theory, possess the linguistic resources and harmony in moral out-

[40] *DIBP* II.2.ii.88.
[41] *DIBP* I.1.xi.23.

looks to enable negotiation of the social contract which allows them exit from the state of nature.

But disagreement about the nature of pre-social man is not the only relevant difference between the Grotian and Hobbesian states of nature. Whereas Grotius treats the development of private property as absolutely central to the development of social order, Hobbes is often portrayed as saying nothing very interesting on the subject. The Hobbesian natural state, in contrast to Grotius, is one of negative liberty in which 'every man has a right to every thing, even to one another's body.'[42] Thus, in the state of nature,

> there be no propriety, no dominion, no *mine* and *thine* distinct; but only that to be every man's that he can get; and for so long, as he can keep it.[43]

A state of negative liberty, then, allows (on the face of it) essentially unrestrained consumption in a way that Grotian positive community does not: uncivilised man and brute beasts compete on the same level for scarce resources; there are in principle no substantive limits to (because there are no rules to limit) the freedom of men and beasts to consume those resources. Distribution is thus completely determined by strength: hypothetically, if one man or group were to acquire everything, no principle of justice or right would stand in the way of his consumption. *Positive* community, on the other hand, emphasises the right of all human beings to participate in the earth's natural resources. As such man's natural *positive* liberty is bounded by the network of participatory rights established by the terms of the original divine grant. The intimate linkage between rights and justice thus places substantive constraints upon man's pursuit of his appropriative and distributive goals.

In addition, however, the assumption of a positive original community presupposes substantive limitations upon consumption which were not foreseen by Grotius or his contemporaries. It is no part of Grotius's thought that animals have rights (Grotius, as we have seen, denied just this); but it is an unconscious assumption of the theory that exercises of the use-right do not threaten to deplete the earth's natural resources beyond a basic level of sustainability for *both* humans *and* animals: if animals form a part of man's common patrimony, not only in the first stages of human evolution but also for future, as yet unborn, generations, then the norm of equality indicates a duty to ensure natural resources are sufficiently plentiful, and habitats adequately protected, so that animals have enough for their needs (whether or not enjoyed as of *right*). In fact, a kind of husbandry ethic is (consciously or otherwise) a quite natural corollary, in Grotius's theory, of the gradual increase in socialisation and technology which characterises human evolution. As social groups become settled in one place, and men no longer wander about nomadically as resources are exhausted in a particular area, the need arises for techniques of environmental management which can

---

[42] Hobbes, *Leviathan* I.14.190 (Page references are, unless otherwise stated, to the Harmondsworth edition, compiled by CB Macpherson 1968).
[43] *Leviathan* I.13.188.

secure sustainable resources over a long period of time. At the same time, the division and organisation of labour which this stable social contact makes possible leads to the development of increasingly sophisticated techniques of farming, agriculture and pasturage. The emergence of social order therefore brings with it a move from basic plunderings of natural resources to a need and desire for cultivation and environmental maintenance.

Despite first appearances, a state of negative original community also has associated with it natural limitations upon the ability of human beings to exploit the natural world. Physical necessity supplies one natural bound upon freedom: though *in principle* one man could assert title to everything, to the exclusion of all others, real-world conditions would effectively preclude any such assertion from being taken seriously. All human beings are limited in their strength, their ability to anticipate the actions of others and to remain alert at all times. Thus the 'right of every man to every thing' is inevitably dictated by what 'he can get; and [how] long . . . he can keep it.' Our ability to acquire property (land, etc) in the state of nature is thus dependent (as Locke would later point out) upon our ability to exercise effective *control* over it. This observation in fact points to a partial revival, in the writings of Hobbes and his successors, of the medieval idea that the ability to bring items within the domain of one's subjective *iura* depends upon the exercise of *dominium*. In taking this line, Hobbes further developed a train of thought which was present in embryonic form in the writings of Grotius: that the extent of one's claim-rights is fixed primarily by reference to human will and action, rather than by reference to the positive prescription of a legislator-deity.

More important, however, is the presence of substantive *moral* restrictions upon negative liberty. The Hobbesian characterisation of the state of nature as a brutal forum of unconstrained freedom upon which conventional standards eventually encroach has obscured the sense in which, and the degree to which, that freedom is structured by substantive moral principles. Initially it seems as if Hobbes's conception of natural rights excludes the possibility of reliable moral assessments of an individual's conduct. For Hobbes cleaves to an extreme notion of subjective right, as defining a realm *outside* that of law:

> The Right of Nature, which writers commonly call *Ius Naturale*, is the liberty each man hath, to use his own power, as he will himself, for the preservation of his own Nature . . . For though they that speak of this subject use to confound *Ius* and *Lex*, *Right* and *Law*; yet they ought to be distinguished; because *right* consisteth in the liberty to do, or to forbear; Whereas *law* determineth, and bindeth to one of them: so that Law and Right differ as much as Obligation and Liberty; which in one and the same matter are inconsistent.[44]

Hobbes seems, in this, to have cast off the last vestiges of the Roman law sense of 'right' as synonymous with 'law' and 'justice.' Men's natural rights consist merely in their freedom to act in the absence of any constraining rules or oblig-

---

[44] *Leviathan* I.14.189.

ations in the state of nature. Rights are not the outcome of divinely promulgated laws but simply reflect the natural conditions in which pre-social man finds himself: as beings we are, Hobbes observes, essentially equal in our intellectual and physical capacities. Though there are natural variations in intelligence and physical strength, 'the difference between man and man is not so considerable, as that one man can thereupon claim to himself any benefit, to which another may not pretend as well as he.'[45] That is, in the state of nature, *your* ability to hurt *me* is roughly on a par with *my* ability to hurt *you*. This equality of ability provokes a natural enmity between men who realise their roughly equivalent natures entail equality of hopes in attaining their ends. Because of the relative scarcity of resources in relation to infinite wants,

> Hereby it is manifest, that during the time men live without a common power to keep them all in awe, they are in that condition which is called War; and such a war as is of every man against every man.[46]

Though Hobbes draws a firm distinction between *law* and *right*, he retains the traditional assumption of synonymy between law and *justice*;[47] in consequence, as long as the state of negative liberty subsists, 'nothing can be unjust. The notions of right and wrong, justice and injustice have no place. Where there is no common power, there is no law; where no law, no injustice.'[48] In the absence of law, in other words, the domain of natural liberty is all-pervading, with the result that there are (apparently) no restrictions, except those imposed by human physical characteristics, upon our freedom to exploit and appropriate the earth and its resources.

Despite the distinctly un-Grotian language of Hobbes's portrayal of natural rights, the extent to which moral considerations encroach on original freedom even at the earliest stages of human existence, is rather surprising. That this has not generally been noticed by Hobbes's commentators is the result of some basic misunderstandings about this aspect of Hobbesian natural law. Although accompanied by a much more subjective psychological theory,[49] the right of nature is yet rooted in the *suum* insofar as it is a right of self-preservation. The lack of imposed limitations on *what* may be used in one's endeavour to survive in such hostile conditions does not imply the total absence of limitations upon the *amount* one may consume. The right of nature thus cannot be conceived as

---

[45] *Ibid* I.13.183.

[46] *Ibid* I.13.185.

[47] He was, however, to employ this equivalence in a radically new way, as supplying the grounds of legitimacy for more-or-less any conventional pronouncement an earthly legislator might make.

[48] *Leviathan* I.13.188.

[49] In a famous passage, Hobbes states that 'whatsoever is the object of any mans appetite or desire; that is it, which he for his part calleth Good: And the object of his hate, and aversion, Evil; And of his contempt, Vile and Inconsiderable. For these words of Good, Evil, and Contemptible, are ever used with relation to the person that useth them: There being nothing simply and absolutely so; nor any common rule of good and evil, to be taken from the nature of the objects themselves; but from the Person of the man [in the state of nature] . . .' *Leviathan* I.6.120. (The core of Hobbes's psychological theory is located between pp 85–130 of the Macpherson text, above n 7)

a perfectly general liberty to appropriate, consume or lay waste to whatever comes one's way. Furthermore, the supervenience of natural laws upon the realm of natural liberty is an *immediate* consequence of possession of the right (whether or not prudentially rational agents are able to spot it):

> And therefore, as long as this natural right of every man to every thing endureth, there can be no security to any man (how strong or wise soever he be) of living out the time which Nature ordinarily alloweth men to live. And consequently it is a precept, or general rule of reason, *That every man ought to endeavour peace, as far as he has hope of obtaining it; and when he cannot obtain it, that he may seek, and use, all helps and advantages of war.*[50]

The first limb of this rule, Hobbes terms the 'Fundamental Law of Nature;' the second encapsulates the right of nature. It follows that Hobbes conceived of the right of nature as everywhere hemmed in by the fundamental law: resort to the right of nature is justified only where attempts to establish peaceful relations have failed, or are likely to fail. As many of Hobbes's modern commentators have pointed out, the 'fundamental' law is not so in the sense of being *basic* in Hobbesian thought; the general consensus among Hobbes scholars is that the grounding rule of Hobbesian natural law, from which all other rules derive, is in fact the Third Law: '*That men perform their covenants made.*'[51] This rule, it is said, enjoys conceptual priority because it forms the moral basis of the mutual renunciation of right men enter into in pursuance of the fundamental law. Prudentially rational agents realise that clinging to their natural liberty means existing in conditions of perpetual hardship, danger and misery. Thus to act in accordance with the injunction to seek peace,

> a man [must] be willing, when others are so too, as far-forth, as for peace and defence of himself he shall think it necessary, to lay down his right to all things; and be contented with so much liberty as he would allow other men against himself.[52]

The embryonic social contract thus established would, if indeed grounded by the third law, point to a conclusion which many political theorists have readily accepted: that Hobbesian natural laws are in fact no more than prudential maxims otherwise devoid of substantive moral significance. Such writers can appeal, in support of their views, to the many passages in *Leviathan* in which Hobbes emphasised the rootedness of natural laws in rational self-interest. 'These dictates of reason,' Hobbes averred,

> men use to call by the name of laws; but improperly: for they are but conclusions, or theorems concerning what conduceth to the conservation and defence of themselves; whereas law, properly is the word of him, that by right hath command over others.[53]

---

[50] *Leviathan* I.14.190. Emphasis in original.

[51] *Ibid* I.15.201. For an instance of this view see M Kramer, above n 7 ch 2. Of course, the third law may well be seen as grounding legal obligations in civil society.

[52] *Leviathan* I.14.190. Original emphasis removed.

[53] *Ibid* I.15.216–17. Elsewhere, Hobbes states that '. . . Keeping of covenant is a rule of reason, by which we are forbidden to do any thing destructive to our life; and consequently a law of

If such a reading were correct, the laws of nature, as a body of rational principles, would have become effectively detached from their traditional moorings in the divine will (a process begun in the writings of Grotius) and rooted instead in mankind's continuing interest in establishing stable and commodious living conditions. While Grotius had emphasised the rootedness of natural law in human nature, he had been careful to show how diversity in the possible forms of social arrangements which could be considered in accord with God's plan did not amount to anything like *boundless* diversity. But if the content of natural law is entirely derived from the conditions upon which men in a state of nature are willing to give up their natural liberty, then the variety of civil laws compatible with the law of nature is in principle limitless.[54] Though certainly representing a further move towards it, Hobbes's writings do not embody a modern theory of subjective rights as interpersonal entitlements. The connection of natural laws with prudence is a feature of their *psychological* necessity for human beings in the state of nature; but as Hobbes pointed out, human desire alone is incapable of supplying coherent guidance for action without the structuring properties of reason: the possibility of exit from the hostile conditions of the state of nature therefore consists 'partly in the passions, partly in [the] reason:'

> The *passions* that incline men to peace are fear of death; desire of such things as are necessary to commodious living; and a hope by their industry to obtain them. And *reason* suggesteth convenient Articles of peace, upon which men may be drawn to agreement. These Articles are they which otherwise are called the Laws of Nature . . .[55]

If the laws of nature were mere outgrowths of prudence, the rule that men should perform their covenants would itself need interpreting purely instrumentally. But Hobbes in fact supplies an alternative moral basis for it in the course of his initial discussion of why men should consider themselves *obliged* to abandon their natural liberty wherever possible: 'This is that law of the Gospel; *Whatsoever you require that others should do to you, that ye do to them.*'[56] Thus, while the laws of nature fully accord with long-term self-interest, it is a rational dictate that men in the state of nature pursue that interest in the way prescribed by those laws. It is true that Hobbes stressed the conventional nature of law to a considerably greater degree than his contemporaries (with the possible exception of Selden); but it would be an oversimplification to read into Hobbes's position a belief in the straightforward supervenience of civil laws of arbitrary content on an otherwise lawless void. The Hobbesian state of nature is thus a state of total freedom only in a notional sense: negative liberty is hemmed in by physical and rational necessity, and as

nature.' (I.15.205); also, 'It is not wisdom, but authority, that makes a law.' *Dialogue Between a Philosopher and a Student of the Common Laws of England* (William Crooke, 1681) 7.

[54] In fact Selden, by whose work Hobbes had certainly been influenced, adopted essentially this position: see Tuck, above n 2 p 62.

[55] Both quotations: *Leviathan* I.13.188. Emphasis added.

[56] *Ibid* I.14.190. Emphasis in original.

pre-civilised men probe and uncover the implications of their unhappy situation the perceived domain of natural liberty will shrink away while the laws of nature gradually come into focus.[57]

If the foregoing argument is correct, Hobbes's writings in *Leviathan* represent a much more limited departure from Grotius's work on natural rights than is generally supposed. Both writers locate the original right to use the earth's resources in the *suum*. But while Grotius saw that right as one ordained by divine grant, and subsequently extended and developed through the positive laws of a civil jurisdiction, Hobbes regarded the right as the area left over to an individual's free will by rational precepts which encroach upon it by laying down (prudential and moral) obligations. Whilst the emergence of private property in Grotian thought is essentially an *amplification* of original natural rights, the same phenomenon in Hobbes's account embodies a set of *restrictions* on man's initial freedom. Thus, whereas the conventional standards which introduce property must, according to Grotius, follow through the implications of the original grant (by, for example, restraining individual owners from committing waste), Hobbesian civil laws are in principle subject to no substantive limitations save those which encroach directly upon the *suum*. But because Hobbesian natural laws represent a rational, as well as prudential, obligation for pre-social men, the rigid distinction Hobbes draws between the realm of right and the realm of law is threatened with implausibility so long as men remain in the state of nature. The seemingly negative use-right characteristic of the Hobbesian state of nature is thus tantamount to a Grotian *ius* with its objective relationship to justice removed and its subjective component strongly emphasised. The main difference between the Grotian and Hobbesian accounts lies therefore in the much greater freedom given to the Hobbesian sovereign to determine the nature and extent of private property according to the *civil* laws.

In emphasising the brutal conditions of the state of nature, Hobbes was following a tradition of analysis which pre-dated Grotius, and which would enjoy further revival in the work of Pufendorf. Hobbes's celebrated lament on the harsh conditions which precede the institution of civil order emphasises, like Grotius, the relationship between the establishment of harmonious relations, technological progress and commodious living:

> In such condition, there is no place for industry; because the fruit thereof is uncertain: and consequently no culture of the earth; no navigation, nor use of commodities that might be imported by sea; no commodious building; no instruments of moving and removing such things as require much force; no knowledge of the face of the Earth; no account of time; no arts; no letters; no society; and which is worst of all, continual

---

[57] There are notorious difficulties associated with Hobbes's juxtaposition of an initially formless social void with the assumption that denizens of that world are in possession of the conceptual and rational means for developing and articulating the law-like propositions which could lead to the establishment of social bonds: in particular the existence of such bonds seems to be a necessary condition for the emergence of exactly the moral discoveries Hobbes sees as pivotal in bringing those relationships about. See (eg) Kramer above n 7 ch 2.

fear, and danger of violent death; And the life of man, solitary, poor, nasty, brutish and short.[58]

But whereas Grotius considered man's need for *culture* as determining the eventual shape of his social arrangements (including property), Hobbes regarded the institution of civil order as the achievement of men who realise their overwhelming desire for *peace*. It follows that the form civil society takes, and the substance of its positive laws, are relatively unimportant in comparison with the establishment of a prior consensus (or social contract) to accede, at least in one's outward speech and behaviour, to whatever the sovereign enacts as law. Hobbes's positivism was a response to the increasing implausibility of the assumption, retained in Grotian thought, that the laws of a community represent the articulation of its amassed wisdom and shared conceptions of the good. Hobbesian civil laws *impose*, rather than embody, shared values around which *individuals* with distinctive and competing outlooks and needs can cluster, and thus coexist in peace. The emphasis on authority, and on law's role as the mainstay of social order in a divided world, of course depends upon the very harmony in moral outlooks and interpretative practices which legal rules (on Hobbes's account) seek to impose: I may have a strong objection to a law which prevents owners of toxic materials from discharging them into the atmosphere, because I champion a moral position which allows owners the freedom to do whatever they like with their property; but if I believe that my assertion of this right could lead to violence or anarchy then I may simply accede to (what I believe to be) an unjust law. Even if I felt that I might prevail through violence on this issue, I might consider that the quite general application of the maxim 'might makes right' would lead to my defeat on issues I cared more about (abortion say).[59] Thus what seems to matter for the rule of law is *not* law's ability to impose concrete standards upon individuals whose moral outlooks utterly conflict, but that the law, taken as a whole, embodies and articulates a moral standpoint with which those individuals are *broadly* comfortable. This basic paradox in Hobbesian thought would later prompt the development, at the hands of Bentham and Austin, of a general distinction between distinctively *legal* standards and the moral values which may or may not underpin them.

Natural rights to property had become, in Hobbes's writings, an aspect of men's subjective *iura* in a hostile state of nature. But these natural rights did not pull Hobbes all the way towards a notion of rights as merely interpersonal claims: this is partly, as we have seen, because Hobbesian natural (and, arguably, civil) rights retain indirect links to the idea of objective *ius* insofar as protection of one's *suum* forms a *rational* as well as prudential imperative; but it is also the result of Hobbes's insistence that an individual's rights delineate the sphere of her (extra-legal) *liberty*. Taken together, these two strands of thought in Hobbes fall short of a resurrection of the Grotian theory of objective *ius* in

---

[58] *Leviathan* I.13.186.
[59] Thanks are due to Dylan Griffiths for suggesting this point.

property, but they do emphasise the much more limited character of Hobbes's departure from the original Grotian theory. It was, ironically, in the writings of the man who, in many people's eyes, tried to rescue the original form of the Grotian theory from its more radical Hobbesian variant, that we find a genuinely modern conception of rights as interpersonal claims with no particular relationship to justice. In his seminal work, *De Iure Naturae et Gentium*,[60] and the shorter *De Officio Hominis et Civis*,[61] Samuel Pufendorf developed a notion of natural rights fundamentally unlike that of either Hobbes or Grotius. Like Grotius, Pufendorf regarded the content of natural law as wedded to the current state of human development. 'Sociality' is the foundation of natural law; thus:

> In this our present state there are a large number of affirmative precepts which seem to have had no place in the primeval state. This is partly because they presuppose institutions which (for all that we know) did not exist in mankind's condition of felicity . . .'[62]

For example:

> . . . we now have among the precepts of natural law: do not deceive anyone in buying and selling; do not use a false length, weight or measure; return borrowed money at the agreed time. But we have not yet clearly resolved the question whether, if the human race had continued without sin, we would practice the kind of commerce that we now practise, and whether there would have been any use for money.[63]

But whereas Grotius had simply assumed the validity of an anthropocentric interpretation of natural law (as embodying a principle of sociality), Pufendorf attempted to show that, if natural law consists of precepts and obligations which bear essentially no relation to human life and action, then our ability to discover, through reason and judgement, what natural law demands of us is taken away. For:

> It has been given to man to become acquainted with the diverse multiplicity of objects that he meets in this world, to compare them, and to form new notions about them. But he has also the ability to envisage his future actions, to set himself to achieve them, to fashion them to a specific norm and purpose, and to deduce the consequences; and he can tell whether past actions conform to the rule.[64]

This is not only an early anticipation of a theory of rule-following behaviour; it also demonstrates the possession by all sound-minded human beings of

---

[60] S Pufendorf, Jean Barbeyrac (ed), B Kennet (tr), *The Law of Nature and of Nations* (London, 1749, (originally published in 1672)); hereinafter cited as LNN. Pufendorf's earlier work, the *Elementorum Jurisprudentiae Universalis* [1660] (Cantabrigiae: Ex officina Joann.Hayes. . .impensis, Joann.Creed. . ., 1672), had been an attempt to resurrect a fundamentally Grotian theory of natural rights.

[61] S Pufendorf, J Tully (ed), M Silverthorne (tr), *On the Duty of Man and Citizen According to Natural Law* (Cambridge, CUP, 1991, (originally published in 1673)), hereinafter cited as DMC.

[62] DMC 12. See also I.3.1.33.

[63] *Ibid.*

[64] DMC I.1.1.17.

sufficient understanding of human nature and of the conditions of the external world in which we live to judge which actions are in accord with general precepts which make for a good and peaceful social life. Although (like Hobbes) Pufendorf regarded human understanding as deeply fallible, he thought (unlike Hobbes) that errors of reason, whether caused by faulty chains of reasoning or by badly selected premises, mostly relate to particular matters and 'rarely [to] general precepts for living.'[65] The most fundamental of these (the 'fundamental natural law') is the requirement that every man must do as much as he can to cultivate and preserve sociality. Indeed, the 'laws which teach one how to conduct oneself to become a useful member of human society, are called natural laws.'[66] This is, on the face of it, a stricter requirement than contemplated by Grotius or Hobbes, for whom sociality is simply the most natural and effective means by which rational individuals can protect and extend the *suum*; but Pufendorf's fundamental law is in fact an outgrowth of man's natural obligation to protect the *suum*:

> Self-love is implanted deep in man; it compels him to have a careful concern for himself and to get all the good he can in every way. In view of this it seems superfluous to invent an obligation of self-love. Yet from another point of view a man surely does have certain obligations to himself. For a man is not born for himself alone; the end for which he has been endowed by his Creator with such excellent gifts is that he may celebrate His glory and be a fit member of human society. He is therefore bound so to conduct himself as not to permit the Creator's gifts to perish for lack of use, and to contribute what he can to human society.[67]

Men thus have a *positive* duty to 'be useful to others insofar as he conveniently can,' which extends beyond the mere injunction against committing waste: rather '[w]e must also give, or at least share, such things as will encourage mutual goodwill.[68] Those who, through indolence, contribute nothing to the development of social life are 'mere numbers born to consume the fruits of the earth' and therefore 'useless burdens on the earth.'[69] Rights to acquire property are thus, on some basic level, tied to *responsibilities* to act for the good of society as part of the divine plan. But from whence do such property rights spring? Pufendorf observed that 'It is the condition of the human body that it needs to take in its sustenance from without, and to protect itself from anything that would destroy its integrity. . .' Hence,

> We may . . . safely infer that it is clearly the will of the supreme governor of the world that man may use other creatures for his own benefit, and that he may in fact in many cases kill them.[70]

---

[65] *Ibid* I.1.7.18. Also unlike Hobbes, Pufendorf thought that reason could, and generally does, 'rise superior' to the passions which afflict men's minds: I.1.14.21.

[66] *Ibid* I.3.8.35.

[67] *Ibid* I.5.1.46.

[68] *Ibid* I.8.1.64.

[69] *Ibid* I.8.2.64.

[70] *Ibid* I.12.1.84.

Though Pufendorf does not draw the inference, it is presumably the divine legislator's will that *all* forms of life depend upon the consumption of others in this way, insofar as this is an inevitable prerequisite for their continuing existence. However, human consumption is in any event presumably a special case, not only because of man's dominant position in the food-chain, but because it is a necessary prerequisite of his ability to carry out the fundamental law of nature (to contribute to human society and refrain from allowing the Creator's gifts to perish unused).

The distinction is an important one: human consumption of the earth's resources is a consequence of a prior obligation and *not*, in Pufendorf's terms, a *right*. For a 'right', Pufendorf states, is 'the moral quality by which we *legally* either command persons, or possess things, or by virtue of which something is owed us.'[71] It follows that, in the state of nature, there can be no rights but merely 'potential rights' or 'indefinite rights' which blossom into proper rights through mutual consent: natural man lives in a state without a common power to keep everyone in line; thus there is no property but merely the potential for its development.[72] The natural state of man is thus characterised as one of negative liberty out of which conventional rights emerge:

> But in the beginning all these things are thought to have been made available by God to all men indifferently, so that they did not belong to one man more than to another. The proviso was that men should make such arrangements about them as seemed to be required by the condition of the human race and by the need to preserve peace, tranquillity and good order. Hence while there were as yet few men in the world, it was understood that whatever a man had laid hold upon with the intention of making use of it for himself should be his and no one should take it from him, but the actual bodies which produced those things should remain available to all without relation to anyone in particular. In the course of time however, men multiplied and began to cultivate things which produce food and clothing. To avoid conflicts and to institute good order at this stage, they took the step of dividing the actual bodies of things amongst themselves, and each was assigned his proper portion; a convention was also made that what had been left available to all by this first division of things should henceforth be his who first claimed it for himself. In this way, property in things [*proprietas rerum*] or ownership [*dominium*] was introduced by the will of God, with consent among men right from the beginning and with at least a tacit agreement.[73]

Despite the superficially Grotian language of this important passage, several key differences had emerged between Pufendorf and the natural rights tradition. The first was Pufendorf's insistence that rights are the product of *agreement*; while Grotius too stressed the conventional nature of private property rights, this was (as we saw) a relatively weak condition insofar as human convention merely *recognised* and *extended* a pre-existing right, rather than actually *constituting* it. A second difference lay in the recognition of property rights, not as

71 LNN I.1.20. Emphasis added.
72 *Ibid* IV.4.3.
73 DMC I.12.2.84–85.

the natural development of mankind's desire for culture (as it had been for Grotius), but a consequence of man's *duty* to seek and establish civil society. Grotian property rights were limited by what could count as a *natural* extension of the *suum*; Pufendorf by contrast limited property rights to that which is necessary to establish harmonious and stable social interaction: 'Things,' he observed, 'were not made property once and for all on one occasion, but successively and as the needs of mankind seemed to require.'[74] Thus 'It would be both inappropriate and unnecessary to set about dividing things' (such as flowing water or remote areas of ocean) 'which, however useful to men, are never consumed, so that they are open for all to use without prejudice to any one person's use of them.'[75] Substantive limitations are set upon man's ability to establish conventional rights to private property by the need to demonstrate a link between acquisition of unowned commons and the requirements of good social order. A third and vitally important difference was Pufendorf's characterisation of full, civic rights within the bounds inside which human convention could operate. This central contribution to the theory of rights emerged from Pufendorf's account of the conditions of the state of nature *before* such rights emerge.

Pufendorf's characterisation of the state of nature was both a profound departure from Grotius *and* an attack on Hobbes. The attack on Hobbes centred on the latter's assertion that the realm of right lies fundamentally outside that of law; whereas, as we have just seen, Pufendorf contended that rights fully emerge only *within* a system of law. If that is true, then the conditions of negative liberty within the state of nature cannot amount to conditions of natural *right*. Rights, in other words, remain separate and distinct from mere *liberties*:

> [I]t is necessary to observe, that not every natural licence, or power of doing a thing, is properly a *right*; but only such as includes some moral effect, with regard to others who are partners with me in the same nature. Thus, for instance, in the old fable, the Horse and the Stag had both of them a natural power or privilege of feeding in the meadow; but neither of them had a *right*, which might restrain or take off the natural power in the other. So man, when he employs, in his designs and services, insensible or irrational beings, barely exercises his natural power if, without regard to other men, we here precisely consider it in reference to the things or animals which he uses. But then, at length, it turns into a proper right when it creates this moral effect in other persons, *that they shall not hinder him in the free use of these conveniences, and shall themselves forbear to use them without his consent.* For 'tis ridiculous trifling to call that power a *right* which, should we attempt to exercise, all other men have an *equal right* to obstruct or prevent us . . . because all men being *naturally* equal, one cannot fairly exclude the rest from possessing any such advantage, unless by their consent, either express or presumptive, he has obtained the particular and sole disposal or enjoyment of it. And when this is once done, he may then truly say he has a *right* to such a thing.[76]

[74] *Ibid* I.12.4.85.
[75] *Ibid*.
[76] LNN III.5.3. Some emphasis added

A 'right' had thus become identical with the set of claims one has over another individual, either excluding that individual from some benefit or requiring that they render one assistance in securing some benefit. This, as Richard Tuck has observed, 'was of course tantamount to the repudiation of the whole history of rights as *dominia*, as active rights expressing their possessor's sovereignty over his world.'[77] At the same time, Pufendorf's departure from Grotius had led him to emphasise the gulf between man's natural and civil states: gone was the Grotian assumption of positive laws encroaching only where needed to structure increasingly complex human relations. For Pufendorf, emergence from the state of nature into civil society was an escape from barbaric and hostile natural world in which man's genteel nature could find nothing but torment, into conditions of sociality which foster and cultivate that nature:

> we may consider the natural state of man, by imaginative effort, as the condition man would have been in if he had been left to himself alone, without any support from other men, given the condition of human nature as we now perceive it. It would have been, it seems, more miserable than that of any beast, if we reflect on the great weakness of man as he comes into this world, when he would straightaway die without help from others, and on the primitive life he would lead if he had no other resources than he owes to his strength and intelligence.[78]

The complete freedom from law and subjection enjoyed by natural man may seem attractive and full of promise, but, Pufendorf warns, 'it is attended with a multitude of disadvantages':

> For if you picture to yourself a person (even an adult) left alone in this world without any of the aids and conveniences by which human ingenuity has relieved and enriched our lives, you will see a naked dumb animal, without resources, seeking to satisfy his hunger with roots and grasses and his thirst with whatever water he can find, to shelter himself from the inclemencies of the weather in caves, at the mercy of wild beasts, fearful of every chance encounter . . . To put the matter in a few words, in the state of nature each is protected only by his own strength; in the state by the strength of all. There no one may be sure of the fruit of his industry; here all may be. There is the reign of the passions, there is war, fear, poverty, nastiness, solitude, barbarity, ignorance, savagery; here is the reign of reason, here there is peace, security, wealth, splendour, society, taste, knowledge, benevolence.[79]

This striking passage, with its image of refined, urban man thrown into the hostile, uncivilised jungle, sets humankind (at least in its social phase) fundamentally apart from the rest of Creation in a way that is essentially divorced from the account of conditions of (relative) natural bounty depicted by Grotius. Laws (including property arrangements) represent a retreat from the untamed

---

[77] *Natural Rights Theories* above n 2,160. But see T Mautner, 'Pufendorf and the Correlativity Theory of Rights' in S Lindstrom and W Rabinowicz (eds), *In So Many Words: Philosophical Essays for Sven Danielson* (Philosophy Dept, Uppsala 1989) 37–59.

[78] DMC II.1.4.115.

[79] *Ibid* II.1.9.117–18.

world into the manufactured realm of civil society. Such an image, of course, trades on the assumption of natural man's possession of essentially modern manners and outlook; but in fact Pufendorf was merely articulating a view of mankind's relationship with nature that had been a central feature of Italian Renaissance humanism, which had emphasised 'the contrast between civilisation, for which (it was believed) a city was essential, and the rude and barbaric life of a pre-civilised people.'[80] The terms on which men emerge from the state of nature thus impose no particular form on social order, but merely lay down some natural boundaries within which human convention must move. Law had thus become the distinctive intellectual product of civil society, part of whose function was to lay down and determine the relative extents of individuals' rights and duties towards one another. Private property rights remained a natural outgrowth of mankind's emergence from the state of nature (and thus part of God's plan); but the analytical emphasis was now upon the interpersonal relationships of right and duty established under the civil law, rather than upon the extent of man's ability to assert *dominium* over aspects of his natural environment.

LOCKEAN RIGHTS AND PRIVATE PROPERTY

The foregoing developments chart the rise of two separate though fundamentally related ideas in late seventeenth century thought, both of which could claim to be rooted in the original Grotian theory of property. The offspring of the eventual marriage between Hobbesian positivism and Pufendorf's subjective rights would be a theory of interlocking private property rights, the extent of which are determined by the purely political concerns of a given society. Restrictions on ownership in the name of the common good would be seen as *conflicting* with individual rights to property. The tension between objective and subjective *ius* was, of course, known to the seventeenth century writers on natural rights, but mainly as it related to the issue of sovereignty: how can people simultaneously possess rights (and thereby claim to be free) yet remain subject to a monarchical authority who seemingly has the power to limit or remove those rights? The response of the natural rights tradition was that, while civic rights are for the sovereign to determine, an individual's fundamental rights derive, at some basic level, from mankind's place in Creation. Man's centrality in Creation was founded upon an inference from certain basic truths

---

[80] Tuck, above n 2, 33. Tuck cites a passage in Cicero's *De Inventione* as the locus classicus for this picture of man's natural existence. More recently, Peter Harrison has argued that 'The story of Adam's fall from grace . . . enabled seventeenth-century thinkers to link the mastery of the passions to the scientific enterprise and the quest for dominion over nature. Control of the passions thus became, for the seventeenth-century, a means of achieving control over the natural world'; P Harrison, 'Reading the Passions: the Fall, the Passions and Dominion over Nature' in S Gaukroger (ed) *The Soft Underbelly of Reason: the Passions in the Seventeenth Century* (London, Routledge, 1997) 49. The implication that thinkers consciously linked these projects is, perhaps, misleading.

about human beings (vulnerability, the need for sustenance, physical capacities etc) and biblical texts which are themselves anthropological attempts to make sense of the place of human beings in the world. This kind of reasoning would later be challenged by Hume. But the failure of the seventeenth century writers to spot the negative environmental implications of their theories is in part a product of the state of social and technological development at the time at which they wrote. Technology was seen by ancient cultures as a means to come to know and understand the world, through the study of mathematics and astronomy; by the seventeenth century, man's interests in pursuing society and technology were perceived as coinciding with the preservation and cultivation of the natural world. The point at which human needs, and the means of achieving them, develop in ways destructive to the natural environment was simply not considered.

The most striking aspect of Locke's *Two Treatises* on the reader is its modernity and significance for the troubles and dilemmas of present-day living. Famously, Locke was far more explicitly concerned than were his predecessors with questions of spoilage and limits to accumulation. He displayed, in general, a much greater sensitivity to the central questions of the theory of property which had been developing in the hands of quite diverse theorists since Grotius. His own remark on the *Two Treatises* ('Property I have nowhere found more clearly explained than in a book entitled, Two Treatises of Government'), is therefore probably accurate as an assessment of the book's objective standing at the beginning of the eighteenth century.[81]

Yet in many ways, Locke's theory was more firmly rooted in classical common law assumptions than were those of Grotius or Pufendorf, and less challenging of them. The emphasis on possession as a significant ground of property is one example: the common lawyers of the sixteenth century had first stumbled upon the importance of possession to political theory as part of their project of reinterpreting Roman law in terms of Roman society. The debate concerning the connection between *dominium* and *ius* had begun to reveal hitherto unplumbed depths of significance in the concept of the *suum* for the central arguments of late medieval political theory, especially those concerning the relationship between the individual and the state. Locke's contribution to this debate was to show how possession, which characterises the natural form of self-ownership in the *suum*, is also a seemingly ineliminable requirement of ownership more generally. In so doing, Locke was effectively articulating the tacit philosophical commitments of the common law's rootedness in empirical forms of reasoning. The common law moves within a conception of justice infused with a strongly historical sense: adjudication is driven by the minute analysis of real-life situations in past cases rather than by what emerges from the

---

[81] J Locke, Letter to Rev Richard King 25 August 1703. Reprinted in Locke, *Works* (London, 1801) vol X 305–9.

'heaven of concepts'.[82] Property, in common law thinking, emerges from sustained possession rather than from abstract assessments of systemic rights. Locke's emphasis was thus ill-disposed towards the distinction between objective and subjective right which had been slowly emerging during the seventeenth century and which had its strongest statement in the writings of Pufendorf. The incongruence of these two positions on property would leave in its wake a considerable problem for common law theory, as the dispenser of justice *and* the guardian of individual rights.[83]

While Locke's theory provided some important philosophical buttressing for the system of agrarian capitalism and the common law rules which protected it, it did so in a way which forced a revision of many of the assumptions on which those established practices were thought to rest. The Exclusion Crisis of 1680 had once again highlighted the deep divisions in English society between those who regarded society as a morally homogenous whole, and those for whom society was made up of morally autonomous individuals, each of whom could be reckoned to be the owners of their persons, attitudes and capacities. The previously little-circulated works of Robert Filmer thrived in this political atmosphere, gaining notoriety in virtue of their support for the Royalist cause through a particular, though largely unoriginal, theory of property and right. Locke's stated aim in the First Treatise is to refute Filmer's polemical contention that the natural state of men is not one of natural freedom, but of subjection to a patriarchal monarch whose authority derives, by direct succession, from Adam's sovereignty, granted by God, over all dominions. Adam's sovereignty is expressed, by Filmer, in terms of *dominion*, not just over the physical world but over life and death, war and peace and so on.[84] Thus, Locke observed, the authority of contemporary monarchs is rooted, on this theory, in a property right which is essentially

> a divine unalterable right of sovereignty, whereby a father or a prince hath an absolute, arbitrary, unlimited, and unlimitable power over the lives, liberties and estates of his children and subjects; so that he may take or alienate their estates, sell, castrate or use their persons as he pleases, they being all his slaves, and he the lord or proprietor of every thing, and his unbounded will their law.[85]

Most of the First Treatise is given over to the dismantling of this view in what is perhaps the most careful and sustained analysis of the Genesis story in the whole natural rights tradition. Locke began by establishing, through textual analysis, that God does not grant Adam private dominion (in Genesis I.28) but only a right in common with all mankind to use the wild creatures and fruits of

[82] K Gray and SF Gray, 'The Idea of Property in Land' in S Bright and J Dewar (eds), *Land Law: Themes and Perspectives* (Oxford, OUP, 1998) 19.
[83] See especially ch 5, below.
[84] R Filmer, 'Patriarcha' in P Laslett, *The Political Works of Sir Robert Filmer* (Oxford, Blackwell, 1949) I.4.
[85] J Locke, P Laslett (ed), *Two Treatises of Government* (Cambridge, CUP, 1988) I.8.148. [Cited as Treatises hereinafter.]

the earth as required for sustenance.[86] This common right is not *property*, but a mere liberty of use which is not exclusive of posterity, 'as [future generations] should successively grow up into need of them, and come to be able to make use of them.'[87] The absence of any natural hierarchy among men led Locke to formulate a fundamental restriction on property rights: God, we know, has not placed any man so at the mercy of another that he may starve him if he so pleases:

> God the Lord and Father of all has given no-one of his children such a property, in his peculiar portion of the things of this world, but that he has given his needy brother a right to the surplus of his goods; so that it cannot be justly denied him, when his pressing want calls for it.[88]

As with Pufendorf, Locke regarded men as bound by a *duty* of charity: no one has a power over the life of another; hence no man may effectively exercise property rights in such a way as to rob another of their existence or liberty by denying them their due in surplusage. In Locke's writings, however, the theoretical basis of the obligation underwent a significant shift. Whereas Pufendorf emphasised the agreed basis of a reciprocal duty of charity to those in extreme need (based on the rationality, in terms of one's long-term self-interest, of submitting to such a rule), for Locke,

> reason plays a more critical role. Natural law's foundation in human nature is for him far less a matter of instincts, and more strongly a matter of reflection on our situation in the universe.[89]

Limitations on the extent of property rights thus derive directly from natural law, and need not be mediated by any agreements forged in the light of self-interest. Like his forebears, Locke considered political power as a function of men's natural rights; but, unlike most seventeenth century writers, he did not regard the form of social arrangements as the product of compacts made between prudentially rational individuals who understand the significance of those rights for achieving the goal of a commodious life. For Locke, natural rights are determined by the logical structure of the state of nature as governed by natural law:

> To understand political power right, and derive it from its original, we must consider what state men are naturally in, and that is the state of perfect freedom to order their actions, and dispose of their possessions and persons as they see fit, within the bounds of the law of nature, without asking leave or depending on the will of any other men.[90]

---

[86] J Locke, Treatises I.24.158. Locke's argument is that the wording of the Genesis passage is revealing only of a particular relationship between human beings and the lower animals, not of any ordering among human beings themselves.
[87] *Ibid* I.39.168.
[88] *Ibid* I.42.170.
[89] Buckle, above n 4 p 143.
[90] Locke, Treatises II.4.269. Emphasis suppressed.

Natural freedom in the Lockean state of nature thus does not betoken unconstrained licence to do what one will, but 'a liberty to follow [one's] own will in
all things where the rule prescribes not.'[91] Locke probably did not have in mind
a *legal* conception of natural liberty, since he went along with Hobbes in supposing the realm of right to define the area in which legal rules are absent;[92] but
his espousal of a form of liberty firmly structured by a network of natural rights
and obligations, themselves derived from natural law, certainly represents a step
towards that notion.

This natural state of liberty is also one of *equality*, 'wherein all power and
jurisdiction is reciprocal' except where God commands otherwise. The Lockean
state of nature is, therefore, one already governed by a network of interpersonal
relationships of right and duty, which Locke perceived as sustaining a much
higher level of affable and successful interpersonal contact than its Hobbesian
or even Grotian counterparts (at least if the passages in which Locke eulogised
the tendency for pre-social men to regard one another with respect, and to
forebear from trespassing upon one another's natural rights, are to be taken as
representative of his reflective position). In fact, a position of original equality
in entitlements cannot of itself guarantee social accord until the substance of
those entitlements is known. Nevertheless, the un-Hobbesian tenor of Locke's
position is evident in the following passage:

> The state of nature has a law of nature to govern it, which obliges every one: and
> Reason, which is that law, teaches all mankind who will but consult it, that being
> all equal and independent, no one ought to harm another in his life, health, liberty or
> possessions.[93]

God's creative act establishes us as His property. Every person has thus a
duty to protect and preserve themselves (as God's property), and a positive
obligation to preserve the rest of mankind insofar as the primary duty of self-
preservation permits. That Locke was dealing with *objective* rights can be seen
in his insistence that we cannot, without injustice, take away 'what tends to the
preservation of the life, the liberty, health, limb or goods of another.' The duty
to preserve mankind is coextensive with the injunction to respect men's *rights*.[94]
Duties are, for Locke, nevertheless logically independent of rights, as is clear
from the fact that the duty of preservation is not a duty merely to other persons:
an individual 'has no liberty to destroy himself, or so much as any creature in his
possession but where some nobler use than its bare preservation calls for it.'[95]
The association of natural law with human self-preservation is thus less direct,
and less total, than in the theories of Grotius or Hobbes. Indeed, Locke explicitly rejected as self-contradictory the Hobbesian belief that the natural law

[91] *Ibid* II.23.284.
[92] J Locke, W Von Leyden (ed), *Essays on the Laws of Nature* (Oxford, Clarendon Press, 1954),
(hereinafter cited as *ELN*), Essay I 111.
[93] *Ibid* II.6.271.
[94] *Ibid* Cf II.7.271: 'all men may be restrained from invading other's rights . . .'.
[95] *Ibid*.

could be simultaneously binding upon human beings *and* traced back, as a whole, to the principle of self-preservation.[96]

Natural law must, of course, be graspable by human minds if it is to represent binding obligations which its addressees are capable of knowing in the absence of direct legislative prescription, in the form of divine revelation; and, indeed, natural rights to property derive, on Locke's account, partly from revealed truth, and partly from general natural law.[97] Locke joined with the mainstream of the tradition in placing the source of human knowledge of the latter in right reason, 'to which everyone who considers himself a human being lays claim.'[98] Natural law, being uniquely addressed to human beings, is uniquely discoverable by them because of the kind of creatures they are. But Locke's talk of 'right reason' disguises a significantly different picture of the kind of knowledge in question:

> By reason, however, I do not think is meant here that faculty of understanding which forms trains of thought and deduces proofs, but certain definite principles of action from which spring all virtues and whatever is necessary for the proper moulding of morals. For that which is correctly derived from these principles is justly said to be in accordance with right reason.[99]

The a priori method had once more come under attack, but in a different way: right reason (that is, knowledge of natural law) does not take the form of logical chains of reasoning based on non-empirical starting-points, nor even of deductions from the natural, if worldly, human condition; rather it draws conclusions from concrete behaviour of particular individuals as they strive to lead the virtuous life. Locke's emphasis on the role of action as a determinant of natural law echoes his strong belief in the necessity of active participation in the constitution of title to property which natural law sanctions. When Adam is turned out of Paradise, it is so that his knowledge, sustenance and well-being will henceforth hinge on his own *actions*. He is commanded 'to till the ground'[100] so that 'In the sweat of thy face shalt thou eat thy bread . . .'[101] The earthly sovereignty which human beings enjoyed prior to the Fall is replaced with servitude: 'God sets [Adam] to work for his living, and seems rather to give him a spade into his hand than a sceptre to rule over its inhabitants.'[102] Locke's intention, admittedly, was to deny Adam's sovereignty over the world's first *human* inhabitants; but it is clear from what Locke says about property in the state of nature that the husbandry ethic implicit in the words of Genesis is one of a participatory and fundamentally active ruler, rather than one of lazily detached majesty.

---

[96] Locke, *ELN*, Essay VI, 181.
[97] Locke, Treatises II.25.285–6.
[98] Locke, *ELN*, Essay I 111.
[99] *Ibid.*
[100] Genesis 3.23.
[101] *Ibid* 3.19.
[102] Locke, Treatises I.45.172.

Like Grotius and Hobbes before him, Locke seems to have believed in the reality of the state of nature as an historical period in human history, at least in the sense that '. . .'tis plain the world never was, nor ever will be, without numbers of men in that state.'[103] Within the state of nature, men remain free and self-determining insofar as the law of nature imposes obligations to act or forebear from acting. In common with the emergent strain of liberalism in the writings of Selden and Hobbes, Locke saw in this natural freedom the basis of all personal capacities and, through them, of property. The very close relationship between the *suum* and the concept of ownership which is a feature of the natural rights theories is elevated by Locke into something approaching an analytic truth: he that 'take[s] away the freedom that belongs to any one in [the state of nature],' Locke wrote, 'must *necessarily* be supposed to have a design to take away everything else, that freedom being the foundation of all the rest . . .'[104] To take away a person's freedom is to rob her of self-determination; the actions of a slave do not, in a sense, 'belong' to the slave but rather to the master who directs him, the benefit of the slave's labour being diverted to his owner. Furthermore, the slave's ability to own property is entirely subject to the consent of the master, and the former's belongings can be removed by the latter at will. The link between labour and ownership which Locke forges here depends upon the running together of two senses of 'labour' which (as shall become clear) Locke repeated in the context of the main theme of his property theory: a philosophical perspective which understands authorship of one's own actions as a kind of ownership of them need not lead to one in which the *products* of that action are also so owned.

Nevertheless, Locke's stance betokens a merging of the two strands of thought on the origin of property rights evident in earlier writers. Grotius and Pufendorf had espoused theories in which property emerges from distinct grounds in the *suum*, on the one hand, and in the need for bodily sustenance, on the other. Though the relationship, if any, between these discrete elements was not made clear by either writer, it *is* clear that there is no logical relationship between self-ownership as a form of property (in oneself) and any claims over the natural abundance which would preserve the life one owns. Locke, in taking one's labour to be both an inevitable extension of the *suum* and the basis for one's claims over external goods in the world, thereby unified these discrete elements into a single theoretical progression.

By emphasising the continuity between property in the *suum* and property in worldly goods, Locke implicitly followed the natural rights tradition in assuming a parallel continuity between human interests and care and cultivation of the environment. Just as the linkage between *suum* and property in the external world is much closer, so the mutually reinforcing relationship between human and environmental values is greatly more intimate. The problem for theorists of

---

[103] *Ibid* II.14.276.
[104] *Ibid* II.17.279.

positive original community had been to explain how, from the supposed fact
of God's grant of the world to mankind in common, we can arrive at the legitimacy of *individual* claims over the earth and its resources:

> God . . . has given the Earth to the children of men, given it to mankind *in common*.
> But this thing being supposed, it seems to some a very great difficulty how any one
> should ever come to have a *property* in any thing.[105]

The Grotian theory had appealed at that point to the self-ownership we enjoy
in our own bodies, and to the need for sustenance, as related though the discrete
ways in which the notion of property arises quite naturally in human affairs.
Through the labour theory, Locke effectively closed the gap between God's
endowment of mankind with a collective right and the titles of individual
members of the human race to acquire worldly goods. Early on in the *Second
Treatise*, Locke had lain out the basic matrix of rights and duties to which men,
even in the state of nature, are naturally subject:

> Every one as he is bound to preserve himself, and not to quit his station wilfully; so by
> the like reason when his own preservation comes not into competition, ought he, as
> much as he can, to preserve the rest of mankind, and may not unless it be to do justice
> on an offender, take away, or impair the life, of what tends to the preservation of the
> life, the liberty, health, limb or goods of another.[106]

This, and like statements, are seen by some as the basis of a much more individualistic approach in Locke to the question of original acquisition: not only
are human beings endowed with a natural *liberty* to preserve themselves, they
are also possessed of rights not to be impeded by others in their quest to survive.
Moreover, this right protects individuals from interruption in their performance
of a religious *duty* to preserve their own lives for God's greater glory. As the
consumption of earthly bounty is a prerequisite for the performance of that
duty, *each man* had a discrete title to use those resources for his sustenance. This
approach indeed emphasises individual *suums* in the context of original takings.
But, just as each individual possesses a right, each individual also owes a duty,
not only to refrain from interfering (in destructive ways) in others' pursuit of
life, but *positively* to sustain them when doing so will not impede one's own
efforts to stay alive. Hence, each individual owed a duty to respect the claims of
others to the use of parts of the world's natural resources which were not
required for their own consumption. In this way, for Locke, the collective entitlement of the God-given grant straightaway ensues in myriad individual rights,
because of the connection of 'external' claims with the *suum* from the beginning
of the argument.

A system of equal rights nevertheless does not, of itself, specify what may be
subjected to appropriation, or the conditions under which takings may be made.
Hobbes had illustrated in graphic terms how individual projects of survival can

---

[105] Locke, Treatises II.25.286. Some emphasis added.
[106] *Ibid* II.6.271.

utterly conflict with one another; thus, one possible picture of equality is of equality in *opportunity* to consume resources based on personal cunning, strength and 'all helps and advantages of war.'[107] Because the Lockean duty of assistance—and even the weaker duty of non-interference—are *conditional* duties, which come into play only where the primary duty to preserve oneself has been, at least for the moment, met, individuals in a world blessed with few resources (or few sustainable resources) would be as likely to find themselves in a Hobbesian war of all against all in which the quest for personal survival demands the attempt to secure and hoard as many resources as possible, to the exclusion of others, or even to dispossess others of bounty they had acquired. Locke, of course, frequently adverted to the plentitude of natural resources in order to show that, at least in the early stages of human existence, there would always be 'enough and as good' left over from individual takings for other human beings to secure what they too required to survive.[108] But (as the Hobbesian example shows) what will count as a legitimate taking (ie what will count as *necessary* for sustaining one's own life), and what will count as leaving 'enough' behind for others, will vary considerably depending upon a range of factors, from the physical characteristics of the world to the psychological traits of human beings and the quality of personal interaction. These questions—of what may be taken, and on what basis—will become especially pressing where individual claims of dominion involve de facto claims over *land* (where, for example, shelter is at stake, or the takings require some form of cultivation of the earth).

The previous attempts to answer these questions had all relied, to some degree, on the notion of human *agreement* in the development of norms of private ownership. Locke's expressed aim, on the other hand, is to show how takings from the original commons can generate private property in men 'without any express pact of all the commoners.'[109] His starting-point is nevertheless familiar: like Grotius, Locke emphasised that the world had been enriched with natural resources for man's sustenance and comfort, to which no individual had a separate and exclusive title, but a common right of use:

> The Earth, and all that is therein, is given to men for the support and comfort of their being. And though all the fruits it naturally produces, and the beasts it feeds, belong to mankind in common, as they are produced by the spontaneous hand of nature; and no body has originally a private dominion, exclusive of the rest of mankind, in any of them, as they are thus in their natural state: yet being given for the use of men, there must of necessity be a means to *appropriate* them some way or other before they can be of any use, or at all beneficial to any particular men.[110]

Despite the absence of private dominion, at least some exercises of the common use-right will (as Grotius had observed) in fact place the consumed

---

[107] Hobbes, *Leviathan* I.14.190.
[108] See eg Locke, Treatises II.33.291.
[109] *Ibid.*
[110] *Ibid* II.26.286.

resources beyond all possibility of use by anyone else. The food which nourishes the wild, uncivilised man 'must be his, and so [much] his, i.e. a part of him, that another can no longer have any right to it, before it can do him any good for the support of his life.'[111] On the back of this proposition, Grotius had charted the emergence of 'de facto' private property: the emergence of the *concept* of private ownership is then a mere recognition of the outcome forced upon us by physical necessity. But for Locke, the *fact* of exclusivity (as a side-effect of resorts to the common use-right) did not successfully explain how such consumption could take place under exclusive *rights*. However, Locke argued, the original, common title vested in mankind excluded the possibility of private dominion in things 'in their *natural* state.' What was required, therefore, for the creation of private property rights, was a means of taking elements of the original bounty out of that state. It was at this point that Locke sought, through the labour theory, to define a connection between the *suum* and external objects which would effectively bring the latter, as *artefacts*, into the realm of 'one's own.'

The world is held in common by all men, Locke observed, 'yet every man has a *property* in his own person. This nobody has any right to but himself.'[112] In tune with earlier versions of the possessive theory, Locke extended the notion of self-ownership which attaches to (and defines) the *suum* to a person's capacities and moral outlooks: just as I am, in some natural sense, proprietor of my own self, so too am I the 'owner' of my actions. The etymology of the word 'property' [*proprietas*, that which is proper] bolstered the perception of a very close relationship between the notions of ownership and authorship. Extensions to the *suum* had been a central feature of property theories since Roman times; but in Locke's hands the ownership of one's actions became the bridge between God's grant to mankind in common and the establishment of rights to private property. 'The labour of his body, and the work of his hands,' Locke said, '. . . are properly his.'[113] Thus,

> whatsoever then [a man] removes out of the state that nature hath provided, and left in it, he hath mixed his *labour* with, and joined to it something that is his own, and thereby makes it his property.[114]

By the introduction of the labour theory, Locke managed to close the gap between original equality and community, and individual title to earthly goods: the *suum*-focused route to the concept of property and the argument based on the need for sustenance had merged into a single ground of property. The labour one mixes with earthly goods (say, by drawing water or picking fruit) creates property in the acquired object because one's actions are, inherently, already

[111] Locke, Treatises II.26.287. Some have pointed out, with justification, that this remark most plausibly concerns the subsumption of appropriated items within the *suum*, as opposed to food which has been literally consumed and digested: see II.28.288.
[112] *Ibid* II.27.287.
[113] *Ibid*.
[114] *Ibid* II.27.288.

within the sphere of 'one's own'; thus, once the article and the labour are mixed, no person save the labourer can have a right to whatever the labour is enjoined to, 'at least where there is enough and as good left for others.'[115]

Although it echoed an established common law idea, based on the Roman concept of *specificatio*, Locke's defence of the labour theory depends upon an ambiguity in his use of the word 'labour', as between directed *actions* and the *products* of that action. The ownership by an individual of her own willed actions gives rise to no problems to anyone who accepts the terms of the possessive theory; but no easy deductive relationship obtains between a physical activity which is, in that rather indefinable sense, 'one's own', and property in the outcome of that activity: a thesis of ownership of *processes* does not yield a thesis of ownership of *products*. Furthermore, Locke could not successfully call upon the doctrine of *specificatio*, since a process of manufacture is not invariably present in original takings (or if it is, the process does not inevitably involve the irrevocable alteration of the acquired object). One who picks apples from the tree mixes his labour, in Locke's sense, and thus gains title to the apples he has picked. One may perhaps assert that an irrevocable change has taken place within the apple as a result of that labour, in that it is no longer attached to and sustained by the tree. But one who picks apples from the ground, which have become severed from the tree by natural forces (by the wind, say), also mixes labour in Locke's sense, but no essential or irrevocable change occurs in the earth-bound fruit. Notwithstanding these logical difficulties with Locke's argument, his justification of the labour theory proceeded largely in terms of a mixture of his religious views and an articulation of the principles governing established patterns of land-holding.

Locke was concerned to refute the traditional assumption that private property rights must emerge from agreement: 'If such a consent as that was necessary,' Locke said, 'man had starved, notwithstanding the plenty God had given him.'[116] He explained this in terms which form the underlying assumptions of a system of agrarian capitalism and enclosure, which was the central feature of English land-economy until well into the eighteenth century:

> We see in *commons*, which remain so by compact, that 'tis the taking any part of what is common, and removing it out of the state nature leaves it in, which begins the property; without which the common is of no use. And the taking of this or that part does not depend on the express consent of all the commoners. Thus the grass my horse has bit; the turf my servant has cut; and the ore I have digged in any place where I have a right to them in common with others, become my *property*, without the assignation or consent of any body. The labour that was mine, removing them out of that common state they were in, hath fixed my property in them.[117]

---

[115] *Ibid*. We will have cause to return to this troublesome remark shortly.
[116] *Ibid* II.28.288–9.
[117] *Ibid* II.28.289.

Only express agreement is mentioned here, but in emphasising the rootedness of property rights in labour, Locke ruled out any form of agreement, express or otherwise, as a ground of private property. Barbeyrac was aware of this distinction between Locke and earlier natural rights theorists as a development of some importance, but it would be wrong to overemphasise the gulf between Locke and his predecessors in the tradition.[118] Though the theoretical emphasis placed upon agreement had always varied, earlier writers on natural rights had, on the whole, employed the notion of an original agreement in a limited way: the Grotian theory merely acknowledged that the particular arrangements within a society for the mutual recognition of property rights (such as agrarian capitalism or agrarian socialism) are the product of social consensus rather than the outcome of natural law. The *form* of those arrangements is determined by agreements forged between human agents, but property rights themselves are natural, in the sense that some form of property is the prerequisite both for human survival in general, and for the protection of individuals' fundamental rights (to life, self-determination etc.) in any stable society. Likewise, Locke was concerned to show how property rights emerge from labour in the state of nature, but acknowledged that the more complex social arrangements of a sophisticated polity would necessitate alterations to existing patterns of rights, and to existing assumptions about how one might acquire (or lose) those rights. Moreover, even if consensus is incapable of supplying the truth of a particular view of property rights, some form of consensus (even if unarticulated) must presumably be in place if such rights are to be mutually recognised and respected.

The labour theory, as noted, supplied the bridge between the original God-given grant of the world to mankind in common and the particular rights of individuals in the state of nature to acquire natural resources to sustain their lives. Acquisitions (which for Locke included *title* to the goods acquired) did not have to be preceded by direct agreement because the mixing of labour with natural resources brought those resources within the scope of one's own, and the limited capability of individuals to exert labour upon external objects thus ensured that there would be, at least 'in the early stages of the world', enough and as good left for others. Just as important as the ability of the labour theory to *generate* claims of right over natural resources is its imposition of natural restrictions upon the exercise and acquirement of those rights. The two main consequences of the labour theory for property rights drawn by Locke are (in modern terminology) the spoilage condition and the sufficiency condition. These conditions, taken together, articulate a concern with sustainable development: for Locke, 'the preservation of mankind (which definitely included future generations) is the ultimate criterion by which any use of resources is to be assessed.'[119] Since the preservation of mankind required the sustainability of

---

[118] Laslett, in particular, overestimates Locke's departure from the Grotian orthodoxy: see Locke, Treatises, 288 fn.

[119] D Schmitz, 'The Institution of Property' in Paul, Miller and Paul (eds), above n 1 p 44.

essential resources necessary to preserve life, the goal of human social flourishing would have seemed, to the seventeenth century mind, to be in complete
harmony with a goal of preserving and enhancing the natural environment.
Property *rights* were thus inherently and intrinsically tied to environmental
responsibilities.

Although it sanctions takings from the original commons, Locke was at pains
to stress that the labour theory did not entail a freedom for any person to take
as much as he or she wanted. 'Nothing,' Locke said, 'was made by God for man
to spoil or destroy':

> The same law of nature that does by this means give us property, does also *bound* that
> property too. *God has given us all things richly . . .* But how far has he given us? *To
> enjoy.* As much as any one can make use of to any advantage to life before it spoils; so
> much he may by his labour fix a property in.[120]

Labour will thus only generate a proprietary title where the acts involved are
improving of the resource acted upon (or at least, where the acts, such as picking fallen apples from the ground, result in a resource being gainfully employed
which would otherwise perish unused.) The spoilage condition clearly applies
to the hoarding of perishable goods, such as foodstuffs, but as Locke was aware,
the 'chief matter of property' is not, in advanced societies, the fruits and creatures of the earth, but the land itself. Yet, Locke observed, it cannot have been
God's wish that the world remain in common and uncultivated; rather, the
world was given 'for the industrious and the rational (and labour was to be
his *title* to it) not to the fancy or the covetousness of the quarrelsome and
contentious.'[121] The enclosure of land from the commons must thus proceed on
the basis of improving acts which issue in products which will actually be used:

> God, when he gave the world in common to all mankind, commanded man also to
> labour, and the penury of his condition required it of him. God and [man's] reason
> commanded him to subdue the earth, i.e. improve it for the benefit of life, and therein
> lay out something upon it that was his own, his labour.[122]

Locke several times emphasised the conjunction between improvement and
utility: 'As much land as a man tills, plants, improves, cultivates and can use the
product of,' he said, 'so much is his property.'[123] Nature sets the extent and
character of property by the limits of individuals' capacities for labour, and their
rational assessments of their needs; each man's possession of portions of the
globe is confined 'to a very modest proportion' because individuals will in general have little taste for labour which furnishes them with goods which go
beyond their needs and wants.[124] From the association between individual needs
and wants and their ability and willingness to toil, Locke drew the conclusion

120 Locke, Treatises II.31.290.
121 *Ibid* II.33.291.
122 *Ibid* II.32.291.
123 *Ibid* II.32.290.
124 *Ibid* II.36.292.

that 'subduing or cultivating the Earth, and having dominion, we see are joined together.'[125] *Dominium* had, of course, traditionally denoted *physical* control over the earth; but Locke was here using 'dominion' as a synonym for *property*. With Locke's labour theory we are therefore back to a theory in which *dominium* and *ius* are intimately linked, a theory which effectively removed the wedge between those two concepts which Pufendorf had so decisively hammered.

The second Lockean proviso relates mainly, though not exclusively, to interpersonal *iura* rather than *dominium*. In the first ages of the world, takings from the original commons did not impinge upon the collective rights of others because each discrete taking hardly diminished the natural plenty left over. Human beings were still relatively few in number, and so each person's acquisition of rights to land and movables (through their labour) would still leave vast spaces of wilderness unclaimed. Each person's discrete taking left 'enough and as good' for others. Thus far the sufficiency condition operates merely as an injunction on rights-infractions in the state of nature: since title to land and natural resources rests on labour and utility, those who take, through labour, only what they need for sustenance and comfort will not be committing any infractions of the original common grant. Now, it is clear that, as human numbers grow, in line with God's command to spread out and people the world, ever fewer wilderness areas will be left over as more takings are made: each (legitimate) acquisition of land by individuals will diminish the land left over, until there is not 'enough and as good' left in the commons for others: future generations will find themselves dispossessed by the historical circumstances of their birth. That argument relies upon an image of ever-decreasing resources: a pride of lions feasting upon a freshly killed wildebeest will, inevitably, end up with nothing but bleached bones as their stomachs fill; those who eat first will tend to grab substantial portions whilst those who come later will find relatively little (and not 'enough and as good') or nothing. Such an image too pervades Philip Larkin's poem 'Going, Going': 'It seems, just now/ To be happening so very fast;/ Despite all the land left free/ For the first time I feel somehow/ That it isn't going to last.'

It may seem that Larkin's lament, that green spaces will live on only 'in books and galleries', while for us there is only 'concrete and tyres', is the inevitable conclusion of the Lockean argument. But in fact this image ignores the assumed relationship between (rational) human wants and needs, and environmental development and enrichment which pervaded seventeenth century thought: legitimate takings from the commons depend upon 'improving' labour which will *increase* the amount of resources available.

> . . . he who appropriates land to himself by his labour, does not lessen but increases the common stock of mankind. For the provisions serving to the support of human life produced by one acre of enclosed and cultivated land, are . . . ten times more than

---

[125] Locke, Treatises II.35.292.

those which are yielded by an acre of land, of equal richness, lying waste in common.[126]

A situation characterised by a general scarcity of resources would thus in fact *require* takings from the commons as a means of increasing the overall level of bounty available for human beings (given Locke's insistence on an obligation to preserve mankind as far as one can). Now, takings of land may well be necessary for the enlargement of natural resources such as food, shelter and clothing, but (it might be countered) hardly for an increase in the amount of *land* left over. In line with his predecessors in the natural rights tradition, Locke acknowledged that the development of human societies would have an effect upon the content of natural law's *specific* injunctions. In the early days of human development, leftover areas of wilderness would raise no interesting problems, since they would not be worth subjecting to claim and counter-claim: they would possess no value unless labour was mixed with them. But the development of even quite crude economic practices would, Locke thought, have the effect of placing a conventional value upon assets which are, in the pre-social stage of human evolution, without worth. The enlargement of individual possessions beyond what was immediately necessary for comfort and sustenance, made possible by the introduction of monetary conventions, 'altered the intrinsic value of things, which depends only on their usefulness to man.'[127] In fact, the economic transactions which confer value upon earthly assets need not involve money at all:

> He that gathered a hundred bushels of acorns or apples had thereby a property in them; they were his goods as soon as gathered. He was only to look that he used them before they spoiled; else he took more than his share, and robbed others. And indeed it was a foolish thing, as well as dishonest, to hoard up more than he could make use of. If he gave away a part to anybody else, so that it perished not uselessly in his possession, these he also made use of. And if he also bartered away plums that would have rotted in a week, for nuts that would last good for his eating a whole year, he did no injury; he wasted not the common stock . . .[128]

The earlier natural rights theorists had emphasised the forging of social links as a primary duty of mankind; basic economic links of the kind presented in the above passage are just the sort of primitive interpersonal links upon which an exit from the state of nature would depend. Without basic bartering and exchange between individuals, mankind would continue to live the starkly hand-to-mouth existence characterised by the earliest human beings living according to the labour theory: each individual (or family group) would effectively remain an economic island unto itself, the comfort and well-being of its members depending entirely upon the capacities of those members to labour successfully and continuously across a range of tasks (farming, building, clothes-making, etc) to provide sustenance and shelter. The bartering system

---

[126] *Ibid* II.37.294.
[127] *Ibid* II.37.294.
[128] *Ibid* II.46.300.

would thus allow for a degree of specialisation in the tasks each sociable individual would necessarily have to perform in order to secure comforts and sustenance for herself and her family, and the general increase in skill within each task that such specialisation would, theoretically, bring would result in a parallel increase in productivity, and thus also bring about an overall improvement in the common good. Locke's argument is, however (at this stage) not one of sociability but of productivity and distribution: for (he says) "'tis labour indeed which puts the difference of value on every thing';[129] and because specialisation yields an overall increase in labour (or at the very least in productivity), economic activity opens up avenues of exchange which allow toiling individuals to effect a much more efficient and useful distribution of the goods they acquire through their work:

> For I ask whether in the wild woods and uncultivated waste of America left to nature, without any improvement, tillage or husbandry, a thousand acres will yield the needy and wretched inhabitants as many conveniences of life as ten acres of equally fertile land do in Devonshire where they are well cultivated?[130]

Locke laboured this point in detail at several other points in the *Treatises*; for example:

> An acre of land that bears here twenty bushels of wheat, and another in America which, with the same husbandry, would do the like are, without doubt, of the same natural, intrinsic value. But yet the benefit mankind receives from the one, in a year, is worth 5 *l.* and from the other possibly not worth a penny, if all the profit an *Indian* received from it were to be valued and sold here; at least, I may truly say, not 1/1000. Tis labour, then, which puts the greatest part of value upon land, without which it would scarcely be worth any thing . . .[131]

Economic activity thus boosts productivity overall, transforming the lives of otherwise 'wretched and needy' individuals into relatively affluent members of a community. The introduction of money is the next step in this process of specialisation. Toilers are able to improve further their output and efficiency, thus enabling them to exchange whatever products are surplus to their needs for imperishable metals and stones, upon which a community of productive individuals has placed a conventional value which far exceeds their intrinsic worth to mankind. The plum-gatherer, instead of finding a market for her goods only when she is herself in need of another commodity (nuts, say), can profitably exchange her fruit for money for which she can later exchange goods and services:

> Again, if [the gatherer of nuts] would give his nuts for a piece of metal, pleased with its colour, or exchange his sheep for shells, or wool for a sparkling pebble or a diamond, and keep those by him all his life, he invaded not the right of others, he might

---

[129] Locke, Treatises II.40.296.
[130] *Ibid* II.37.294.
[131] *Ibid* II.43.298.

heap up as much of these durable things as he pleased; the exceeding of his just property not lying in the largeness of his possession, but in the perishing of anything uselessly in it.[132]

The advance constituted by the development of a rudimentary monetary economy would simultaneously improve the welfare of mankind (or, at least, that of discrete economic communities) *and* promote the best practices for cultivation and development of the natural environment. The optimal model for human enrichment is thereby one of rational environmental management and improvement. The anthropocentric tenor of Locke's argument thus does not (or would not, to contemporary eyes) detract from a goal of environmental welfare, least of all promote an ethic of brute plunder. But the conventional values conferred upon earthly assets by the more sophisticated economic practices would, as Locke was at least partially aware, entail a fundamental shift from the idea that title to property is the direct product of labour. As Locke noted, labour puts value into the land, but in any sophisticated community:

'tis not barely the ploughman's pains, the reaper's and thresher's toil, and the baker's sweat, [that] is to be counted into the bread we eat; the labour of those who broke the oxen, who digged and wrought the iron and stones, who felled and framed the timber employed about the plough, mill, oven, or any other utensils, which are a vast number requisite to this corn, from its being a seed sown to its being made bread, must all be charged on the account of labour, and received as an effect of that . . . all [of] which, 'twould be almost impossible, at least too long, to reckon up.[133]

Such developments, then, put a strain on the notion that property in goods is the result of the improving acts of the individuals who work upon them. In a sophisticated trading community such as Locke described, the owner of a holding may have no especial relationship with the bricks which make up his house other than that he paid for them with (imperishable) currency; nor does the possession of amassed currency entail prior labour on the part of an individual once a society develops a principle of inheritance and succession. Labour, of course, will remain the engine which drives the economic transfers which occur (and will continue to be the predominant means by which most individuals procure hard currency); but the largely untraceable relationship between discrete acts of labour and the products of that labour, and the conventional values money places on those products, will entail a shift away from the perspective that the constituent acts of labour which produce distinct goods also constitute title to those goods, towards a perspective of abstract rights. Goods become worth whatever particular individuals are prepared to pay for them in monetary terms; thus the relationship between people and their property will become broadly economic: assessments of ownership will inevitably depend upon assessments of individual *iura* rather than concrete examples of *dominium*. Because the value of money is purely conventional, the original emphasis tying acquisition to

[132] *Ibid* II.46.300.
[133] *Ibid* II.43.298.

labour and dominion is submerged beneath a welter of interpersonal relation-ships of entitlement and duty. Moreover, as Matthew Kramer has pointed out, though individuals in the Lockean state of nature acquire goods through their labour, Lockean individuals (both in the state of nature and, more particularly, in civil society) owe one another extensive obligations, and thus enjoy extensive entitlements in respect of one another, regarding the way in which those goods are to be distributed.[134] Possession (*dominium*) thus remains as a curious but important determinant of ownership now understood predominantly in terms of *ius*.

That said, the primarily economic relationship between human beings and land within sophisticated communities sublimates, rather than supplants, the original Lockean theme of possession as a necessary condition of ownership: monetary transactions 'by compact and agreement *settled* the property which labour and industry began.'[135] The specialisation of labour increases greatly the yield of natural resources thus ensuring 'enough and as good' for an increasingly large population; but the first Lockean proviso, forbidding waste, forces the retention of actual (and eventually legal) possession as a necessary condition of ownership. Locke saw no tension between these two routes to ownership, roughly split between *dominium* and abstract rights, as he hinted that monetary transactions make for effective distribution and land-use: individuals, thought Locke, will in general only purchase what they will actually use, or derive ben-efit from, thus reducing waste at least in areas of land taken from the original commons. Locke's ongoing commitment to possession as a necessary, but not sufficient, condition of ownership is illustrated by passages, such as the follow-ing, which are drawn from the midst of his discussion of the second proviso:

> The same measures [as applied to takings of nature's spontaneous products] governed the possession of land too: Whatsoever he tilled and reaped, laid up and made use of, before it spoiled, that was his peculiar right; whatsoever he enclosed, and could feed, and make use of, the cattle and product was also his. But if either the grass of his enclo-sure rotted on the ground, or the fruit of his planting perished without gathering, and laying up, this part of the Earth, notwithstanding his enclosure [of it], was still to be looked on as waste, and might be the possession of any other.[136]

The elimination of such waste, through economically directed distributions of goods, was an important reason for labour-specialisation and the develop-ment of community and economic ties between working men and women. Just as the development of such ties ensured a better distribution of resources than the bare and atomistic world of original takings, so the environment is well-tended and cultivated to the maximum possible extent by those individuals with most knowledge of agricultural techniques. Rotting fruit and stagnant grass are less likely in a world in which specialised farmers ply their skill over the land,

---

[134] MH Kramer, *John Locke and the Origins of Private Property* (Cambridge, CUP, 1997) 29.
[135] *Ibid* II.45.298.
[136] *Ibid* II.38.295.

than one in which amateur labourers endeavour to fend for their families in isolation, without firm knowledge of techniques of cultivation and in the face of rotting and diminishing natural resources. For Locke, as for his predecessors in the natural rights tradition, human flourishing and a thriving and well-managed environment went hand in hand; property rights were rooted in an intimate knowledge of, and intensive and sustained labour in, the natural world.

CONCLUDING REMARKS

The foregoing discussion began by observing a distinction, between property *rights* on the one hand, and collective *controls* on the extent and exercise of those rights, on the other. The relationship between rights and restrictions can be, and is, presented in various different ways: rights might (for example) be regarded as delimiting a realm of individual interest or autonomous choice which must be subjected to curbs where the overwhelming needs of the common good so demand; alternatively, individual rights can be represented as a structure of horizontal relationships between private individuals, whose ability to deal with each other is limited by vertically-imposed statutory controls for reasons of policy. In the former example, an individual's penchant for burning rubber tyres in her garden might be outlawed because of a recognition of a greater social interest in maintaining a healthy and pollution-free environment. In the latter case, a fisherman's right to ply his trade to acquire and sell fish might be subject to restrictions or quotas which are designed to stabilise the market price of fish for the benefit of all fisherman, or to ensure that fish stocks are not entirely or dangerously depleted in a certain area. In either case (even if the motivation for introducing restrictions is environmental rather than social or economic), the curbs set upon individual rights are perceived as extrinsic to the rights themselves, rather than as, say, deductive consequences of the possession of rights, or a fundamental constituent of the idea of those rights as such.

The assumption that collective goals or substantive moral principles are related to individual rights instrumentally rather than intrinsically is not inevitable. The preceding discussion was intended to show that the intellectual, political and philosophical currents which led to the emergence of individual ('subjective') rights in fact perceived the extent of an individual's rights to be *essentially* limited and determined by the nature of those rights themselves. The great seventeenth century theories of natural right and property had their origins in Quattrocento Italian debates about monastic poverty, and the compatibility of the use and consumption of goods and land with a general renunciation of earthly possessions. The political positions on property which emerged from those debates were explored and refined in the fifteenth and sixteenth centuries by scholars who wished to uncover the significance of the Roman concepts of *dominium* and *ius* by reference to their role in Roman *life*. Unsurprisingly, the Renaissance humanists emphasised the urban cityscape as the horizon within which human flourishing must take place, and saw in property the prerequisite of its existence. The Grotian natural rights tradition would likewise place stress upon the idea of sociability, and the technological know-how in terms of farming and cultivation which make social relations sustainable and worth having. The linkage of these two issues (agrarian development and sociability within an urban setting) is attested to most forcefully and consciously in the writings of Pufendorf. In the meeting-place of those ideas, the modern conception of interpersonal, subjective rights is indeed close at hand.

In England, theories of natural rights and property were fundamentally tied to debates concerning individual freedom and the relationship of citizens to powerful forms of state authority. Theories about the origins of property and the idea of natural rights were exploited variously to justify totalitarian or absolutist government (Filmer, Hobbes) and to promote the notion of legally limited sovereignty (Locke). The concept of property both shaped, and was shaped by, the struggle between liberalism and absolutism which constituted one of the flashpoints of the civil war, and the attendant political instability which characterised much of the seventeenth century. For these writers, originary theories of property served as an essential precept in explanations of how, and to what extent, individual members of a sophisticated polity might possess fundamental rights to their self-determination as individuals. An individual's attitudes, outlooks and moral stances were no longer seen as products of the interpretative, linguistic and moral practices of the whole community, but instead as the outpourings of an individual's thoughts and experience (and thus 'owned' by the individual). The *suum* was seen as something simultaneously requiring protection and sustenance; as both a ground of property rights in worldly goods *and* a reflection of essential limits upon those rights. Individuals, as autonomous agents, were likewise perceived as owing one another obligations (not to impinge upon each other's essential rights) and thus as the bearers of extensive interpersonal rights and privileges. Whereas the Grotian tradition had perceived the role of civil government as protecting and preserving the essential structure of rights and duties established in the state of nature, both Hobbes and Locke regarded the practices of any mature society as the outcome of consensus. Thus, an individual's civil rights would tend to be seen less in terms of mastery over one's affairs, but rather as defining a realm of freedom from interference by others.

Within the English canon, Locke's labour theory stands out as a genuinely original and troubling offshoot from the mainstream of thought about property. The implications of it continue to present a problem for a system of property conceived in terms of interpersonal right. By emphasising the rootedness of property in labour, Locke overturned the idea, which had been developing in the works of Grotius and Pufendorf, that property rights derived from convention in the state of nature. Property rights even in a sophisticated civil society could thus never be seen in wholly socio-economic terms, but as expressions of mankind's relationship to the world. Ironically, for a theory with close links to the Roman *dominium*,

> The different and opposed definitions of Pufendorf and Locke embody two radically dissimilar views of the relation of man to the world. For Pufendorf, property expresses man's right to dominate the world . . . For Locke, it expresses man's privilege to use a world which is not essentially his own and which is to be used, and not abused, for purposes not his own, of preservation and enjoyment.[137]

Sustained possession remains an important determinant of legal rights to property at common law. These patterns in common law thought are, however, heavily overlaid by the characterisation of the law of property as a conceptual framework of estates and interests, wherein an individual is held to enjoy no direct proprietary relationship with the physical features of land, but rather owns, in effect, a bundle of rights over the land. It is this conception of property which is most familiar to students of real property, and which finds expression in the English 1925 property legislation. In the next chapter the developments which led to the modern legal conception of property will be followed in some detail. In the course of that study it will become clear that the development of a law of property which stands in no particular relationship to wider moral or environmental questions is not inevitable. Whilst 'subjective' interpersonal rights are always detachable from categorical impositions in the name of environmental protection (at least where those impositions do not reflect purely social concerns about collective well-being), a regime of interpersonal entitlements need not develop in isolation from a wider moral perspective on the nature of property. Rights to property can be regarded as hemmed in by prior limitations which derive from a philosophical understanding of property itself.

The natural rights theories constitute a corpus of scholarship (albeit an eclectic one) which stands out as unique in western thought. Whilst the terms in which we talk about property have remained fairly constant since Roman times, the thought of Grotius, Pufendorf, Locke and their contemporaries transformed the significance of the central concepts of property in ways that are still felt. It is nevertheless important to understand those theories as themselves the product of historical, religious and political forces. The seventeenth century constitutes a high watermark in the theory of property; the early twenty-first is likely to engender the beginnings of another. Like all sea-changes they are crisis-driven: the proper use and implications of concepts long in use and taken for granted suddenly take on a new and urgent significance which requires their articulation and theorisation. The seventeenth century writers advocated a conception of property which placed social man at the centre of God's injunctions, in perfect harmony with the needs of the natural environment. Twenty-first century notions of property *responsibilities* as well as rights, contain the echo of these assumptions, but those old truths seem no longer to constitute a suitable

---

[137] J Tully, *A Discourse on Property: John Locke, and his Adversaries* (Cambridge, CUP, 1980) 72.

framework within which to work out the matrix of obligations and entitle-ments: the seventeenth century supposition of unqualified harmony between the environment and human interests is no longer sustainable.

3

Commerce, Capitalism and the Common Law

THE NATURAL RIGHTS theories had extended and refined the Roman jurists'
perception of a close relationship between property and right, and between
right and autonomy. Human interests were regarded as inevitably wedded to
the acquisition of property (whether through labour or social convention) and
the pursuit of society built on individual rights; and those same interests
appeared, to the seventeenth century mind, to be fully in harmony with the care
and protection of the natural environment. There is thus a clear and pervasive
drive in those theories towards an instrumentalism which borders on conse-
quentialism: property rights emerge and develop in ways which, ideally, best
serve the goal of human flourishing. Because not *inherently* coupled to an envi-
ronment-preserving perspective, a society's institutions of property can develop
in ways which place no special emphasis on the goal of environmental protection or development. In the eighteenth century, the theory of property was
broadly concerned with the increasingly complex and sophisticated relationships between individual property rights, emergent forms of commerce and the
idea of public virtue. This interplay of ideas elevated the connection between
property and *ius* to something approaching an analytic truth, whilst under-
mining the significance of the Roman notion of *dominium* as one concerning the
physical capacity of human beings to alter and control the external world.

The refinement and expansion of the language of rights during the late seven-
teenth- and early eighteenth centuries brought about profound changes in the
theory of common law, for which Hobbes and Selden had argued philosophically decades earlier. Classical common law theory, which had shaken itself free
of the natural law theories of the medieval period to achieve its most profound
expression in the writings of Coke and Hale, understood the rules and practices
of the common law as expressions of a community's shared conceptions of the
good. The authority of propositions of the common law derived not from their
congruence with the universal postulates of right reason, but from their rootedness in the community's established practices and on-going reception of those
propositions as embodying rational and just solutions to the problems of
collective living.[1] The nature of those propositions thus consisted not in any
correspondence with transcendent standards of reasonableness which the wise

---

[1] M Hale, *A History of the Common Law*, 5th edn (London, W Clarke & Son, 1794) 17.

commend as true or desirable, but rather in their *articulation* of standards of reasonableness and justice which underpin the community's conceptions of the good. The value placed upon historical pedigree in the common law is thus inexorably connected with the value placed upon reason and justice: the ability of a rule or practice to endure over time depends upon its soundness being repeatedly confirmed in the collective experience of the community.[2]

Rights, by contrast, will tend to become very important only in a society characterised by entrenched moral, political and religious divisions. The language of rights emerges quite naturally out of the theory of property, but the notion of liberal rights typified by a pervasive concern with possessive and individualistic ideas will largely gain a hold on the collective imagination in contexts which place a high value on individual self-rule. Liberal rights *essentially* mark off aspects of an individual's life from the interests and aspirations of the collectivity. It is this aspect of individual rights, and not Locke's labour theory of value, which is of most importance, in political terms, in the eighteenth century. The nexus of thought about rights and virtue connecting Harrington to the Whig movement is chiefly concerned with rights as defining individuality and concretising intellectual, moral and political independence from collective interests.[3] But if the Lockean conception of rights failed to gain a purchase in the prevailing political debates on virtue, it nevertheless remained a significant determinant of property at common law. The Lockean theory had prized *dominium* as a prerequisite of virtue in the ethics of ownership; but the forms of interpersonal *iura* which were developing in the hands of Harrington's successors would have a major impact both on the form of common law and upon the intelligibility of a theory of property rooted in conceptions of nature and the environment.

PROPERTY AND LIBERAL RIGHTS

The language of rights introduced into the common law ideas which were at once largely alien to the traditional forms of common law theory, and broadly attractive to the positivists. In terms of the classical theory, a body of common law rules need not exhibit any overarching concern with systematicity or coherence, except insofar as consistency is understood as a virtue essential to rationality. A community's legal rules form a body of thought continually adapting to experience, rather than a system of deliberately interlocking standards deriving from a limited number of axioms or organising principles. A system of rights, by contrast, will tend to derive from a collection of ideas about how individuals should be free to determine their lives, and in what respects their freedom and interests must be curtailed in the name of the collective good. (A

---

[2] See G Postema, *Bentham and the Common Law Tradition* (Oxford, Clarendon Press, 1986) 7.
[3] J Harrington, *The Art of Law-Giving in Three Books* (London, Henry Fletcher, 1659).

mature theory of rights will, of course, distinguish between 'rights' in the sense of 'claims' and mere *liberties*, but both claim-rights *and* liberties are always intimately connected with an individual's freedom of action: claim-rights secure freedom by outlawing interference by the duty-bearer in the right-holder's privileged activity, whereas a liberty merely allows the liberty-endowed individual to engage in that activity.) Such a system will effectively regard liberal rights as being in tension with the mechanisms through which a society's collective interests are advanced: an individual's rights demarcate a sphere of liberty within which she can act in ways which actually or potentially damage, or fail to enhance, the common good. Unlike propositions of the common law, therefore, statements of an individual's rights will usually be predicated on a collection of abstract principles aiming at a *systematic* treatment of horizontal and vertical relationships within a state. An individual's rights and duties will be understood as a function of a larger network of relationships forged between individuals and between the state and its citizens, and of the rules regulating those interactions.

Among the various ways in which the law might attempt to balance individual freedom and the collective good is by reference to a norm of equality. The law might be seen as being concerned with ensuring that all individuals in society remain essentially free to engage in their own projects, and to develop their own interests and live their lives according to their own conceptions of the good. Such a standpoint will require legal rules which endeavour to maximise the degree of freedom each person enjoys, whilst simultaneously placing restrictions on that freedom in the name of equality. Law would, on this conception, both define and regulate the boundaries between essentially competing interests. Alternatively, the law might be seen as primarily concerned with setting out duties and rules of conduct which allow for the possibility of harmonious social interaction in a morally diverse world, and as thereby only indirectly establishing a sphere of individual autonomy removed from the pressure of collective interests. Which of these approaches we choose to adopt (for want of better labels, we can refer to these as 'egalitarian' and 'positivist' respectively) will impact upon the common law in a way which undercuts its traditional connection with shared values and customary usage: the egalitarian approach because of its presentation of common law as a deductive system of rules and formally regimented interests; positivism because it forces us to see the common law as essentially concerned with the interpretation and application of formally created black-letter rules rooted in the legislative will. The former account represents the law as a particular cross-section of interests, frozen in time, whereas on the latter, the common law loses its autonomy vis-à-vis collective goals and public policies.

The impact that these developments would have upon the legal idea of property requires careful explanation. Two broad issues can nevertheless be identified in general terms. The drive towards an understanding of common law in terms of a structure of horizontal relationships defined by liberal rights (which was soon to be given a philosophical underpinning in Kant) gave further weight to the idea that 'property' signified a technical and specifically legal concept distinct from other rights possessed by individuals merely in that it was enforceable against society-at-large and not, as with contractual rights, against particular persons. At the same time, the form of positivism which would emerge in Bentham's writings would complete the journey towards a standpoint which viewed a person's property rights as standing in direct opposition to collective needs and interests. Individual rights were increasingly perceived as defining a realm of private entitlement free from official interference in the name of public welfare. The common law came to be seen as displaying a distinctive concern with individual rights and duties, in opposition to, and hemmed in by, the realm of posited law which aimed at the regulation, curtailment and adjustment of those rights in the light of the common good. The requirements of sociability, agrarian development and 'natural' limitations on property came to be looked upon, not as essential determinants of the very notion of property, but as legislated restrictions upon property *rights*. The gradual slide towards this perspective was simultaneously a retreat from the notion that property might be invested with intrinsic theological and moral significance. Rules defining the extent of property rights were viewed as the political choices of an enlightened polity, and the rights themselves as deriving from law rather than morality.

The Transformation of Property

The notion of liberal rights emerged from the writings of the natural lawyers as an expression of man's *sociability*. One's natural rights (to one's person, and to that which was essential for survival) prompted reflection upon, and participation in, forms of social interaction which would promote and underpin those rights. Philosophical reflection on the state of nature had shown how a state of total freedom would in fact decrease the net ability of individuals to act in life-enriching ways. In the state of nature, the lack of social ties and consequent need for constant vigilance forced pre-social man to live a life dominated by the short-term quest for food, shelter and survival. A society's positive laws, by placing restrictions upon original freedom, extend and preserve individual rights, allowing individual citizens to concentrate on improving their lives in a world of scarce resources without trespassing on the rights of others to maximise their lot. Later writers would see in this project a significance wholly alien to the thought of the seventeenth century theorists. The foundations of private property lay, for Kant and Hegel, not in any reflections upon mankind's place in the world, but in the individual will. The essential desire of each person for freedom, both from forms of collective control and vis-à-vis her neighbours, would *itself* be regarded as requiring the existence of private property rights. In terms of this conception, the law is best understood as guided by the ideal of equal freedom, in which the imposition of rules of conduct, looked upon as undesirable in itself, is nevertheless required as a means of ensuring that individual choices are not exercised in ways which retard the freedom of others.

Concern with individual liberty and equality promotes the conception of a state's property arrangements as the product of elaborate social rules, and de-emphasises the 'natural' aspects of property explored by the seventeenth century writers. For the egalitarians, property is but one aspect of the individual's striving for freedom, and not the necessary foundation of that freedom. By placing an emphasis on social rules, the egalitarian stresses property's situation in the ebb and flow of historical pressures which determine a society's political culture. Property rights are thus explored in terms of their contingency and artifice, and regarded as matters essentially for legal determination. The egalitarian viewpoint tends therefore to form part of a political perspective which echoes the juristic language and assumptions which grew out of civic republicanism. For the later republicans, true involvement in political society derives not from Aristotelian assumptions about the active life of the *vir civilis*, but from the possession of rights and obligations. Man was seen as essentially a political animal (and not naturally a denizen of a state of nature). Thus the conception of liberty within republican accounts differed from the starkly negative version of liberty found in the natural rights theorists and, most predominantly, the writings of Hobbes.[4] Hobbesian liberty marked out a domain distinct from that of law, so that an individual's liberty consisted in her rights to be free from legal interference in her private projects. The republican conception of liberty, by contrast, stressed the freedom of citizens to participate in the legal order itself, by forging an active role in public life. But unlike their humanist successors, the early republicans saw fidelity to the public good in terms of rights and duties.

The humanists had voiced their conception of political participation in terms of virtue. In the writings and arguments of the republicans, this humanist language was wedded to conceptions of justice firmly rooted in the tradition of possessive individualism: the 'right' (ie liberty) of a citizen to engage in public life stemmed from his interests as a *proprietor*. Accordingly, '. . . a particular mode of participation might be seen as appropriate to the specialised social individual: to be proper to him, to be his propriety or property'.[5] The political values of the republicans and their successors thus favoured independence as a key moral virtue. Freehold ownership of land was seen, by Harrington and his Whig descendants, as the mainstay of political independence (independence, that is, from the projects and interests of others). Those who must sell their labour in exchange for essential goods depend upon another's will, and thus seem, in this view, to lack the essential moral self-rule required for political life. The debate over property in the eighteenth century was not one of increasing industrialisation *vs* environmental welfare, but of culture *vs* virtue. Political

---

[4] See J Pocock, *Virtue, Commerce and History* (Cambridge, CUP, 1985) 37–42. The following argument is heavily influenced by Pocock, but falls short of complete agreement with him on the matter of humanist views on liberty.

[5] *Ibid* 42.

virtue was seen as having an agrarian base, since landowners (unlike merchants and investors) could be expected to display a direct concern in the political stability and general welfare of society.

The changing attitude towards property is perhaps most clearly seen in the mature work of Rousseau. First of all, Rousseau described the state as a network of horizontal and vertical relationships of right and duty, governed by a:

> general will . . . which always tends to the preservation and well-being of the whole and of each part, and which is the source of the laws; is, for all members of the state, in relation to one another and to it, the rule of what is just and unjust.[6]

Rousseau's account of public virtue proceeds in terms of a distinction between the realm of public good and that of private interests. Good government consists, Rousseau said, in following the general will in all things, which is nothing else than having the good of the people at the centre of one's political deliberations. But to follow the general will, the virtuous citizen must sharply distinguish it from the particular will beginning with himself. To do so requires the 'most sublime virtue', and a precondition of that virtue is moral and political independence:

> Since one has to be free in order to will, another, no lesser difficulty is to secure *both* public freedom *and* governmental authority. Inquire into the motives that have led men united by their mutual needs into the great society to unite more closely by means of civil societies; you will find none other than that of securing the goods, the life and the freedom of each member through the protection of all . . .[7]

The distinction Rousseau draws in this passage—between public freedom and governmental authority—is one dimension to the changing nature of the debate over property in the eighteenth century. In that debate we find some indication of a general shift in perspective towards property's connection with personality, or the will, and away from the notion of property's 'natural' or 'environmental' dimension. The main participants in that debate were themselves aware of the transfiguration of property in political culture, choosing to explain the heady rise of mercantile capitalism as a genuinely new form of property, the commitments and consequences of which would demand a revision of traditional assumptions and theories of what property *is*.[8] In particular, capitalist production and competition were seen as giving rise to a mode of boundless and unconstrained acquisition which lay beyond the comprehension of traditional moral assumptions, with the result that the relationship between property rights and sovereignty, lately expounded in the writings of the natural rights theorists, had become unintelligible in terms of their theory of absolute (or intrinsic) value. **Property came to be regarded as the cornerstone of person-**

---

[6] J Rousseau, 'Discourse on Political Economy', in V Gourevitch (ed), *The Social Contract and Other Later Political Writings* (Cambridge, CUP, 1997) 12.6. (Hereinafter, *Discourse*.)

[7] Rousseau, *Discourse*, 19.9. Emphasis added

[8] Pocock, above n 4 p 108.

ality, and the centre of the debate became the question whether that personality should be 'affirmed in liberty or governed by authority'.[9] Rousseau's distinction, then, pointed to a fundamental and self-consciously articulated problem for eighteenth century property theorists:

> how can men be forced to defend the freedom of one of them without infringing on the freedom of the others; and how can the public needs be met without disturbing the particular [or private] property of those who are forced to contribute to them?[10]

The two parts of this question focus on distinct forms of social relation. The question of compossible freedoms[11] relates to the horizontal relationships which structure interpersonal interaction within society; the question of public and private realms pertains to vertical relationships between individuals and the state. Taken this way, Rousseau's question becomes that of how the law, which strives to safeguard freedom, can nevertheless place restrictions on that freedom in the name of the common good. Kant would later answer this question in terms of the categorical imperative. Mutual respect for individuals (the argument goes) requires that a state seek to maximise individual freedom; but because freedom can be exercised in such a way as to trammel the freedom of others, the law can impose limitations to individual liberty for the purposes of securing *equal* freedoms. Rousseau's interest, on the other hand, lay not in the distributive mechanisms of the law as such, but in the question of what grounds the political legitimacy of those mechanisms in the first place. His answer echoed the ideals of civic republicanism: individual liberty consists not merely in the immunity from law given by rights conferred by that law, but in the *active* participation of the virtuous in the determination of the law. 'The [state]', he said, 'cannot endure without freedom, nor freedom without virtue, nor virtue without *citizens*.'[12] Rousseau was here using the term 'citizen' in its true political sense, to denote the *vir civilis*, the man who possesses an active voice in the governance of the state and who therefore serves the public good. The essence of citizenship, in *this* sense, is moral and political independence, understood in firmly possessively individualistic terms. If a society does not possess citizens, Rousseau said, 'you will have nothing but nasty slaves, beginning with the chiefs of state'.[13] For Rousseau, then, what defines the true citizen is *property*:

> It is certain that the right of property is the most sacred of all the rights of citizens, and more important in some respects than freedom itself; either because it bears more directly on the preservation of life; or because goods being easier to usurp and more difficult to defend than persons, greater respect ought to be accorded to what can be more easily seized; or finally because property is the true foundation of civil society, and the true guarantee of citizens' commitments: for if persons were not answerable

---

[9] *Ibid* 70–71.
[10] Rousseau, *Discourse* 19.9.
[11] See generally: H Steiner, *An Essay on Rights* (Oxford, Blackwell, 1994) 2ff.
[12] Rousseau, *Discourse* 36.20. Emphasis added
[13] *Ibid*

in their goods, nothing would be so easy as to elude one's duties and scoff at the laws.[14]

Only those with fixed property in land, the argument runs, should be able to participate in the political life of the state. Ownership of property guarantees that the citizen will act for the common good, since his interests are fundamentally tied to the health and wellbeing of the body politic. Continuing respect for, and enjoyment of, permanent rights requires stability and prosperity in society as a whole; and since the prudent citizen desires to pass on his estates to his descendents, he will thereby have the long-term interests of society in mind—will, in short, act in the name of the general will, and not his own, narrower private interests. In contrast, the capitalist, whose wealth lies not in land but in moveable property (mostly in the form of currency and bonds) will act in ways which promote his own personal interests in acquisition and accumulation, and which stem from corruption rather than virtue. Hence, when Rousseau spoke of 'the conformity between the authority of law and the freedom of the citizen' he was referring to the appropriateness (the propriety, or *property*) of the landed class as the ruling class within the state.

Property rights therefore came to be regarded as constituted by social rules, their character and scope being determined, in general, more by developments and changes in economic practice than in relation to the effects of industrialisation and capitalism on the natural environment. The development of forms of property unknown to the seventeenth century writers served to undermine the idea of *dominium* as a principal determinant of property in political theory. Property was increasingly conceived in terms of *ius*, and law a matter of the safeguarding and regulation of interpersonal *iura* through deliberately crafted rules. The idea of property rights as being subject to intrinsic limitations, in relation to the norm of sociability or the needs of the natural world, gave way increasingly to a conception of property rights as fully determined by the juridical characterisation of individual liberty and social obligation. 'What a man loses by the social contract', Rousseau wrote,

> . . . is his natural freedom and an unlimited right to everything that tempts him and he can reach; what he gains is civil freedom and property in everything he possesses. In order not to be mistaken about these compensations, one has to distinguish freely between natural freedom, which has no other bounds than the individual's forces, and civil freedom which is limited by the general will, and between possession which is merely the effect of force or the right of the first occupant, and property which can only be founded on a positive title.[15]

The move from the pre-social to the social world therefore represents a move from a formless social void into the world of rules and stable practices. The lineaments of property rights derive entirely from those social practices and

[14] Rousseau, *Discourse* 42.23.
[15] J Rousseau, 'The Social Contract', in V Gourevitch (ed), *The Social Contract and Other Later Political Writings* (Cambridge, CUP, 1997) 12.61.8.2.53–54.

conventions: 'the social contract . . . serves as the basis of all rights within the State'.[16] In Rousseau therefore one sees the convergence of two ideas which were to exert a powerful influence over the subsequent legal treatment of property. The first saw the continuing focus on (and respect for) agrarian values and fixed agricultural property transform from a naturalistic moral doctrine into an argument about political virtue vis-à-vis the 'corrupt' pursuit of money through commercial activity. The second embodied a faith in the legislative will as the means through which to regulate and organise property and rights in ways which would foster the inculcation of political virtue and promote the welfare of the whole society. In the meeting-place of these ideas would be waged the ideological battle between capitalism and socialism which came to dominate western political debate, and which would see property as both central to that debate *and* morally significant only within the terms set by the conflicting arguments of the opponents. Rousseau's recognition that social reality, and not nature, determines our political focus opened up an immense ideological battle-ground over how society itself should be structured. If human nature is reflected in our social arrangements (and not vice versa) then social change ceases to be an inherent threat to security and stability, and becomes the means through which we express our distinctiveness as civil and political beings. Property arrangements would be, not innately subject to teleological limitations, but malleable, alterable social relations. This dynamic aspect of property and right, and its connection to the will, would become the main focus of the Kantian theory of justice.

In Rousseau's writings were to be found the beginnings of a conception of juridical equity which would fundamentally change the way common lawyers looked at individual rights. 'While [men] may be unequal in force or in genius', Rousseau had said, 'they all become equal by convention and right'.[17] This idea (or rather *ideal*) of juridical equality was, in Kant's philosophy, directly grounded in the individual will. Rights emerge not from philosophical reflection upon the rational processes of nature, but from the will's striving after freedom in the face of social reality. 'We know our own freedom', Kant said,

> —from which all moral laws and consequently all rights as well as all duties arise—only through the moral imperative, which is an immediate injunction of duty; whereas the conception of right as a ground of putting others under obligation has afterwards to be developed out of it.[18]

In Kant therefore, relationships of right and duty are *essentially* interpersonal. Having noted that 'right and duty refer to each other', Kant went on to consider whether juridical relations could obtain between human beings on the one hand, and beings not possessed of rights or duties: 'There is no such relation, [he said] for such beings are irrational, and they neither put us under obligation, nor can

---

[16] *Ibid* 1.9.1.54.
[17] *Ibid* 1.9.8.56.
[18] I Kant, W Hastie (tr), *Philosophy of Law* (Edinburgh, T & T Clark, 1887).

we be put under obligation by them.' By contrast, in the case of juridical relations between man and beings who have both rights and duties, 'There is such a
relation, *for it is the relation of men to men.*'[19]

Rights, then, became the artificial product of social interaction. But property
itself, in Kant's terms, ceased to denote a distinctive kind of right, instead
becoming a near-synonym for the term 'right' itself. Freedom, which consisted
in not being limited by an opposing imperative, 'constitutes a moral right as a
warrant or *title* of action *(facultas moralis)*'.[20] Such rights are comprehended
through the categorical imperative; juristic thought therefore considers rights in
terms of their systemic properties, by detaching the *form* of those rights from
their substance:

> Acts of will or voluntary choice are thus regarded only in so far as they are free, and
> as to whether the action of one can harmonize with the freedom of another, accord-
> ing to a universal law. Right, therefore, comprehends the whole of the conditions
> under which the voluntary actions of any one person can be harmonized in reality with
> the voluntary actions of every other person, according to a universal law of freedom.[21]

Rousseau's insight, that a form of human association itself supplies a source
of moral and philosophical reflection, is difficult to combine with a concern with
systematicity. When the substance of rights is seen as deriving from abstract
principles, moral philosophy becomes the project of articulating universal
truths which specify the necessary form of social relations, rather than specu-
lating upon the philosophical import of those relations.[22] Kant's self-conscious
concern with grounding rights in categorical principles removes the science of
right from the historically extended practices through which rights emerged.
The quest for a 'pure' science of right renders impossible the reflective project of
exploring rights in terms of the social practices which thinkers first identified as
important and distinctive, and as requiring recognition through the rubric of
'rights'. By detaching the form of rights from their substance, the Kantian
conception of *jurisscientia* becomes 'the theoretical knowledge of right and law
in principle, as distinguished from positive laws and cases':

> The science of right thus designates the philosophical and systematic knowledge of the
> principles of natural right. And it is from this science that the immutable principles of
> all positive legislation must be derived by practical jurists and lawgivers.[23]

Such a conception of legal science was unknown to the natural rights theorists
of the seventeenth century. Their writings display a concern with socially

---

[19] All quotations *ibid* Emphasis added

[20] *Ibid,* Emphasis added

[21] Kant, 'Metaphysical Principles of the Science of Right' in *Philosophy of Law* (above n 18) para
C Paragraph break suppressed

[22] See also: NE Simmonds, 'Rights at the Cutting Edge' in MH Kramer, NE Simmonds and H
Steiner, *A Debate Over Rights* (Oxford, OUP, 1998) 119–20; A Rosen, *Kant's Theory of Justice*
(Ithaca, Cornell University Press, 1993) 8.

[23] Rosen, above n 22 p 111.

embodied phenomena firmly ingrained in the course of history. Accordingly, they represent an attempt to identify what is distinctive in patterns of thought which emerge over extended periods of time. The substance of the social relations identified by the name of 'right' determine the distinctive form those relations would take in the scholarly imagination. The concepts of freedom, right and law derived from what seemed to those writers as fundamental truths about human nature and the human condition. The Kantian conception of justice, by contrast, treats rights as the instruments through which individual choices are recognised and protected. Rights (on this view) play a central role in structuring societal relations according to a set of higher principles which transcend the historical formation of the social reality they are intended to order.

This picture of the juridical realm is one which contemplates human beings as shapers of their own destinies. The Kantian conception of justice is accordingly both formal and abstract: what is important for law and ethics is not the ever-shifting pattern of goals and desires which drive individual agents, but the *form* of interpersonal relationships structured by vying and competing wills. Considered as a formal realm of juridical equality, the purpose of law is to maximise individual freedom insofar as it is compatible with the freedom of others. The analysis of social relations, which had traditionally been grounded in highly particular features of social life, thus required articulation at a considerable degree of abstraction in terms of general principles which could present men as fundamentally equal. Ironically, the emergence of a specifically *juridical* conception of justice presented a basic challenge to traditional forms of common law scholarship. For Kant, justice amounted to the restriction of each person's freedom so that it harmonises with the freedom of others within the framework of a common law.[24] The depiction of fundamentally unequal individuals as possessing equal rights in an abstract realm of juridical equality hence required the representation of law as a systematic body of principles establishing and regulating specifically legal relations.

In the history of jurisprudence, little has been said about the way in which Kantianism supplies a ground of positivism. For positivists, the proper emphasis for legal scholarship is on the conventional nature of legal rules, and on the fundamental importance of legislation for the determination of rules and rights. Although often contrasted with legal positivism, Kantian jurisprudence nevertheless implies a concern with positivity by emphasising systematicity. The idea that law constitutes a doctrinally coherent whole introduces into legal thought a concern with fixed rules of considerable generality which stand in need of interpretation in individual cases, but which do not emerge from those cases. Once the juridical realm is thought of as establishing a network of juridical relationships, it is easy to see legal rules as concerned with structuring and regulating individual interests and collective choices. Since individuals can be expected

---

[24] I Kant, 'On the Common Saying: This May be True in Theory, But it Does Not Apply in Practice', in H Reiss (ed), *Kant's Political Writings* (Cambridge, CUP, 1985) 289–90/71.

to prioritise their own freedom over curbs and restrictions in the name of the common good, the identification of public goals and the imposition of legal duties becomes a matter of legislative will. The content of particular rights and duties cannot be expected to drop out of individual interaction, with the result that positive rules are required to define and delineate the boundaries of individual freedom against the pressures of collective interests.

The character of social life thus comes to be recognised as a matter for legislative deliberation and determination, and at the same time fundamentally linked to the nature and quality of individual lives. The medieval dichotomy of agrarian capitalism and agrarian socialism is replaced by the view of society as determined and shaped by individual rights and collective duties, arrived at not by natural or historical processes but by the exercise of the collective will. The Grotian and Lockean traditions had regarded social arrangements as deriving from the nature of property; now, the idea that those arrangements could be altered in numerous ways in the light of diverse moral visions fuelled the conception of property rights as themselves variable according to alternative distributive projects. The recognition of property rights as alterable in line with underlying collective goals and policies in turn encouraged the idea that the nature, scope and extent of those rights are fully determined by the social relations in which they figure.

Positivism and Public Values

Under the influence of Rousseau and Kant, property rights came to be seen not as expressions of man's relationship with the external world, but as manifestations of the internal life of the will. The content of individual rights and liberties was regarded as the product of artifice and contrivance rather than as deriving from nature. The drive towards a conception of private law as a system of legal relations between competing wills conferred a high value on interpretative viewpoints which aim to expound a coherent legal vision.

As we have seen, the presentation of law as a *system* was reflective of a general shift in intellectual life towards legal positivism. Doctrinal legal science emerges at the point where law ceases to be regarded merely as oil for the wheels of social life, but purports to constitute a focal centre for moral life generally. Instead of seeking to reconcile and adjudicate between rival standpoints in situations where individuals' pursuit of their moral projects conflict, the law comes to embody an authoritative body of rules and precepts considered as *applying* to the concrete particularities of social life rather than emerging from them. When our moral beliefs and propensities give way to legally established rules, rights and obligations, positivism provides an attractive explanation of the provenance and legitimacy of legal standards. For if the universal law of freedom is to become something other than an abstract ideal, positive rules will be needed in order to specify what that principle requires in concrete cases where freedoms conflict, and to come to definite conclusions about the boundaries between private choices and collective interests. When legal scholarship favours the systematic exposition of hard-edged rules and principles over the gradual elucidation of customary precepts of no fixed formulation, the gap between the interpretation of specific rules and their *determination* will erode considerably. Articulated rules will, of course, be viewed by the Kantian theorist as shaped by and responsive to an underlying corpus of rational principles; but in presenting law as a system of legal relations guided by articulated rules, the Kantian theory of justice paves the way for versions of positivism which retain the focus on the willed origin of rules but eschew the idea that those rules emerge from precepts of natural reason. Accordingly, the move towards highly articulated bodies of systematic rules will be accompanied by a flourishing concern with questions of legal reasoning of a distinctly positivist hue.

Blackstone was perhaps the first eighteenth century jurist to take these questions seriously. Though conceived as a robust defence of traditional common law values against the doctrine of Parliamentary supremacy, Blackstone's *Commentaries* in fact wages its war in an intellectual context whose assumptions and ideas were already firmly, if unconsciously, positivist. Bentham would later articulate those underlying assumptions with characteristic zeal; but Blackstone's endeavour should itself be understood as representing, not the zenith of traditional common law scholarship, but a symptom of its inevitable decline.

Blackstone's views on property in this transitional period repay close scrutiny. On the face of it, the *Commentaries* sided with the traditional common lawyers on the question of the relationship between law and reason. At various points in the text, Blackstone emphasised the common law's association with a society's collective experience and usages. Not reason alone, but 'a familiar acquaintance with legal writers' are necessary to identify the laws of England.[25] The right understanding of those laws, property laws among them, will therefore depend upon a thorough grounding in legal studies as much as upon excellence in the moral sciences. English law reflects, not universal moral truths, but the traditional arrangements of the English people and their folkways. To stress the connection between rules and social practice was to recognise rules as the artificial product of the society which generated them. Since their authority depended upon their ongoing reception rather than any transcendent moral force they might possess, a society's laws—including its laws of property—must be regarded as determined by the conditions of civil society rather than inherently shaped by nature. 'For the authority of these maxims [of the law of England]', wrote Blackstone,

> rests entirely upon general reception and usage: and the only method of proving that this or that maxim is a rule of the common law, is by showing that it has always been the custom to observe it.[26]

[25] W Blackstone, *Commentaries on the Laws of England 1765–69* (various editions) vol. I, 14, 17.
[26] I *Comm* 68.

The property rights of a given legal order will thus, in general, derive from attempts to structure interpersonal relationships of individuals within society, and will not intrinsically reflect the sort of 'environmental' conceptions charted in the previous chapter. Accordingly, Blackstone's celebrated characterisation of property rights presented them in terms of mankind's essentially unlimited power over the external world:

> There is nothing which so generally strikes the imagination, and engages the affections of mankind, as the right of property; or that sole and despotic dominion which one man claims and exercises over the external things of the world, in total exclusion of the right of any other individual in the universe.[27]

The 'sole and despotic dominion' was not, evidently, intended by Blackstone as a reflection of the reality of property rights in English law; but he arguably *did* intend the phrase as a serious representation of the philosophical framework within which those rights are expressed.[28] The 'absolute' right of property is, as Whelan put it, 'a contingency which might or might not be provided for by law', but it is a form of ownership legislatively or customarily limited, not intrinsically so. For Blackstone, then, property rights were things determined by the particular political and legal arrangements of a state. But despite his adherence to the traditional common law assumptions of Coke and Hale, the *Commentaries* would effectively lead to a view of property rights as limited and shaped by positive law. The resultant shift in conceptions of the relationship between public and private law would, in turn, render any attempt to view property rights as intrinsically limited by substantial moral concerns highly problematic.

In one clear sense, of course, Blackstone was committed to a rejection of the Hobbesian positivism of the previous century, for whereas Hobbes sought to reduce the types and instances of speculation about written rules, Blackstone saw the written rules of a legal order as mundane and merely exemplary and partial. A man who goes through the motions of a legal education, Blackstone observed, will of course know the law as it is written; but,

> if he be uninstructed [also] in the elements and first principles upon which the rule of practice is founded, the least variation from established precedents will totally distract and bewilder him: *ita lex scripta est* is the utmost his knowledge will arrive at; he must never aspire to form, and seldom expect to comprehend, any arguments drawn *a priori* from the spirit of the laws and the natural foundations of justice.[29]

The idea that all (written) law was ultimately situated within the customary precepts of the common law corpus, and subject to them, had been expressed in seventeenth century thought through the idea of the antiquity of common law

---

[27] II *Comm* 2.
[28] I see no textual evidence for FG Whelan's assertion that Blackstone's remarks should be viewed as ironical. See FG Whelan, 'Property as Artifice: Hume and Blackstone', in JR Pennock and J Chapman (eds), *Nomos XX: Property* (New York, NYU Press, 1980) 119.
[29] I *Comm* 32.

principles and their origin in an 'ancient constitution'.[30] Since the fundamental principles of the law derived from immemorial custom, the integrity of the common law as the prime determinant of social arrangements would transcend the political thought of any given historical period, including one which viewed the royal prerogative or parliamentary enactments as the principal source of legal and social rules. Blackstone's extended discussion of legal history in Book I of the *Commentaries* was thus simultaneously an attempt to affirm the antiquity of common law principles *and* to contain the forces of statutory consolidation by establishing the common law's primacy over forms of political arrangement incompatible with the nature of the ancient constitution. But the intellectual framework within which Blackstone situated his philosophy of law was already deeply indebted to positivist ideas, and had a clear ancestor in the political thought of Hobbes.

> [I]nasmuch as political communities are made up of many natural persons, each of whom has his particular will and inclination, these several wills cannot by any *natural* union be joined together, or tempered and disposed into a lasting harmony, so as to constitute and produce that one uniform will of the whole. It can therefore be no otherwise produced than by a *political* union; by the consent of all persons to submit their own private wills to the will of one man, or of one or more assemblies of men, to whom the supreme authority is entrusted, and this will . . . [is] understood to be *law*.[31]

Such a move presented an apparently insurmountable problem for the traditional common law scholarship Blackstone favoured, since it entailed the view that the possibility of harmonious social relationships rests upon shared acceptance of a sovereign whose explicit rules *forge* social consensus. In order to reconcile these apparently incompatible positions, Blackstone resorted to a naturalist conception of property.

In common with the republican jurists, Blackstone regarded legal rules as essentially involving asymmetric relationships of power. A law is a rule of action, prescribed by a superior, which an inferior is '*bound* to obey'; hence, the notion of legal obligation excludes *a priori* that of (political and moral) independence. Man's obligation towards the law of nature likewise stems from *dependence*: the extent of one's obligation is the extent of 'all those points wherein [one's] dependence consists', since an independent being lives by his *own* rules. So, 'as man depends absolutely upon his maker for everything, it is necessary that he should in all points conform to his maker's will.'[32] On the face of it, Blackstone's reliance on the language of dependence, and not of property (as in Locke), reveals a philosophical preoccupation with liberty and virtue as the grounds of legal science, rather than ownership. The language of dependence and liberty does not *inevitably* reduce to that of property, but it will do so

---

[30] J Pocock, *The Ancient Constitution and the Feudal Law* (Cambridge, CUP, 1957) 46ff. But see J Cairns, 'Blackstone, the Ancient Constitution and the Feudal Law' 28 (1985) *Historical Journal* 711–17.

[31] I *Comm* 52. Emphasis in original.

[32] I *Comm* 39.

where liberty is conceived of in possessive terms. To be of any explanatory value, the notion of 'dependence' must amount to more than a mere synonym for 'obligation'; but it is equally clear that Blackstone's remarks cannot be directed at our physical dependence upon the Creator for life and the means to sustain it, for that would not establish the *moral* dependence required for the notion of obligation. The republican tradition had forged strong links between dependence on another's will and forms of moral and political corruption, and it was precisely stable *property* which guaranteed the independence essential for political virtue. In a passage which makes clear the proprietary nature of God's relationship with man, Blackstone reversed this line of thought by regarding human dependence upon the life-creating will of the Almighty as a source of *virtue*:

> Considering the Creator only as a being of infinite *power*, He was able unquestionably to have prescribed whatever laws He pleased to His creature, man, however unjust or severe. But as He is also a being of infinite *wisdom*, He has laid down only such laws as were founded in those relations of justice that existed in the nature of things, antecedent to any positive precept.[33]

Since God's will is the *sine qua non* of both human life and the means to sustain it, our recognition of God's commands as a source of binding obligations is simultaneously a recognition of God's grant as a property-creating act.[34] Moreover, our dependence upon our Creator for sustenance invoked, for Blackstone, originary property rights more readily understood in terms of *dominium* rather than interpersonal *iura*:

> In the beginning of the world, we are informed by holy writ, the all-bountiful Creator gave to man 'dominion over all the earth; and over the fish of the sea, and over the fowl of the air, and over every living thing that moveth upon the earth'. This is the only true and solid foundation of man's dominion over external things, whatever airy metaphysical notions may have been started by fanciful writers upon this subject.[35]

The 'natural' form of property implicit in this argument has often passed unnoticed in the shadow of Blackstone's more celebrated conception of property rights as the artificial product of a civil polity. Faced with the problematic relationship between these two conceptions, the historian of legal thought might feel that the matter can readily be interpreted as symptomatic of a work imbued with contradictions. In fact, the apparently janus-faced conception of property and that of the basis of the authority of law itself achieve some measure of synthesis in Blackstone's conception of the way in which reason permeates legal standards.

---

[33] I *Comm* 40.
[34] In common with the major natural rights theorists, Blackstone wrote explicitly in terms of men as owners of their rights and liberties, hence evincing a deep commitment to the notion that human life fundamentally consists in relationships of property. See eg I *Comm* 53–54.
[35] II *Comm* 2–3.

The idea that the municipal laws of a state—including its property arrangements—might have a contractarian basis, rooted in powerful sovereignty, had been a feature of political thought since the time of Grotius. The seventeenth century had seen a continuum of thought on which property rights slid further and further away from their theocratic beginnings as natural consequences of man's worldly situation, and closer towards a view of them as constituted by the positive municipal legal arrangements of a mature political order, whilst never wholly relinquishing their political origins in either extreme. The relationship between the natural law and the hard-edged standards of municipal legal orders had been characterised in various ways by members of the natural rights tradition, according to the perceived luminosity (or otherwise) of the former's promptings and the degree of dependence (or independence) of the latter upon the clearly articulated pronouncements of a sovereign will. Common to both of these strands of theory was the notion of reason: our ability to identify, with any degree of accuracy, the requirements of natural laws depended upon our rational comprehension of human nature and of the means and prospects of communal living and striving; at the same time, the success of that interpretative endeavour variously stressed or downplayed the need for a contractarian solution to our problems in the shape of a powerful sovereign whose express commands would put an end to the ceaseless competition between rival conceptions of the demands of reason.

Blackstone's distinctive solution to the problem of political origins was essentially Hobbesian with a common law twist. As with *Leviathan*, a persistent theme of the *Commentaries* is 'the frailty, the imperfection, and the blindness of human reason' in the face of the task of discovering the dictates of the laws of nature.[36] Though the basis of obligation to natural laws is human 'dependence' upon God's will, our reason for uncovering and following those laws is *prudential*. 'If the discovery of . . . first principles of the laws of nature depended only upon the exercise of right reason', Blackstone wrote, then:

> mankind would have wanted some inducement to have quickened their inquiries, and the greater part of the world would have rested content in mental indolence . . . As therefore the Creator is a being not only of infinite *power* and *wisdom*, but also of infinite *goodness*, He has been pleased so to contrive the constitution and frame of humanity that we should want no other prompter to inquire after and pursue the rule of right, but only our own self-love, that universal principle of action. For He has so inseparably woven the laws of eternal justice with the happiness of each individual, that the latter cannot be attained but by observing the former; and, if the former be punctually obeyed, it cannot but induce the latter.[37]

Hobbes had shown that the prudential attractiveness of the laws of nature would not of itself overcome the bitter and hostile conditions of the state of nature, given the weakness of the human intellect (in such conditions) in

---

[36] I *Comm* 41.
[37] I *Comm* 40.

distinguishing between our rational needs and wants and our passion-fuelled desires. The ability of individuals to grasp the laws of nature is thus likely to be limited to the perception that (as Kant might have put it) peace can only emerge through formal agreement, rather than substantive moral consensus. The foundations of communal living, for Hobbes, do not emerge from the unmediated laws of nature, but require the institution of powerful political authority. The realisation of social union is thus contingent upon that of a political union which *imposes* moral consensus through articulated rules. By contrast, Blackstone's perception of the 'mutual connection of justice and human felicity' revived the classical idea of man as *essentially* a political animal, and of politics rather than war as the natural state of humanity. '[M]an', said Blackstone, 'was formed for society; and . . . is neither capable of living alone, nor indeed has the courage to do it.' [38] Though siding with Hobbes on the issue of the conventional origins of the political state, Blackstone nevertheless regarded man's political arrangements as preceded by a stable social life. Such a conception of humankind's existence prior to the emergence of political institutions (Blackstone explicitly denied the existence of a 'state of nature' in the sense of a pre-*social* mode of existence) clearly implies basic agreement in judgements about the conditions in which human beings should live alongside one another, and it comes as little surprise to find Blackstone portraying that life in terms of agrarian communism.[39] The rudimentary social existence of pre-political man depicted in the *Commentaries* is rooted in basic agreement over values, signifying Blackstone's greater confidence in the ability of human reason to uncover moral truths.

Traditionally, views concerning human access to the propositions of natural law emphasised either the mind's logical faculty, and the construction of chains of reasoning from the mundane and particular to the abstract and sublime, or what might be termed the 'living tradition of ethics', the idea that perceived values derived not from the putative universals beloved by platonists and theologues, but from the very social practices such values were meant to evaluate and to 'structure'. Broadly speaking, the former view was championed by the natural lawyers and by Hobbes (the former praising the human capacity for metaphysical speculation, the latter stressing the seamless continuity between individuals' rational speculation about their condition and their powerful wants and desires). The second, inductive, approach was the one favoured by the common lawyers, who saw reason in terms not of abstract philosophical speculation, but of *experience*. Though ideologically closer to the common lawyers,

---

[38] I *Comm* 41, 43, respectively. (In the latter extract, Blackstone took himself to be following Pufendorf's views on human nature.) The alert reader will have begun to realise that the true tension in Blackstone's views on property lies not in the dichotomy of naturalness vs artifice, but in the conflict between his implicitly possessive individualist assumptions about natural rights and obligations and his rejection of those assumptions in the notion of man as essentially belonging to, and shaped by, society.

[39] I *Comm* 47.

Blackstone's position more closely mirrored that of the former group. The common lawyers understood the rationality of law as arising out of the reasonableness of particular decisions and doctrinally established rules. Law's connection with reason was not a matter of the conformity of particular rules and decisions with abstract principles, but of their continuing confirmation as reasonable and just solutions to recurrent social problems. The common law conception hence embodied a belief that the standards of rationality at work in the law defy reduction to a set of universal principles. The reason of the law is, on this view, 'the reason not of rules and principles, but of cases.'[40] The idea that social rules might principally derive from experience was also a feature of Blackstone's argument: 'the foundation of what we call ethics, or natural law', he said,

> ... amount[s] to no more than demonstrating that this or that action tends to a man's real happiness, and therefore very justly concluding that the performance of it is a part of the law of nature; or, on the other hand, that this or that action is destructive of man's real happiness, and therefore that the law of nature forbids it.[41]

Yet the empirical standpoint which is implicit in the traditional view gave way in Blackstone's thinking to a view of moral philosophy as essentially a deductive activity:

> But in order to apply this [law] to the particular exigencies of each individual, it is still necessary to have recourse to reason: whose office it is to discover ... what the law of nature directs in every circumstance of life; by considering what method will tend the most effectually to our own substantial happiness. And if our reason were always, as in our first ancestor before his transgression, clear and perfect, unruffled by passions, unclouded by prejudice, unimpaired by disease or intemperance, the task would be pleasant and easy; we should need no other guide than this. But every man now finds the contrary in his own experience, that his reason is corrupt, and his understanding full of ignorance and error.[42]

The intellectual background to Blackstone's political thought is therefore reminiscent of Hobbes's, in that both thinkers took ethics and legal science to be rooted in a faculty of deductive reason regarded as flawed and problematic. But whereas the Hobbesian argument drew from the premise of the fragility of human reason a conclusion that espoused the need for extreme positivism, Blackstone's legal vision emphasised law's rootedness in moral reflection. Once we become aware of the paucity of our ability to understand and uncover metaphysical truths, a central reason for the perpetuation of solipsistic conflict is removed as we no longer regard ourselves as uniquely privileged in our moral insights; hence, social co-operation and discourse replace the competitive strivings of Hobbesian natural man. The authority of law, then, derived in Blackstone's account not from social contract but from 'the law of nature, and the law of revelation', the latter originating in the Holy Scriptures, the former in

[40] Postema, above n 2 p 31.
[41] I *Comm* 41.
[42] *Ibid*

reflective activity. The only difference between these two 'foundations' of the law lies in the degree of certainty that attaches to them:

> These precepts, when revealed, are found upon comparison to be really a part of the original law of nature, as they tend in all their consequences to man's felicity. But we are not from thence to conclude that the knowledge of these truths was attainable by reason, in its present corrupted state; since we find that, until they are revealed, they were hid from the wisdom of ages. As then the moral precepts of this law are indeed of the same original with those of the law of nature, so their intrinsic obligation is of equal strength and perpetuity. Yet undoubtedly the revealed law is of infinitely more authenticity than that moral system which is framed by ethical writers, and denominated the natural law. Because one is the law of nature, expressly declared to be so by God himself; the other is only what, by the assistance of human reason, we imagine to be that law.[43]

Along with the common lawyers, then, Blackstone viewed the authority of law as deriving principally from reason rather than the will. Unlike the common law theorists, however, he tended to conceive of the standards of reason as transcendent rather than immanent. Accordingly, Blackstone placed much greater emphasis on articulated, posited standards where the voice of reason was silent:

> Upon these two foundations, the law of nature and the law of revelation, depend all human laws; that is to say, no human laws should be suffered to contradict these. There are, it is true, a great number of indifferent points, in which both the divine [ie revealed] law and the natural leave a man at his own liberty, but which are found necessary for the benefit of society to be restrained within certain limits. And herein it is that human laws have their greatest force and efficacy; for, with regard to such points as are not indifferent, human laws are only declaratory of, and act in subordination to, the former. . . . But with regard to matters that are themselves indifferent, and are not commanded or forbidden by those superior laws, . . . here the inferior legislature has scope and opportunity to interpose, and to make that action unlawful which was not before so.[44]

Insofar as it allowed a greater role for speculative reason, Blackstone's conception of legal science brought about an intellectual climate in which ideas congenial to positivism were allowed to thrive. For once the law is conceived as a rational science, the focus of scholarly attention is removed from particular decisions and transferred to general principles from which those decisions are then presented as deductions or instances. Individual judgements are not perceived as just or unjust purely on their own terms, but insofar as they conform to or depart from a conception of justice, or a set of universal principles. The task of the legal commentator became that of presenting the various rules and decisions of the law in a way that revealed the justifying principles which underlay them.[45] There had, of course, been legal treatises before; but whereas Coke's

[43] I *Comm* 42.
[44] I *Comm* 42–43.
[45] See also Postema, above n 2 p 33, and AWB Simpson, 'The Rise and Fall of the Legal Treatise: Legal Principles and the Forms of Legal Literature' (1981) XLVII *University of Chicago Law Review* 632–79.

Institutes and Bracton's *De Legibus* were little more than alphabetised compendiums of legal rules, Blackstone's *Commentaries* presented the law by treating the subject thematically in terms of its discrete areas, each possessing its own doctrinal coherence. His 'first endeavour' was

> to mark out a plan of the laws of England, so comprehensive as that every title might be reduced under some or other of its general heads, which the student might afterwards pursue to any degree of minuteness.[46]

This new form of legal scholarship,[47] with its suggestion that law was at least potentially transformable into a deductive science, was disposed to regard law as a *system* rather than a set of procedures. Whereas the classical formularies, abridgements and glossaries treated the law (in the words of Sir William Jones) as 'merely an unconnected series of decrees and ordinances', Blackstone's systematic presentation attempted to explain particular rules and decisions against the background of the general principles under which they were allegedly subsumable. This concern with system and coherence had the consequence of forcing out into the open ideas about *stare decisis,* and encouraging the formulation of so-called 'rules of precedent'.[48] The role of speculative reason in formulating and refashioning the principles upon which like decisions were based came to be regarded, by Blackstone's successors, as the project of unearthing and articulating *rationes decidendi.* As with the classical common law theory, universal juridical principles came to be seen as immanent to law, but the focus had shifted from the content of those principles to their 'source' in legal judgments. At the same time, the increasing use of legislation as a means of regulating social and economic life provided an undeniable source of authoritative general principles from which particular decisions could be fashioned. Although private law retained its doctrinal integrity as an interlocking *system* of horizontal entitlements, public law was increasingly seen as the major source of legal rules and principles, and private law as the realm in which those rules are interpreted and applied.[49] The integrity of private rights thus came progressively to be regarded as threatened by the aggregative and distributional goals expressed in legislation.

It is within the context of this changing conception of the nature of law that Blackstone's views on property must be seen. Despite this loss of faith in the immanence of reason, Blackstone portrayed property as a largely customary

[46] W Blackstone, *An Analysis of the Laws of England, to Which is Prefixed an Introductory Discourse on the Study of the Law* (1771) (reprinted William S Hein & Co, 1997)
[47] Though, as Simpson notes (above n 45 p 634), works such as Littleton's *Tenores Novelli* (translated as Littleton on Tenures) (1481, reprinted Fred B Rothman & Co, 1991) are early examples of the form.
[48] 'The doctrine of the law', Blackstone said, 'is this: that precedents and rules must be followed, unless flatly absurd or unjust; for though their reason be not obvious at first view, yet we owe such a deference to former times as not to suppose they acted wholly without consideration.' (I *Comm* 70).
[49] I *Comm* 61. As Blackstone put it, private law is the realm within which 'the reason and spirit of [the laws]' is explored

institution. In common with Grotius, he regarded original community in things as 'sufficient to answer all the purposes of human life' only as long as men remained in 'a state of primeval simplicity',[50] and hence the property rights of a mature political order are essentially a matter of human convention. The terminology, however, had changed. When describing the use-right, Blackstone wrote of the dawning recognition that

> he who first began to use [a thing] acquired therein a kind of transient property, that lasted so long as he was using it, and no longer; or, to speak with greater precision, the *right* of possession continued for the same time only as the *act* of possession lasted.[51]

Here, then, was property equated with *ius*. Individual *iura* arose, to be sure, from individual acts of possession, but *dominium* alone (without *ius*) did not constitute property, which is a right, but only the *fact* of possession. The extent to which Pufendorf's terminology of subjective right had permeated Blackstone's thinking is revealed in the focus of the latter's ruminations. What chiefly interested Blackstone was the notion of property as a right one has *against* other people. The import of the discussion of the use-right was that the *right* to possess (ie exclude others from the use of some object) lasts only so long as dominion is exercised; but it is (to speak, as Blackstone said, *precisely*) the *right* rather than the *fact* of possession which constitutes property.

The means by which use-rights crystallise into full property rights in things was analysed in largely the same way in the second book of the *Commentaries* as in the writings of Pufendorf. Stable dwellings, and ultimately agriculture and commerce developed as a response to the increasing complexity of social life in each *municipum*, and hence property law took shape within municipal law rather than the law of nature: 'the permanent right of property . . . was no *natural*, but merely a *civil*, right'.[52] Yet his attachment to the Lockean philosophy that property rights had a lot to do with *possession* pulled Blackstone's thought in a direction which would later be seized upon by the positivists. For if property is rooted in *dominium*, it is tempting to see ownership as involving a brute, factual and in principle unlimited relationship between a person and a thing, and individual *iura* as later grafts constituting limitations to that basic relationship. Hence Blackstone's 'absolutist' conception of property treats property rights as legislatively, rather than intrinsically, limited:

> [A person's property] consists in the free use, enjoyment, and disposition of all his acquisitions, without any control or diminution, save only by the laws of the land.[53]

These 'modifications under which we presently find' property rights were, in Blackstone's view, 'some of those civil advantages, in exchange for which every individual has resigned a part of his natural liberty.' From this position

---

[50] II *Comm* 3.
[51] *Ibid*
[52] II *Comm* 11.
[53] I *Comm* 138.

Blackstone was led to formulate one of the key ideas which would come to dominate property theory from the mid-eighteenth century onwards: the idea of private property rights as vying and competing with the common good.

> So great . . . is the regard of the law for private property that it will not authorise the least violation of it; no, not even for the general good of the whole community. If a new road, for instance, were to be made through the grounds of a private person, it might perhaps be extensively beneficial to the public; but the law permits no man, or set of men, to do this without consent of the owner of the land.

In the Grotian tradition, property rights were grounded in objective morality and were never so fixed that the wider distributive needs of society could not modify or restrict them. For Blackstone, however, the shape of private rights was 'modelled by the municipal law', and thus only the use of legislative power could alter them. It is clear from the *Commentaries* that Blackstone thought that any such power ought to be used sparingly, since it would involve (in his view) an unequal economic bargain between an individual and the state in which land is traded for compensation. This conception would itself become important during the intense period of infrastructure-building prompted by the Industrial Revolution. Blackstone's legal science had produced a framework within which private rights and public goods conflicted, and in which philosophical discussions about the nature and origin of property rights would be seen by practising lawyers as inessential insofar as they had no bearing upon the grounds of judicial determinations or the interpretation of statutes.

PROPERTY AND LEGAL 'SCIENCE'

The seventeenth century rights theorists had explored property principally in terms of its theological origins and its role in human social life. These accounts proceeded in largely anthropocentric terms, but insofar as human development and nurture of the environment were seen as being in complete harmony, the writings of the major natural rights theorists constituted a body of scholarship which viewed property rights as emerging from, and shaped by, humankind's relationship with the natural world. By the mid-eighteenth century, these 'philosophical' issues of property rights had come to be viewed as extraneous to legal determinations of the extent of an individual's rights. Property was seen as a creation of law, constituted by the existence of contingent social rules and practices. In contrast to the attempts of the natural rights theorists to show why human societies must have property rights of a certain kind, the idea of necessary moral truths was regarded by the eighteenth century lawyers as inimical to the historical variability of conventional rules which change and adapt in relation to shifting social conditions.[54] Moreover, the conception of legal science

---

[54] See Whelan, above n 28 p 123.

which had grown out of the works of Blackstone and his successors in the text-book tradition viewed the wider moral questions as essentially separate from legal argumentation concerning rights, which hinged upon the articulation and interpretation of distinctively juridical *dicta*.

The evolution of this systematic legal science, it has been argued, encouraged explanation of the grounds of law in positivistic terms. Where individual decisions of the court are perceived as owing their justification to underlying principles, the task of the lawyer or the treatise writer is seen as that of uncovering those principles by an examination of the judicial pronouncements through which they receive expression. It is the nature of the common law that no particular pronouncement can claim to express the rule in its final, unalterable form, and that attempts to formulate a general rule are always partial and open to modification, amendment or variation by a later court. Nevertheless, the treatise writer's mission is to interpret the law in such a way as to reveal the underlying coherence of a body of rules found in statutes and judicial decisions. The natural law interpretation of eighteenth century legal science, most eloquently captured by the oft-quoted remarks of Lord Mansfield, thus held that the 'Law does not consist in particular cases, but in general principles which run through the cases and govern the decision of them.'[55] To the positivists, the activity of legal reasoning seemed more like the 'business [of arranging] yesterday's results in whatever way will be most convenient for those working on today's problems.'[56] From that point of view, Lord Mansfield had stood matters on their head: should we not cut through the mystique of theological language and see the law as consisting in the statues and judgments, and dismiss the 'underlying principles' as mere phantoms?

Such a view, to Bentham's empiricist mind, was inescapable. Accordingly, his writings dealt the death-blow to the natural rights theories which had, a century earlier, grounded property rights in nature. Now, property was seen as created and determined exclusively by (positive) *law*. Any moral questions one might raise about property or property rights might be debated by the philosophers (and contrary to Bentham's occasional belief, the moral and political status of the principle of utility ensured that such debates would be at least *intelligible*, however confused) but would have no effect upon what property rights, legally speaking, are. In Blackstone's conception of absolute ownership, the view of property rights as possessing no intrinsic moral properties is already close at hand; in Bentham's thought this view would receive its definitive expression. That Bentham held this view, however, is of less importance than the impression which formed among his nineteenth century successors, and which Bentham was keen to promote, that the principle of utility was in fact no more than a scientifically acceptable reworking of the view of property and rights held

---

[55] *Rust v Cooper* [1774] in Cowper's Reports of Cases in the Court of King's Bench p 632.
[56] SFC Milsom, 'The Nature of Blackstone's Achievement' (1981) 1 *Oxford Journal of Legal Studies* 1.

by Locke. Property rights, in the hands of Bentham and his successors, became *purely* interpersonal in nature, and conceptually resistant to limitation in the name of environmental protection.

From Blackstone to Bentham

The version of legal positivism to be found in Bentham's writings is very often associated with the view that law and morality are discontinuous intellectual realms. As we have seen, the 'positivism' implicit in the works of the eighteenth century legal and political thinkers, including Blackstone, consisted not in any theses about the separability or otherwise of these two spheres of human thought, but in a conception of legal science which encouraged a concern with *articulated* rules and principles. Bentham's positivism, likewise, emerged not from a desire to purify law of all moral thinking (since the principle of utility was to be the governing principle behind legislative reform), but from a deeply empiricist conception of legal science. Bentham's remarks on the purpose of definition has given the impression that his main aim was to identify a rigid distinction between law, on the one hand, and morality and politics on the other. Definitions are employed, he wrote,

> [i]n the first place to convey to our apprehension some idea as signified by the word defined, and to teach us to distinguish the idea so signified by that word from any other idea that can be signified by any other word.[57]

Yet the substance of Bentham's definition of law was entirely consistent with the notion that legal standards might identify moral precepts. His concern was not with questions of 'moral purity', but with establishing conceptual priorities:

> Law is a term of the collective kind, signifying at pleasure the whole or any part of an assemblage of objects, to each of which, if the term be taken in its natural and obvious meaning, should be applicable the individual appellation *a Law* . . . To know then what is meant by law in general, we must know what is meant by a law; and if we know what is meant by a law, we cannot but know what is meant by law in general.[58]

The point being made was that we must be acquainted with particulars before we can possess an understanding of any general concept (such as 'law'). This is not the absurd suggestion that we must know what individual laws are before we can grasp the concept of 'law', but rather that our ability to frame a general concept is an ability to place an intellectual structure upon the uneven texture of our social life, and hence depends upon our prior acquaintance with the phenomena in question. Firm ideas about how a social phenomenon might be

---

[57] J Bentham, *A Comment on the Commentaries* I.1 in J Burns and HLA Hart (eds), *A Comment on the Commentaries and A Fragment on Government* (London, Athlone Press, 1977) 3. [Hereinafter, *Comment*.]

[58] *Ibid* 7.

classified emerge upon the intellectual plane only as we gradually become aware of that phenomenon as distinctive in our *experience*. Had Bentham lived a century later, he might have quoted Russell:

> The discussion of indefinables . . . is the endeavour to see clearly, and to make others see clearly, the entities concerned, in order that the mind may have that acquaintance with them that it has with redness or the taste of a pineapple.[59]

Quite clearly, no such empirical acquaintance is available in respect of the laws of nature. Our ability to frame a concept of law will thus be dependent upon our experience of statue law and judicial decisions: 'a law', Bentham said, '. . . is an assemblage of words. Of any words, then? No: but of such words alone as are signs of, as serve to express, we may say, a volition.'[60]

Law is, then, an expression of will. But whereas the positivism of Hobbes and Selden resided principally in the notion of *will*, Bentham's thought centred on the necessity of *expression*, that is, on the necessity, for something to count as a law, of its verbally articulated, posited status. Since the human will can be so expressed (in words either written or spoken), a law is thereby the expression 'of something real: of something the reality of which we have the testimony of our senses.'[61] Such a conception of law effectively placed beyond reach any plausible reference to natural law or natural rights. Accordingly, Blackstone's remarks on the laws of nature were dismissed as 'composed of the choicest and most current phrases of theological grimgribber.'[62] In accordance with his empiricist postulates, Bentham launched an attack on the meaningfulness of passages (predominantly in the *Commentaries*) which referred to natural rights. 'There are no such thing,' he wrote,

> as any '*precepts*', nothing 'by which man is commanded' to do any of those acts pretended to be enjoined by the pretended law of nature. If any man knows of any let him produce them. If they were producible, we should not need to be puzzling out the business of 'discovering' them, as [Blackstone] soon after tells us we must, by the help of reason.[63]

The kind of knowledge referred to by Bentham is, of course, knowledge in the sense of empirical acquaintance. Thus Bentham removed at one stroke the intellectual foundation of the natural rights theorists' account of property. The philosophical context in which questions of property rights had been raised and explored were regarded by Bentham as utterly redundant. Of Blackstone's treatment of the subject he remarked:

---

[59] B Russell, *The Principles of Mathematics* (London, Routledge, 1903) xx.

[60] Bentham, *Comment* I.1.7.

[61] *Ibid* Bentham's empiricism here consisted in a form of deflationism which fell short of the materialism of his later writings. In the *Comment* he was content with individuated meanings; the position in *Of Laws in General* was to attempt an outright reduction of meanings to mere signs and symbols, and of words to ink marks on the page: JH Burns & HLA Hart (eds) *Of Laws in General* (London, Athlone, 1970) I.1.

[62] *Ibid* I.1.10.

[63] *Ibid* I.2.13–14.

Why did he not write in verse? It can certainly only be from an undue deference to modern prejudices that he condescended to tread the career of humble prose. Verse is what his oracles, like those of the ancient sages, would have appeared in to best advantage.[64]

Bentham was here not merely contrasting the verse style with that of the ideal form of legal writing ('a science of which precision is the very life and soul . . .'), but suggesting that the metaphorical richness traditionally associated with verse would put readers on guard against assuming the entities discussed were in any way real. Putative laws of nature were to be shown, on this account, either to be empirically false generalisations (ie false in law; such as the proposition that 'we should hurt nobody'), or else in fact rules of municipal law, or mere tautologies. Take, for example, one Blackstonian candidate for a law of nature, the proposition that 'we should render every man his due'.[65] Of this proposition, Bentham said,

> the meaning, I suppose, is either that we ought to render him what we ought to render him, we ought to do, once more, what we ought to do (for this edifying and instructive sense is all that belongs incontestably to any [putative natural law]); or else that we should forbear to violate his property: that is, should forbear to deal with anything which *the law* (as I should call it, *the municipal law* as [Blackstone] calls it) shall have declared to belong to him, in a manner which the law shall have commanded us not to deal with it. For how impossible it is that anything can be a man's property, but by virtue of this same municipal law . . .[66]

Whatever its value as a piece of Blackstone exegesis (the latter, after all, regarded property as a *civil* right), this line of thought put an end to the suggestion that the philosophical ideas of the natural rights tradition had any consequence for legal determinations of property rights. Indeed, the revisionist intellectual histories of the nineteenth century jurists would endorse the view of Blackstone as the muddled natural lawyer.

Had the impossibility of natural law been, for Bentham, the same thing as the non-existence of moral values *tout court*, his critique of the natural rights theories would not have enjoyed the lasting influence it has over legal thinking. The problem was not the inexistence of moral values (since the teachings of Jesus and the Apostles clearly state moral rules)[67] but rather the category error in supposing moral values to be *laws*. Revealed law (or divine positive law) admittedly consisted in specific commands laid down at a specific time for a certain people, and hence might be counted as 'genuine law'. But revealed law mediated by 'natural theology', Bentham said, 'cannot furnish . . . a *precept*: what it may furnish is a *sanction*.'[68] That is, the attempt to elevate the specific legal commands of,

[64] *Ibid* I.2.11. Bentham's reference to 'oracles' related to a passage in Blackstone which referred to judges as 'living oracles of the law' (I *Comm* 69).
[65] I *Comm* 40.
[66] Bentham, *Comment* I.2.16.
[67] See *Comment* I.3.23.
[68] *Ibid* I.3.22–23.

say, the law of Moses into universal laws is to mis-categorise those commands as something they are not; as if *reason* could elevate the English doctrine of assumpsit into a universal truth for all nations and for all time.[69] By the same token, moral rules which make any pretence of general validity should not be mistaken for the *legal* rules of some jurisdiction. 'Politics' and 'theology' are discontinuous intellectual realms precisely because theological propositions are aimed at the afterlife, not the 'temporal felicity of the state'.[70] A modern critic of natural law might have phrased this in terms of the popular conception of politics as the art of the possible rather than the necessary truth: 'natural' universal precepts, however necessary for guiding human souls towards their everlasting reward, are (he might say) no good guide to the political good.

Bentham's argument, then, did not eliminate conceptions of moral value but dethroned reason and conceptions of the good as central determinants of legal rules and rights. Moral conceptions might, of course, exert an indirect influence on the shape of legal rights insofar as a legislator has particular ends in mind when formulating new law; but such conceptions must vie and compete with rival conceptions which present themselves as best able to promote the *political* good. Bentham clearly thought that that end was best served, not by abstract notions of distributive justice or the theocentric epiphenomena of the natural rights theorists, but by the principle of utility:

> Besides, if we lay it down as a fixed principle that whatever laws have been given by the author of revelation were meant by Him to be laws subservient to the happiness of present life, that this subserviency is an indispensable evidence of the authenticity of what are given for such laws, that is, of their really coming from Him, to know whether a measure is conformable to the dictates of the principle of utility is at once the readiest and surest way of knowing whether it is conformable to the dictates of revelation.[71]

Passages such as this one reinforced the view among Bentham's nineteenth century interpreters that the principle of utility, as the master criterion for guiding law-making, was an ingenious intellectual reworking of Lockean natural rights theory, whose principal assumption had been the necessary congruence between natural law and rational self-interest.[72] Might we not, they argued, put all such discussions on a scientific footing by eliminating obscure and inferential

---

[69] Phrased as a canon of interpretation, Bentham was arguing that one should opt for the narrowest possible construction of a written rule–a theme he would later apply to the whole of common law.

[70] *Ibid* I.3.27.

[71] *Ibid* I.3.27–28.

[72] Locke's *Essay on Human Understanding* (ed) PH Nidditch (Clarendon, Oxford, 1989) had referred to '[t]hat which we call Good, which is apt to cause or increase pleasure, or diminish pain in us; or else to procure or preserve us the possession of any other good, or absence of any evil, and on the contrary we name that Evil which is apt to produce or increase in us any pain . . .' (II.20). But other passages, in the Essay and elsewhere, refute the Utilitarians' interpretation that good and evil were relative to pleasure and pain. Further down the same page, Locke observed that 'Pleasure and pain, and that which cause them, Good and Evil, are the things on which our passions turn' (*ibid*, emphasis added).

talk about natural laws, and demonstrating that the purported consequences of those laws are no more than the results of applications of the principle of utility? Bentham certainly encouraged this interpretation:

> The question concerning the truth of the sacred history in general is a very compli-cated and difficult question of evidence, and another very complicated and difficult question in every case is whether the sense we put upon a given group of passages be the true one. The question concerning the utility of a measure of government, of an article of conduct in the subject, is a question of fact: a question concerning a matter of fact that depends upon experience, and is to be collected by observation.[73]

The view of the principle of utility as a tacit ground of earlier theories was not original with Bentham or his supporters. Decades earlier, Hume had observed that the rational force of arguments concerning natural rights lay in the appeal to considerations of utility. The claim that property rights naturally reflect man's need for society and social development was, Hume thought, just another way of saying that rights are shaped according to prevailing conceptions of the pubic good.[74] The part played by the naturalistic, theological assumptions, on this view, was simply to emphasise the deontic quality of the rules which estab-lish property rights as distinct from mere prudential precepts. Once those assumptions were stripped away, we can see that property rights are not deduc-tions from fixed moral rules, but instead serve utility. Unlike Bentham, however, Hume thought it possible that our conceptions of property *could* serve other values apart from utility. Indeed, he perceived in established forms of juridical reasoning the tendency to present rights in a way which severed any obvious links to utility: 'there are,' he observed,

> no doubt, motives of public interest for most of the rules which determine property; but still I suspect that these rules are principally fixed by the imagination, or the more frivolous properties of our thought and conception.[75]

The point of Hume's reflections was not to show that *every* attempt to define rules of property according to an abstract conceptual scheme tacitly invokes utility, but rather that property rules are most beneficial where they are delin-eated in line with explicitly utilitarian ideals:

> We shall suppose that a creature, possessed of reason, but unacquainted with human nature, deliberates with himself what rules of justice or property would best promote the public interest, and establish peace and security among mankind: His most obvi-ous thought would be, to assign the largest possessions to the most extensive virtue,

---

[73] *Ibid* I.3.28.

[74] See Hume, *A Treatise of Human Nature* (ed) DF Norton (Oxford, OUP, 2000) 3.2.2.8ff. Later, Hume restated his claim in more uncompromising language: 'Examine the writers on the laws of nature; and you will always find, that, whatever principles they set out with, they are sure . . . to assign, as the ultimate reason for every rule which they establish, the convenience and necessities of mankind.' (*Enquiry Concerning the Principles of Morals* (ed) TL Beauchamp (Oxford, OUP, 1998) III.II.156).

[75] *Treatise* above n 74, 3.2.3.4n.

and give everyone the power of doing good, proportioned to his inclination. In a perfect theocracy, where a being, infinitely intelligent, governs particular volitions, this rule would certainly have place, and might serve to the wisest purposes: But were mankind to execute such a law; so great is the uncertainty of merit, both from its natural obscurity, and from the self-conceit of each individual, that no determinate rule of conduct would ever result from it; and the total dissolution of society must be the immediate consequence. Fanatics may suppose *that dominion is founded on grace*, and *that saints alone inherit the earth*; but the civil magistrate very justly puts these sublime theorists on the same footing as common robbers, and teaches them by the severest discipline, that a rule which, in speculation, may seem the most advantageous to society, may yet be found, in practice, totally pernicious and destructive.[76]

Bentham, by contrast, viewed any attempt to provide an intellectual basis for property rights other than utility as not only misconceived but utterly incomprehensible. Hume's subtle point was thus replaced in Bentham's writings with a typically stark dichotomy between establishing property rights as instruments of social utility or talking arrant nonsense.

Thus, despite the attempt to create a favourable intellectual legacy, Bentham's cardinal principle in fact constituted a genuinely new departure in thinking about legal rules and rights. The dichotomy Bentham drew between the purely factual nature of utility and the interpretative complexity of rival moral viewpoints is, of course, unacceptably constraining, and disguised the way in which his philosophical framework relegated moral thinking from a central to a commentating role in legal thought. The *moral* properties of legal rights were, in Bentham's philosophy, entirely independent of, and secondary to, their legally determined content. You and I may disagree about the moral desirability of a certain kind of right, but the existence or otherwise of the right must be seen as entirely unrelated to such disagreements. The nineteenth century jurisprudents were, by and large, happy to accept Bentham's depiction of the principle of utility as uniquely verifiable against everyday experience, other moral principles and standpoints remaining forever locked inside the endlessly 'complicated and difficult' interpretative controversies of ethics.

The destruction of the idea that property rights derive from God's divine plan for his Creation did not, in and of itself, involve a rejection of the main ideas of the natural rights theorists as to what those rights were composed of. The belief that property rights were inevitable outgrowths of the need for human sustenance; that there might be an intimate relationship between human flourishing and the protection and cultivation of the environment; even that human labour thus has a determining role in the recognition of such rights: all of these ideas 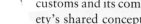 might have emerged, over time, as conventional beliefs about human nature, and become reflected in the social fabric of a community through its social customs and its common law. For it is plausible to see the common law as a society's shared conceptions of the good, and its laws as attempts to promote the

---

[76] *Enquiry* above n 74, III.II.154.

welfare of the community in general. Hence, ideas about the relationship between property rights, on the one hand, and human welfare and social wellbeing, on the other (both those of the natural rights theorists *and* rival conceptions) might constitute the philosophical and intellectual basis of property law in a given community. Attempts by legal commentators to expound the property law of their society might then resort to such conceptions both as the starting point for *systematic* accounts of the complex body of rules and concepts which confront the lawyer, and as an explanation of the aims and purposes which the rules and concepts serve. The beliefs of the natural rights theorists about the character of property might represent the intellectual commitments of a society's property law *and* the moral project which the laws promote: they will embody 'the heart of a legal system as well as its brain'.[77] Those beliefs will normally constitute just one way in which the mass of rules, principles and doctrines can be regimented for the purposes of coherent exposition of an area of law; but the possibility of such an explanation highlights the centrality of moral thought about property to the recognition and delimitation of property rights.

Bentham's scepticism towards natural values alone could not thereby rule out the possibility that moral values are constitutive and explanatory of property rights, rather than simply evaluative. The conception of doctrinal legal science held by the seventeenth- and eighteenth-century common lawyers was one which regarded legal concepts, rules and rights as fashioned and shaped according to a deeper philosophical vision. The considerable escalation in legislative activity during the first half of the eighteenth century rendered this view of legal science increasingly difficult to maintain. The response of the traditionalists, such as Blackstone, to the growing encroachment of the will onto the time-honoured preserve of reason, was to seek to integrate the traditional doctrinal scholarship with the medley of legislated rules. Bentham's reaction, by contrast, was, roughly speaking, to perceive 'the traditional learning as a circuitous fiction, and demand that the law should more directly represent the realities'.[78] Hence, the idea of legal rules and rights as the products or consequences of a deeper moral vision was supplanted by the notion that the form and substance of legal rights were something determined by statute. Common law came to be seen as the forum in which legislated rules are applied, and less and less as an autonomous body of principles.

Bentham and the Critique of Common Law

Bentham was perhaps not the first thinker to see law as two intersecting systems of horizontal and vertical relationships: such an idea had, after all, enjoyed a central place in the civic theories of both Selden and Hobbes. But Bentham was

---

[77] NE Simmonds, *The Decline of Juridical Reason* (Manchester, MUP, 1984) 1.
[78] See Milsom, above n 56 p 3.

the first to present this conception in a way which utterly undermined the idea that the legal characteristics of rights are determined by their supposed intrinsic moral properties. The extreme positivism of Bentham's view can be clearly seen in a passage in which he lampooned Blackstone's account of rights as grounded in juridically determined general precepts:

> A right then to a thing is, as I understand it, the relation a man is in with respect to a thing, which that man is left free to convert to the purposes of his own pleasure, punishment being denounced against any other man who shall impede him from so doing, or does the like as the first man with respect to that thing, without his consent.[79]

Within this picture, the horizontal entitlements we enjoy as against other individuals are determined by legal rules which impede a person from trammelling a right by laying down a punishment on occasions on which the right is infringed. Bentham took his account of individual rights to differ from Blackstone's precisely in that the former, and not the latter, is duty-led: whereas for Blackstone, rights are brought into existence by general rules which have nothing essentially to do with the provisions which establish what happens when the right is infringed, Bentham maintained that 'rights, duties and offences all arise out of one and the same law. Nay that no right can arise out of a law but a duty and an offence spring with it.'[80] The nature and extent of our horizontal relationships, in other words, are determined not by any universal conceptions of the intrinsic value or purpose of rights, but by vertical rules placing limits on protected action. Bentham explained:

> The law gives Titus the *right* to [his field]. How? By making it the *duty* of other men not to meddle with it, and by making it an *offence* in them if they do . . . For that is what the law itself does. The affair of its having *prescribed* a *duty* and *created* an *offence* is the only language we use in speaking of what the law has done. They are different terms of expression of our own concerning what the law has done at *one* operation, by *one* expression of will: not different operations.[81]

The law establishes and protects rights by *making* offences, and *conferring* duties through acts of will. The suggestion that the contours of property rights are determined by vertical rules imposed by authority was thus simultaneously a rejection by Bentham of the Blackstonian account of the nature of common law. For the latter, the central task of the doctrinal writer was the systematic reconstruction of areas of law in terms of general rules from which the rights could then be deduced. Bentham, by contrast, regarded any such attempt to frame general precepts from particular decisions or statutory rules upholding claims of right as misconceived and ungrounded. 'Whether it be expedient or no for the legislature to institute any such plan of interpretation *ex ante facto*', Bentham argued,

---

[79] Bentham *Comment* I.8.87.
[80] *Ibid* I.8.88.
[81] *Ibid*

one thing cannot be otherwise than expedient: and that is to narrow the *occasion* for such interpretation, by transforming the rule of conduct from common law into statute law; that is, as I might say, into law from no-law: to mark out the line of the subject's conduct by visible directions, instead of turning him loose into the wilds of perpetual conjecture.[82]

The 'wilds of perpetual conjecture' were, in Bentham's view, what one ended up with if one followed Blackstone's advice that the interpretation of statutes should proceed according to their words, context and purpose, in other words, 'the spirit and reason of the law.'[83] Blackstone had assumed that a body of jurisprudence of this kind must build up around a statute if we are to avoid the intolerable situation of having to ask Parliament to decide particular disputes. In providing the necessary intellectual conditions in which statutes could be *applied*, the common law's traditional role in establishing coherent principles by which cases are decided would be, in some form, preserved. Equity would, it was thought, temper the excesses and illogicalities of the statute law in its purest form through the medium of reason. Such a role was, for Bentham, unthinkable: for it traded on the assumption that judges could pronounce on the reasonableness or unreasonableness of already posited rules. The fallacy of this view, Bentham thought,

> consists in supposing [the words 'reasonable' and 'unreasonable'] to stand for something that is fixed and certain, and that all men are agreed about, and think that it could be told by certain indications independent of opinion, whether a given course of conduct was reasonable or otherwise.[84]

But what is 'unreasonable', for me, but that of which I disapprove? From this Hobbesian premise followed the inevitable Hobbesian conclusion:

> [W]hen all comes to all, reasonableness or unreasonableness is nothing but conformity or nonconformity to, at least can be decided by nothing but, opinion. The question here then is, whose opinion shall be the standard? That of the Legislature, or that of the judge? Of him whose office is to *make* his will be law, or of him whose office is no other than to find out that will and carry it into effect?[85]

The very idea of 'law' had become, in Bentham's philosophy, a set of individuated, canonical rules, 'that had for its archetype some sensible symbol of the legislator's *will*'.[86] Law consists in expressed *commands*, and hence of individual rules laid down at specific points in time. The legal universe is composed, accordingly, of statutory provisions and the individual decisions handed down by judges to the parties to a dispute. The idea of common law as a body of general rules and principles gave way to the stark reality of particular commands handed down to specific individuals. We should not, in other words, be misled

---

[82] *Ibid* I.9.95.
[83] Blackstone I *Comm* 58–59.
[84] Bentham *Comment* II.2.159.
[85] *Ibid*
[86] *Ibid* II.1.118–19.

by the word 'common' into believing in the reality of a corpus of shared standards; 'for what one individual object was there', Bentham asked, 'to which it could be applied? As a system of general rules, the common law is a thing merely imaginary . . .'[87]

Under the influence of the natural rights theorists, the common law had taken on the appearance of a coherent system of universal principles which depicted a body of individual rights. In presenting the common law in such terms, the treatise writers saw their task as that of reporting the particular rules and decisions encountered in legal practice in the light of those general principles, and as *deductions* from those principles. What struck the common lawyers as a rational necessity was, in fact, historical contingency; for the possibility of presenting the common law as a body of rational principles is closely tied to literary forms in which coherence and abstraction are perceived as important and profound.[88] But such a view of law is far from inevitable. As Hobbes had shown, in societies characterised by moral, political and religious diversity, or during periods of political instability or civic strife, the view of law as a body of express commands is likely to supplant the view of law as the repository of shared conceptions of the good. In such contexts one could expect greater faith to be placed in hard-edged, written rules to offer stability and guidance, than in abstract formulations of the 'rational' or the 'just' solution. The common law itself had only lately escaped from the confines of reports and treatises which had presented the legal material as a series of technical rules and procedures arranged for the convenience of legal practice within the system of writs.[89] Only with the rise of the possessive theory of rights did questions of coherence and systematicity come to be perceived as pressing. For if individuals are the owners of their persons, abilities and moral capacities, law becomes more than a collection of technical rules for deciding issues of standing and redress, but comes to embody 'an immutable realm of legal concepts, natural rights, and so forth, that is merely *described* by the lawyer's technical propositions'.[90]

Bentham regarded this conception of legal science as both confused and distortive of law's true nature. Legal commentaries, he argued, are either *historical* or *argumentative* in nature. Whereas the former 'purport . . . simply to relate such and such particular transactions as having passed in the Courts of Justice', the purport of the latter 'is, from the consideration of those particular transactions, to lay down general rules of law as either having taken place or being likely to take place'.[91] While Bentham viewed both forms of scholarship as potentially distorting of our perceptions of the law, it is the second, the treatise, which misleads the unwary over the very nature of the subject. Reports of court decisions may of course be inaccurate or misleading; but the degree of veracity

---

[87] *Ibid* II.1.119.
[88] See Simpson, above n 45 p 633.
[89] See Simpson, above n 45 p 634ff; see also Simmonds, above n 77 p 51.
[90] Simmonds, above n 77 p 73.
[91] Bentham *Comment* II.6.206.

possessed by a report will in general be a matter of *fact*. The authority of a treatise, by contrast, depends on whether we think the legal rule laid down in a given passage should be deemed the legitimate *conclusion* from decisions on a particular subject, and hence depends upon its argumentative, rather than factual, validity. On the face of it, both historical and argumentative texts expound the law; but, in a celebrated passage, Bentham firmly assimilated the role of treatise writer to that of *censor*:

> There are two characters, one or other of which every man who finds anything to say on the subject of law may be said to take upon him;—that of the *Expositor*, and that of the *Censor*. To the province of the expositor it belongs to explain to us what, as he supposes, the law *is*: to that of the censor, to observe to us what he thinks *it ought to be*.[92]

These roles, Bentham added, embody 'perfectly distinguishable functions'.[93] It was in this thesis of separability of the roles of 'expositor' and 'censor' that Bentham's critique of the common law had its source. Bentham repeatedly insisted that our perception of 'general rules' beyond the particular decisions of the courts resulted from the tendency of the treatise writer's definitions and explanations to be couched in expository form. The treatise writer purports to be our guide through the otherwise unruly mass of decisions, rules and concepts. How easy it is, then, to mistake his statements *about* the law for statements *of* law. The legal order thus takes on the outward appearance of a body of general rules, principles and doctrines requiring systematic exposition; but the expository form of the definitions, distinctions and rules which make up much of the common law's business (such as those relating to ownership and possession, or the making of contracts), and the treatise writer's subsequent attempt to arrange them into a logical order, obscure the law's true, imperatival character.[94] In such situations, Bentham said, 'all traces of the imperative character seem at last to have been smothered in the expository'.[95]

The view of common law as a set of particular decisions effectively put an end to the idea that property rights might derive from underpinning philosophical principles. Indeed, in terms of Bentham's positivistic conception of legal science, individual rights are not *deductions* from general rules at all, but are rather conferred and established by canonical provisions which aim to regulate legal relationships between individuals and secure certain distributive outcomes. Whereas the natural rights tradition and its Kantian offspring had placed rights

---

[92] J Bentham, 'Preface', to 'A Fragment on Government', in J Burns and HLA Hart (eds), *A Comment on the Commentaries and A Fragment on Government* (London, Athlone Press, 1977) 397 [Hereinafter *Fragment*.] 'The [expositor]', he went on to observe, 'therefore is principally occupied in stating, or enquiring after *facts*: the [censor], in discussing *reasons*'.

[93] Bentham, *Fragment* 398.

[94] Simmonds, above n 77 p 73.

[95] J Bentham, J Burns and HLA Hart (eds), *Introduction to the Principles of Morals and Legislation* (London, Athlone Press, 1982) 307. Also quoted in Simmonds, above n 77. (Compare Bentham *Fragment* 417.) As Simpson commented *a propos* of Coke's *Institutes*, 'The text came to be treated as though it were *itself* law' (above n 45 p 635, emphasis added).

at the heart of their accounts of law, the attention of positivist legal science centred, not on rights, but on the rules that conferred them. Rather than seeing rights as intrinsically valuable or necessary, the positivists tended to regard rights as instrumental in securing wider distributive or aggregative goals. The latter may, or may not, entail explorations and assessments of the impact of the exercise of property rights on the natural environment, but the moral argumentation involved in such assessments would be both instrumental and indirect. Moral reasoning might seek to influence the shaping of prospective legal rules for the regulation of property, but cannot alter the character of property rights by deductive arguments from conceptions of property or purpose.

Seventeenth-century conceptions of property purported to derive the character of property rights from their alleged origin in mankind's relationship to the rest of Creation. Those accounts were deeply rooted in theocentric and anthropocentric values, but regarded individual rights to property as intrinsically valuable (and indeed necessary) for both man and the natural world he inhabited. The form of property rights was seen as determined by the interdependency between the basic human need to acquire and consume natural resources and the environmental knowledge and responsibility necessary to ensure the sustainability of those resources. Hence, the natural rights theories tended to regard varieties of agrarian communism or agrarian capitalism as the inherent form of property law. By the mid-eighteenth century, the conception of property rights as the product of natural law had largely given way to a view of property as socially constructed civic rights. New kinds of commercial activity had moved the conception of value beyond that of the agrarian paradigm; and the rise of systematic industry and capitalist production exposed the assumption of complete harmony between social welfare and environmental values as naïve and over-simplistic. Conceptions of property centred less on the nature of man's relationship to his natural surroundings, and ever more exclusively upon the growing number and variety of interpersonal relationships between individual citizens. Bentham's contribution was therefore not the perception of property rights as purely interpersonal, but the claim that individual rights took their shape not from the nature of society, but from the positive law. Rights thus do not possess any inherent form, but are the contingent product of the legislative will. Rights are not intrinsic to human beings, but instrumental in the pursuit of social goals.

The shift from an intrinsic to an instrumental conception of rights fundamentally alters the moral framework within which one thinks about rights. For the instrumental conception portrays individual rights as inevitably competing with social goals which impose limitations upon those rights in the name of collective welfare. The idea of intrinsic limitations to property rights is supplanted by the idea that rights can be interfered with only on the basis of their potential to cause social harm. Rights, that is, 'shrink' rather than 'grow' as they do in the Lockean account. Bentham's nineteenth century reputation as the expounder of a scientifically respectable version of Locke's theory thus significantly underestimates the impact of his work upon the subsequent theoretical treatment of property.

Private Right and Public Law

Positivistic legal science of the kind outlined above heralds a shift in legal thought from the centrality of *rights* to the centrality of *rules*. The focus of legal thinking naturally moves from a private law orientation to a public law one. The horizontal relationships of right and duty between individuals are seen as determined by, and shaped according to, vertical rules imposing duties between individuals and the state. Commenting on the changing relationship between public and private law, SFC Milsom had this to say about the possibility of depicting private law as an autonomous realm of legal principles, distinctively concerned with horizontal relationships of entitlement:

> . . . a mixed economy has generated two intersecting systems. There are the horizontal relationships between citizens, in which private rights are conceived of as having some absolute existence. And there is the vertical system of social regulation and dependent benefits, in which the citizen can have only claims or expectations as against authority rather than abstract rights. If, as seems likely, the vertical system is superseding the horizontal, perhaps a new *Commentaries* is indeed impossible until the process is complete. Or perhaps the very attempt would hasten its completion. Imagine the reaction of a new Bentham if a new Blackstone were successfully to integrate the traditional learning about land law with planning, rent control and the like, or indeed the traditional learning about property in general with taxation and national insurance. Might he not pillory the traditional learning as circuitous fiction, and demand that the law should more directly represent the realities?[96]

Perhaps, Milsom considered, a good conservative ought to hold back from giving such an account, lest it hasten the common law's demise. Milsom's remarks might be seen as reflective of a growing perception among lawyers that the traditional terms in which the public-private distinction are framed no longer fit the realities of legal life and practice. What is the point (they might say) in attempting to sustain a conception of private law and private rights as forming a coherent system based on philosophical principles, when the overwhelming majority of curbs and limitations to the exercise of rights derive from specific statutory rules? Ought one not to see the values involved in shaping rights as instrumental rather than deductive, pragmatic and incremental rather than systematic and settled? It is not inevitable that a legal culture must embody a belief in the value of coherence and rational order. In a society of considerable size and complexity, lawyers and public alike may feel that if piecemeal rules secure and advance the pubic interest, then that is all that can be asked of them. Where such

---

[96] Milsom above n 56 p 3.

+| measures succeed, what extra value is served by 'internal coherence' or the
ability to reduce the rules to a set of rational principles?

To such questions there is, of course, no simple answer. Rather, we should
become aware of the reasons which drive the questions in the first place. For the
attractiveness of pragmatism is something which itself requires the existence of
certain social conditions. In a society characterised by diversity over conceptions of individual welfare and social good (and of the relationship between
them), it will seem less important that the law strive to create a system of
entitlements derived from abstract principles, and more pressing that there are
rules which succeed in regulating individuals' pursuit of their own interests
where otherwise market forces would be the determining factor in all interpersonal transactions. Because, within a market society, individuals often pursue
their interests at the expense of others, the rules of a legal system will be perceived as rational if they allow for the protection of important or vulnerable
interests and choices, and would appear artificial, contrived and unnatural if
they attempted to impose on social relations an inclusive framework based on
abstract notions of formal equality. Pragmatism and its rivals therefore *all* imply
a wider vision of the purpose of law within society, which is to say that rampant
pragmatism is itself a moral standpoint. The issues raised by pragmatism are
thus unexpectedly deep (although, perhaps, we should have expected this), as a
form of legal practice will inevitably involve ideas about the nature of law, and
its place within society, which go to the heart of philosophical debates about the
nature of society itself.

Despite Bentham's attack on the genre, the legal treatise survived the intellectual shift away from rationalist theories of legal reasoning to theories which
stressed the central importance of authority. One major reason for this is no
doubt the massive volume and extreme complexity of the legal rules governing,
say, contract or property from the mid-eighteenth century onwards.[97]
Legislative interference in traditional common law areas, and judicial attempts
at clarification and application of a vastly inflated law, had resulted in the need
for expository works to guide the practitioner through a subject no longer capable of easy inculcation and understanding organised around principles of practice and procedure. Another is the perennial attractiveness of a belief in law as
a coherent body of rational precepts, an attraction partially explained by the
inherent pull of the abstract over the particular in spheres of thought in which
the mind is confronted with a large volume of normative standards apparently
crying out for classification and systematisation. But the general shift towards
positivism did have an impact on the way legal treatises were conceived and
regarded. Whilst they retained the belief that private law was composed of

---

[97] For interesting reflections on the reception of Bentham's and Austin's legal philosophy in the
late-19th-to early 20th century see N Duxbury, 'When We Were Young: Notes in the Law Quarterly
Review 1885–1925' (2000) 116 *LQR* 474. See further R Cosgrove 'The Reception of Analytic
Jurisprudence: the Victorian Debate on the Separation of Law and Morality 1860–1900' (1981) 74
Durham University Journal 47.

systematic underpinning principles, of which judicial decisions were merely the
expression, the treatise writers of the late eighteenth century onwards displayed
an awareness of the increasing role of the notion of authority.[98] Loss of confidence in the idea that the allegedly underpinning principles were of universal
validity prompted a reassessment of the importance and significance of treatises,
according to which the opinion expressed by the author of a treatise does not,
in general, possess legal authority. This shift in the treatise writers' perception
of their task led, as AWB Simpson noted, to a shift in attitude towards the
formal status of treatises generally:

> To writers who claimed to be formulating universal principles, the lack of personal
> authority was not particularly significant; it was what they wrote, not the identity of
> the author, that mattered. But with the decline of this spirit the treatise writer's formal
> status inevitably declines as well, for what he says then appears to matter only to the
> extent that it can be supported by judicial authority . . . He who has no authority him-
> self comes to rely on authority and not on pure reason.[99]

Legal writing and thinking on property at this time reflects this change in
approach. Lord Camden, for instance, expressed the opinion that the business
of common law judges 'is to tell the suitor how the law stands, not how it ought
to be', going on to remark that:

> I hope judges will always copy the example [of Lord Chief Justice Lee], and never
> pretend to decide upon a claim of property without attending to the old black letter of
> our law, without founding their judgment upon some solid written authority,
> preserved in their books or in judicial records.[100]

The natural rights theories of the eighteenth century, it has been argued, were
already underpinned by assumptions which were unconsciously positivist.
Blackstone's attempt to synthesise his speculative conception of legal science
with his portrait of law as an historically extended practice resulted in his
emphasising the role of custom in the formation of firm title to property. His
positivist successors had little difficulty in jettisoning the speculative element in
Blackstone's thought, in favour of a conception of property as an institution
determined by rules rather than reason. Unlike their Kantian counterparts, the
positivists regarded rights as the product of the *legislative* will, not the 'common
will'. The moral foundation of property rights thus shifted significantly in the
eighteenth century, from a conception of rights as grounded in, and limited by,
man's ability to assert *dominium* over parts of his surroundings, to one which

---

[98] Although the Bentham/Austin axis in legal theorising continued to supply the basic
framework for juristic thought well into the 20th century, the stark terms in which Bentham (in
particular) viewed the common law were far from wholeheartedly absorbed by ordinary common
lawyers. It is no accident that Pollock's attack on Austin's jurisprudence cited aridity and lack of
historical sense as its primary failings. It is also no accident that Pollock sought to correct perceived
shortcomings in judicial reasoning by the pursuit of principle: see Duxbury, above n 97 p 488.

[99] Simpson, above n 45 p 668.

[100] Cobbett: Parliamentary History XVII 998–99, quoted in D Lieberman, *The Province of
Legislation Determined* (Cambridge, CUP, 1989) 98.

saw rights as determined by rules for the regulation of competing *iura*. Because
of their hostility towards universal principles, and their concomitant tendency
to focus on *posited* rules, the positivists naturally gravitated away from conceptions of rights which favoured the will theory, and instead articulated versions
of the interest theory: rights were seen as protecting individual interests, both
from encroachment by competition from other individuals, and from curtailment in the name of general social goals. The decline of the will theory was
hence accompanied by a decline in the importance of systematic jurisprudence.
Legal treatises became less concerned with establishing internally consistent theories of individual rights, and instead centred on questions of the grounds on
which the legislature might interfere with individual rights in the promotion of
the public interest. Moral debate about rights became the construction of arguments about the relationship between public and private interests, rather than
speculation about the intrinsic worth and significance of rights.

   Yet the view of rules concerning property as overwhelmingly instrumental did
not inevitably reflect any straightforward acceptance among legal practitioners
of the principle of utility as the ground of property rights. Accordingly, writing
on property law during this period may be a better indicator of the degree of per-
meation of positivist dogma into the legal consciousness than the writings of that
tradition's most famous spokesmen. The principle of utility itself might be
thought rather congenial to common law thinking. The traditional scholarship
had always stressed the openness of rules of common law to later revision or
rejection. No rule or doctrine, it was thought, was immune from modification,
reformulation or qualification by later courts in the light of countervailing
reasons. Ronald Dworkin would later point to a similar fluidity in the utilitarian
view of rights. Utilitarians, Dworkin argued, perceive individual interests as
perennially vulnerable to marginal shifts in utility; hence, utilitarian ethics elim-
inates the possibility of rights when the latter are understood as legally protected
interests. For the purpose of rights is to *shield* those interests which are identified
as worthy of protection from encroachment by considerations of general utility.[101] But if the rules which define those rights are themselves open to potential
revision, the utilitarian has a strong prima facie case for believing that the view
of rights as conceptually immune from assessments of utility is anyway false.

   In fact, treatises on the law of property during the late eighteenth and early
nineteenth centuries articulated a conception of property in which individual
rights *were* shielded from marginal shifts in utility. The right to property was
not understood as a constitutionally protected right in the traditional sense that
courts have a power of review over legislation pertaining to the exercise of property rights. Rather, property rights were seen as 'fundamental' in that they constituted an unwritten ethical limitation on Parliament's power to interfere with
an individual's property.[102] According to this principle, the state is not free to

[101] R Dworkin, *Taking Rights Seriously* (London, Duckworth, 1977).
[102] T Allen, *The Right to Property in Commonwealth Constitutions* (Cambridge, CUP, 2000) 13.

modify an individual's property entitlements on the basis of wider welfare-orientated or distributive goals, even where the public good considerably outweighs individual utility. Hence, in cases where the state does so interfere, the individual is entitled to compensation for loss of property.[103] Such a conception of the relationship between individual rights and public utility had been articulated by Blackstone in volume II of the *Commentaries* on the basis of the 'absolute and despotic dominion' involved in the relationship of ownership between a person and a thing. Later treatises on property saw this limitation not as a substantive characteristic of property rights, but effectively as a canon of interpretation of property statutes. This was, inevitably, something of a fiction, as most treatises of the time, in practice, treated the assumption of non-interference and the requirement of compensation as a substantive principle.

Property law had abandoned the Lockean natural rights theory as its theoretical underpinning, but retained its empiricism. The idea of possession as a central determinant of property rights continued to be regarded as a natural feature of property rights, in the sense in which 'natural' and 'commonsense' are synonyms, and hence as something which should not be lightly overridden even in the public interest. By the end of England's 'century of law', property rights were conceived as both necessary for individual utility and as inherently competing with aggregative policies for securing general welfare. The very sameness of the conclusions of the utilitarians and natural rights tradition concerning property rights was very effective in channelling moral discourse about property along quite specific lines, whilst making relatively little impact on established legal definitions and rules. Although the utilitarians rejected the metaphysical arguments of the natural rights scholars, they shared a common belief in the distributive ambitions of a civil property regime. This amounted, roughly, to 'a moderate inequality coupled with a large number of middle-sized fortunes' distinctive of middle-class liberalism.[104] Philosophical debate about property during the nineteenth century thus concerned the implications which followed from a utilitarian reworking of the Lockean natural rights theory; for it was recognised by many contemporary writers that a straightforward interpretation of that theory suggested that the existing pattern of landholding in England was undermined, rather than supported, by a strict application of the utilitarian ideal. Utility (it was argued) seemed to demand what the natural rights theorists had argued was anyway intrinsic to the concept of property: the retention by each individual of the right to exclusive use of the products of her labour.[105] But the substantial disparity between the fortunes of those who owned land and those who merely laboured upon it suggested to contemporary commentators that the existing rules effected distributions which were neither natural nor utility-maximising. The debate was conducted between those who, like Mill and

---

[103] *Ibid* 14.

[104] R Schlatter, *Private Property: The History of an Idea* (London, Unwin, 1951) 249.

[105] *Ibid* 249. For a critique of this position see MH Kramer, *John Locke and the Origins of Private Property* (Cambridge, CUP, 1997) esp ch 4.

Herbert Spencer, endeavoured to find a way out of the apparent impasse, and those, such as Proudhon and Marx, who embraced fully the implications of the theory and advocated communism and the abolishment of private property.

At the same time as the philosophical debate addressed the problem of the extent of a state's power to interfere with individual property rights to effect a just distribution, legal commentators considered the need for regulation of private property use in the name of public interest, manifested through both legislation and the expansion of the private law of nuisance.[106] Individual rights to property were thus forced to compete with the aggregative and distributive needs of the collectivity. The tendency to see this situation in terms of a competition between the public and private realms (or, equivalently, of the increasing encroachment and penetration of public law into the traditional preserve of private law) is both a natural and a powerful one. But the corresponding account of the relationship between public and private law will remain credible only as long as the relevant legislative provisions are identifiable with regulatory and policy-implementing goals. A considerable portion of the 1925 legislation, for example, is not restricted to the role of what Nigel Simmonds has termed 'public project pursuit'.[107] Rather, it establishes principles, definitions, distinctions and procedures for the recognition, creation and transfer of property rights in a quite general sense. It would therefore be premature to conclude that the distinction between a 'private law subject', such as property, and a 'public law subject' such as administrative law can be rendered in terms of a division between statute and common law rules. The validity of accounts of the public-private distinction is something which requires justification in the light of prevailing legal conditions.[108]

It is testimony to the enduring appeal of legal positivism that the terms in which legal and political thought about property are framed largely reflect the assumptions of the eighteenth century jurists. As we have seen, the assumptions of positivistic legal science made increasingly problematic the presentation of common law as a body of rational precepts. The authority of the textbook writer's propositions was seen as deriving not from their reasonableness but from their reflection of judicial pronouncements. Hence law took on the appearance of intersecting realms of horizontal and vertical entitlements in which private property rights collide with public goals. Such is the extent to which this picture of law is embedded in the legal consciousness, a leading authority on modern land law can state, without anachronism or absurdity, that his book:

> examine[s] the way in which the land lawyer uses and manipulates technical concepts in order to describe the accumulation of wealth and security. It discusses the way in which the underlying ideology of property law interacts with key issues of priority and efficiency. Above all, it depicts property law as a network of jural relationships

---

[106] For a full treatment see ch 4 below.

[107] NE Simmonds, 'The Possibility of Private Law' in J Tasioulas (ed), *Law, Values and Social Practices* (Aldershot, Dartmouth, 1997) passim.

[108] See ch 5 below.

between individuals in respect of valued resources, and land law as a body of rules which ultimately governs the distribution of utility in the particularly significant resource of realty.[109]

The dominance of this picture, it has been argued, has led to a narrowing of moral thought about property to questions of the relationship between private rights and public projects. This has, in turn, lent much force to the presentation of such projects as instrumental and transitory. The effect of such thinking has been, according to the same authority, to impede significantly the construction of novel moral standpoints on property.[110] It is not difficult to think of examples of arguments which are deeply coloured by a preoccupation with the collision of private right and public utility. The prevalent image of environmental law as a rag-bag of legislative measures aimed at the restriction of private property use for the sake of public health and wellbeing is one illustration. Overwhelmingly, legislative invasion of private property rights requires justification not because the invasions entail loss of individual liberty (to act within one's rights), but because they reduce the *value* of the rights. In a free market society, the question of individual liberty becomes, to a large extent, submerged beneath questions of value, as utility will centre upon the freedom to amass wealth in the face of competition, rather than upon individual liberty more generally construed. Free market societies tend not to thrive within the rigid social structures perpetuated under totalitarian regimes, so the question of liberty will become most pressing in the context of commercial freedoms and actions rather than in traditional political senses. The moral thinking which accompanies arguments about the extent of legislative curtailment of individual rights will, in general, view the debate as one concerning the desirability of preferring one kind of value over another or, in a more abstract version, of the long-term distributive or socio-political effects of imposing those preferences on existing socio-economic structures. It will, on the whole, form no part of such argumentation that the moral basis of individual rights might be *inherently* shaped by community-directed obligations, or substantive limitations upon exploitation of limited natural resources.

CONCLUSION

The natural rights theorists of the seventeenth century constructed accounts of property which were rooted in natural values, but had varied over the extent to which human convention played a determining role in the specification of property rights in civil society. Under the influence of Rousseau and Kant, on the one hand, and the legal positivists, on the other, property became gradually

---

[109] K Gray and SF Gray, *Elements of Land Law*, 3ed edn (London, Butterworth, 2001).
[110] K Gray and SF Gray, 'The Idea of Property in Land', in S Bright and J Dewar (eds), *Land Law: Themes and Perspectives* (Oxford, OUP, 1998) 39.

detached from its basis in theological reflection on the order of the world, and came to be viewed as the product of rules whose origin lay not in reason but in the legislative will. At the same time, the growth in the types and complexity of mercantile activity gave rise to conceptions of property more readily associated with commercial value than with natural rights or liberty. This shift in intellectual attitudes greatly narrowed the kinds of moral argument which might hope to demonstrate any practical relevance for the way in which property rights are legally regulated and determined. Debate about property rights centred increasingly upon the relationship between public and private interests, and upon the relationship between a society's institution of property and its social, economic and political arrangements. Legal measures for the regulation of private property came to be regarded as related to property rights instrumentally rather than intrinsically. At the same time, changing socio-economic conditions highlighted the falsity of the seventeenth century assumption that property rights and environmental interests went hand-in-hand. The growth in industrial processes and intensive agricultural and farming methods demonstrated that human social and economic interests and environmental protection often lay along quite different paths. The law came to articulate a conception of property which stood in no particular relationship to environmental values.

The truth of the latter proposition has often been taken as support for another: the proposition that a conscious concern with environmental protection is both new and purely instrumental. Environmental law is, on this view, at once predominantly reactive and (consequently) a piecemeal affair. Prior to relatively recent legislative involvement in environmental matters, the argument continues, the law neither articulated nor pursued any coherent position on environmental matters. Typical of, though somewhat more considered than, such attitudes is the following passage from a recent essay on the foundations of land law:

> The notion of land as scarce and fragile is relatively new . . . Blake's dark, satanic mills were terrible to behold, but local. It is only relatively recently that we have realised that our transport systems, our power stations, our industrial processes, and our intensive agricultural methods have the potential utterly to destroy this green and pleasant land. The private law of nuisance, the historical role of which was to control annoying activities as between one neighbour and another, cannot sufficiently express the social interest in the safety of this scarce resource.[111]

In the next chapter, we intend to some extent to falsify this conclusion. For a close examination of legislative activity and the law of torts during the late eighteenth century and the nineteenth, demonstrates a body of legal rules which *do* recognise and articulate environmental values in the context of property use, and which do *not* inevitably reduce those values to utilitarian calculi.

With its roots in the common law of nuisance, legal protection of the environment began as an attempt to situate property rights within a moral

---

[111] P Birks, 'Five Keys to Land Law' in Bright and Dewar, above n 110, 458.

framework which distinguished 'natural' and 'non-natural' uses of property on the basis of their *environmental* setting. Although the law's treatment of the issues was far from consciously systematic, it was, we argue, nevertheless consistent. If the texture of the common law is woven from juridical argument as well as judicial rulings, a conception of property becomes visible in which tensions between private right and public interest were keenly felt and understood by contemporary judges. In giving expression to a legal standpoint which broadly favoured private property, they nevertheless displayed acute awareness of the impact which the exercise of property rights have upon the environment. The 'locality' of nuisance actions did impose limitations on legal principle, but did not prevent some quite striking argument about property rights and the environment. As a result, the presentation of environmental law as a wholly modern, public law-orientated affair, is (we shall see) misleading.

4

Legal Regulation and
Environmental Values

THE FOREGOING CHAPTERS chart the rise of a conception of property which was broadly positivist and utilitarian. The early natural rights theories had offered an understanding of the moral and religious significance of property, but had advanced an effectively utilitarian account of the basis of property rights. Once the connection of property rights with human interests was recognised as holding independently of its supposed theological underpinnings, it was possible to conceive of property rights as standing in no particular relationship to environmental values. Property rights came to be seen as determined by reference to the tension between individual and collective interests. Awareness of this conflict in turn suggests a picture in which rights to property do not *emerge* from the need for the development and protection of the natural environment, but often *clash* with those ends.

In the present chapter, we begin to explore the ways in which legal regulation of the environment in its modern form began to take shape. These developments have their roots in a legal order already steeped in the assumptions and preoccupations of legal positivism. The growth of a specific concern with environmental issues in their own right tended to be associated with legislative innovations, emphasising the deliberate choices of a society and the manipulation of social arrangements for political ends. The focus on legislation would eventually obscure the political significance of those choices: speculation about the nature of property and rights, of the kind explored in the previous two chapters, would come to be seen as quite separate from the interpretative preoccupations and practices of the environmental lawyer, and of interest only to the philosopher or theologian. Yet the emergence of regulatory regimes was the result, not of the *irrelevance* of juristic debate about property and rights, but of its central importance.

The case-law of the late-eighteenth and the nineteenth centuries displays a concern with the nature and limitations of property rights that is startling in its political astuteness and sophistication. A close study of that case-law, which forms the main business of this chapter, reveals a concern with the social and environmental impacts of property rights which at once embodies an attempt to work out a philosophical theory of property of the kind lately explored *and* forms the intellectual backdrop to the emergent statutory regimes with which the modern environmental lawyer is familiar. The emergence and development of environmental law represents a shifting conception of the relationship between property and environmental values ultimately removed from the utilitarian framework inherited from the eighteenth century positivists. As will emerge more fully in chapter 5, a deep understanding of the political significance of the modern law on protection of the environment requires an understanding of the intellectual assumptions of the traditional doctrinal categories and principles of private law.

A Brief Conspectus

Law has been used to manipulate the shape and use of the environment for political ends for a surprisingly long time. Initially, government action was focused on agriculture. Later initiatives broadened the scope of action to the improvement of communications by making provision, first, for the development of toll roads, then canals and later still railways. However, it was only with the advent of the Industrial Revolution and its side effects that state intervention in environmental matters in a more specific sense fully emerged. Principally important among these effects were urbanisation and pollution. In the eighteenth century, industrial activity was characterised by fairly dispersed domestic outworking. The Industrial Revolution first harnessed water power, resulting in the concentration of manufacturing activity in relatively small-scale and topographically confined factories. Later, the advent of steam power largely freed industry from physical constraints of location and of scale, and facilitated the concentration of factories in cities. The environmental pollution that was the inevitable by-product of industrial activity was experienced on a greater scale, and in a more complex and concentrated form, than ever before.

By the nineteenth century, industry was characterised by labour-intensiveness and the growth across the country of large conurbations. Some settlements expanded with unprecedented rapidity whilst others, so-called 'shock towns,' grew from nothing. In both, sanitary conditions deteriorated rapidly with disastrous effect. Epidemics of typhoid and cholera were commonplace; and even in the absence of particular crises, infant mortality was high and adult life expectancy was low in the urban population. Social reformers began to latch on to the need to exercise deliberate control over the urban environment in order to tackle the atrocious living conditions of the urban poor.[1] The reforms which eventually resulted from such initiatives, although obviously anthropocentric in their intention, also generated incidental benefit for the environment as they focused on cleaning up the surroundings of urban dwellers.[2]

---

[1] For example, the nineteenth century author JP Kay-Shuttleworth, *The Moral and Physical Conditions of the Working Classes Employed in the Cotton Manufacture in Manchester* (Manchester, Morten, 1969), called for the 'judicious management' of urban evils, including poor housing and sanitation in order to improve the lot of the working classes.

[2] Though as we shall see, absent from such a conception was any assumption of a necessary relationship between environmental welfare and human flourishing, characteristic of Lockean thought: see ch 2 above.

Legal regulation of the environment began as a series of attempts at the reconciliation of diverse groups of interests: a body of principles concerning property rights grew up around the resolution of clashes between private users, between private owners and commercial industrial interests, and between private or commercial interests and collective goals and interests. The conceptual framework which emerged from these cases would embody a set of principles essentially different from the utilitarian ideas which had developed in the eighteenth century. Property came to be seen as bounded *in principle* (rather than exclusively on the basis of *interests*). The principles involved often related (roughly speaking) to conceptions of harm and wellbeing; yet the courts articulated such conceptions in terms of the notion of 'natural use': the extent of an owner's entitlement to use property in his own way was conceived as depending on the nature of the environment over which the rights are exercised. From these ideas would emerge a juridical framework in which property rights are restricted and shaped according to goals and interests essentially un-utilitarian in nature. The body of case-law which developed during the eighteenth- and nineteenth centuries, and the legislative regimes which followed, would embody a moral context for property, in which proprietary rights are thought of as being hemmed in by countervailing moral ideas and needs.

Initially, however, environmental legislation was closely and explicitly associated with human welfare, with Parliament and the courts only willing to interfere in private property rights where necessary for securing important social benefits. Yet developments in legislation, as much as in the patterns of common law thinking which evolved to deal with nuisance claims, sometimes exceeded a purely instrumental approach to environmental protection. The evolution of legal responses to environmental problems, charted below, reveals a body of thought of increasing sophistication: the impact of human activity upon the natural environment is seen as constituting, not merely a conflict between individual rights and collective interests, but a complex moral problem invoking notions of value and responsibility which cannot be fully articulated within a framework of interpersonal rights and duties. The resulting picture is one of a complex body of thought which exceeds the bounds of the positivistic and utilitarian assumptions most closely associated with interventionist legislation. Environmental law, it will turn out, is the product of a distinctive moral theory: one which attempts to address the significance of property, rights and nature.

COMMON LAW RESPONSES TO ENVIRONMENTAL PROBLEMS

. . . there is no particular reason why the common law should comply with environmental principles except to the extent that they are embodied in customary international law or in the ethical values of the community from which the law derives it authority.[3]

[3] J Alder and D Wilkinson, *Environmental Law and Ethics* (London, Macmillan 1999) 220.

Statements such as this reflect an underlying positivism about law. The term 'positivism', here, does not refer to any specific theory about the relationship between law and morality, but to the idea that the form and substance of our legal practices emerge through social interaction rather than reflective engagement with a rational order which transcends those practices. Legal concepts such as property may invoke or entail important philosophical or moral ideas; but legal rules can exist and develop without reference to such ideas. Social mores do, of course, respond to the situations in which they are played out, and the values of British society in the nineteenth century were certainly reshaped by new social, economic and environmental forces to an unprecedented degree. The concerns raised by these new circumstances in everyday life eventually made their way before the courts, where they were dealt with employing a degree of deliberation and sophistication that is often surprising to the modern reader. In fact, the common law by its very nature is uniquely placed to give expression to underlying societal values and priorities in dealing with novel problems that have been brought before it, and was thus particularly well-suited to fill the gaps in the legal system that were becoming ever more apparent as the nineteenth century progressed, by applying established general legal principles to novel situations.

The common law, through its case-driven approach to property law, necessarily exhibited a piecemeal approach towards environmental pollution. Nuisance served to address the adverse environmental consequences of industrial activity to land. Water pollution and flow considerations were addressed under the land law pertaining to riparian rights. In contrast, atmospheric pollution was not recognised as a justiciable issue in its own right in the context of the common law of property.[4] That said, nuisance in particular rapidly proved extremely valuable in the context of dealing with some of the undesirable side-effects of the Industrial Revolution. It is, however, worth noting that the classes of interference that could be addressed by nuisance were limited to physical damage to the land itself, and interference with the use and enjoyment of that land. Other, less tangible, interference was not actionable: for example, legal protection did not extend to protecting amenity.[5] These limitations also characterise the modern law of nuisance.

---

[4] Property rights can apply to the atmosphere insofar as airspace above a property is concerned, though such rights are limited to those ordinarily incident on everyday enjoyment of the property: see *Bernstein v Skyviews* [1978] QB 479. Where pollution is concerned, legal intervention is yet more limited: *Merlin v British Nuclear Fuels* [1990] 3 All ER 711 confirmed that atmospheric pollution does not of itself constitute property damage in the absence of mental or physical injury or physical damage to property. Where atmospheric pollution does damage property, *Blackburn v ARC* [1998] Env LR 469 demonstrates that it can be accommodated in damages.

[5] *Aldred*'s Case (1610) 9 Co Rep 57b (77 ER 816).

Private Nuisance

For centuries, nuisance had served to deal with disputes between property owners whose lands were adversely but indirectly affected by the activities of their
neighbours. The focus of the action was not, of course, the protection of the
environment as such, but rather the vindication of property rights. In *Malone v
Laskey* [1907],[6] the plaintiff, who shared a house of which her husband held the
tenancy, was injured as the result of vibration from machinery in neighbouring
premises which caused the WC cistern to fall off the wall. She was denied an
action in nuisance because she did not hold a legal interest in the property
affected. The link between interests in land and an action in nuisance continues
to be required, despite an ambitious but ultimately abortive attempt by the
Court of Appeal in *Khorasandjian v Bush* [1993][7] to introduce a much more
expansive approach to standing to sue, freeing it from the ties of property interests. The plaintiff had been harassed by repeated phone calls made by an ex-
boyfriend to the homes of her parents and grandmother. The plaintiff was
granted an injunction despite her lack of a proprietary interest in the properties
affected. This expansive approach to the entitlement to bring an action in nuisance was also followed by the Court of Appeal in *Hunter v Canary Wharf Ltd
London Docklands Development Corporation* [1996].[8] However, the House of
Lords, in a majority judgment in the case in 1997,[9] returned to the orthodox
position, overruling the Court of Appeal on the right to sue in nuisance and reaf-
firming the requirement that a plaintiff possess a proprietary interest in the
property affected in order to bring an action. The case involved actions by several hundred local residents whose television reception had been adversely
affected over a period of years by the Canary Wharf Tower in London, and
actions against the London Docklands Corporation in respect of nuisance
caused by dust during the construction of the Limehouse Link Road. Many of
the plaintiffs were the spouses or children of those holding proprietary interests
in affected properties, but lacking such interests in their own right. Several arguments underpin the majority decision, including an unwillingness to expand a
tort against land in such a way as to transform it into tort against the person.
The decision has met with criticism as a retrograde step,[10] though it can equally
be regarded as ensuring that the law of nuisance remains tightly bound to its
historical roots and justification.

   The recent line of authority thus confirms that the purpose of the law of nuisance remains that of achieving a balance between conflicting property interests
by ensuring that the activities of one individual on his own land do not interfere

---

[6] *Malone v Laskey* [1907] 2 KB 141.
[7] [1993] QB 727.
[8] [1996] 1 All ER 482.
[9] [1997] 2 All ER 426.
[10] See, for example, P Cane, 'What a Nuisance' (1997) 113 *LQR* 515.

unreasonably with those of his neighbour, and in so doing, it achieves a degree of incidental protection for the environment.

Prior to the Industrial Revolution, British society was relatively homogenous, at least as regards the groups equipped with sufficient wealth to seek recourse to law to vindicate their interests, and the law of nuisance had proved itself over several centuries more or less equal to the task of adjudicating the fairly narrow range of disputes that came before the courts. Cases such as *Bryant v Lefever* (1878–79),[11] where one householder brought an action when alterations to his neighbour's house adversely affected the use of the fireplace in his own, were fairly typical. The Industrial Revolution brought about a more complex and fragmented society, with conflict beginning to emerge between land uses which were increasingly at variance with each other.[12] A classic example of the type of case that arose from these new social circumstances is found in the well-known case of *St Helen's Smelting Co v Tipping* (1865).[13] In June 1860 the plaintiff purchased an estate in the Black Country a mile and a half from the defendant's copper smelting works. In 1861 Tipping threatened litigation in respect of alleged physical damage to his crops, cattle and gardens and to his own and his servants' health, allegedly caused by acid deposition from the defendant's plant, in what would now be classed as a classic example of an 'environmental tort.'[14] The defendant scaled down production and, for a time, all was well between the parties. In 1863 the defendant intensified the operation of the smelting plant, and further damage to the plaintiff's property ensued; this time Tipping initiated legal proceedings. Though the plaintiff was ultimately successful, the juridical context out of which the decision emerged is worth exploring in some detail.

St Helen's v Tipping presents an early example of the courts being called upon to adjudicate on the emerging conflict between the interests of those holding land, traditionally protected by the common law, and the interests of industry. It was, despite the antecedents of the law of nuisance, far from self-evident that the courts would adopt a stance that favoured traditional landowning interests over those of emerging industry, as evidenced by the decision in *Hole v Barlow* (1858).[15] *Hole* seemed to protect industrial plants operating within normal parameters from actions in nuisance even where they interfered with the interests of neighbouring landowners. The facts demonstrated an industrial context,

---

[11] (1878–79) 4 CPD 172.

[12] See generally JPS McLaren 'Nuisance Law and the Industrial Revolution–Some Lessons from Social History' (1983) 3 *Oxford Journal of Legal Studies* 155 and R Cocks 'Victorian Foundations?' in J Lowry and R Edmunds (eds), *Environmental Protection and the Common Law* (Oxford, Hart Publishing, 2000).

[13] (1865) 11 HL Cas 642. This case has been the subject of extensive and varied comment and analysis, see, in particular, AWB Simpson, *Leading Cases in the Common Law* (Oxford, OUP, 1995) ch 7 and Cocks *ibid*.

[14] C Gearty, 'The Place of Private Nuisance in the Modern Law of Torts' (1989) 48 *Cambridge Law Journal* 214.

[15] (1858) 4 CB (NS) 334, 140 ER 1113.

albeit a limited one, in that the defendant, preparatory to embarking on a housing development, was firing bricks at a brick kiln on his property, generating emissions and smells that adversely affected his neighbour's new home and garden. At trial Byles J told the jury that 'no action lies for the reasonable use of a lawful trade in a convenient and proper place, even though someone may suffer inconvenience from its being so carried on.'[16] By way of explaining his reasoning on this point the judge observed that:

> it is not every body whose enjoyment of life and property is rendered uncomfortable by the carrying on of an offensive or noxious trade in his neighbourhood, that can bring an action. If that were so . . . the neighbourhood of Birmingham and Wolverhampton and the other great manufacturing towns of England would be full of persons bringing actions for nuisances arising from the carrying on of [such] trades in their vicinity, to the great injury of the manufacturing and social interests of the community.[17]

This goes to the heart of the dilemma which faced the courts when trying to balance traditional property rights against emerging industrial interests. It was left to the jury to decide, as a question of fact, whether or not the location, in this case the outskirts of the expanding city, was 'proper and convenient' for the activity in question. In addition, the courts often showed willingness to find, in such commercial activities, a wider public interest in the benefits of industrial activity (for example in electricity, fuel and so on).[18] They found for the defendant. Willes J succinctly summed up, having drawn parallels with defamation and privilege and Crown takings of land for defence in wartime, 'In these and such like cases, private convenience must yield to public necessity.'[19] The question was, how far did the category of 'such like cases', in which the rights of the individual could be subjugated to commercial and, by extension, wider public interest, extend? The categories in which such an explicit trade-off had been employed in the past were quite distinctive in character and relatively confined in scope: the same could not necessarily be said for extending this type of approach into the sphere of the environment.

The position adopted in *Hole* did not, however, survive for long[20] and the Court of Exchequer Chamber in *Bamford v Turley* (1862)[21] took a contrary and arguably more predictable approach that protected the interests of private property where these were interfered with to an unreasonable extent by neighbouring industrial uses. In this case, the Court was prepared to protect individual

[16] Quoted at p 1113.
[17] Quoted at p 1114.
[18] Some, though not all, industrial activities might indeed be said to be linked to wider public interests in this way. Yet one should not overstate this tendency to elide and obscure the different types of interest involved: often the courts displayed an awareness of distinctions between commercial interests and public benefits which arise from them, even if, by the end of the century, the implicit link between them became a settled feature of most judgments.
[19] P 1118.
[20] Hole was confined to its facts in *Stockport Water Company v Potter* (1861) 7 H & N 160.
[21] (1862) 3 B & S 62, 66; 122 ER 25.

interests in property despite the defendant's argument that they were carrying out their activities for the benefit of the public. Bramwell B took issue with the public benefit argument for a number of reasons, not only through reluctance to inflict loss on the individual without compensation on such grounds, but also because he felt that a public benefit argument was misplaced in the context of what he viewed as one individual attempting to call upon it to aid in protecting their commercial endeavours from legal control.[22] He further distinguished infrastructure-based enterprises from broader commercial ventures, conceding that the former were truly in the public interest, in that they were, on balance, productive of greater gain than loss to those individuals who made up the public. But even then they were required to 'pay their way' by compensating those whose interests in land were interfered with in order to produce this net benefit. Public interest considerations were also argued as a reason to control lawful but malicious use of land in *Bradford Corporation v Pickles* (1895)[23] where the defendant proposed to divert a spring on his land that fed one of the plaintiffs' reservoirs providing water to the metropolis, rendering it useless. Pickles's motivation was to extract payment from the Corporation to forgo his plans. Nonetheless, both the Court of Appeal and the House of Lords were of the view that the plaintiffs were not entitled to an injunction to prevent Pickles from acting as he chose, despite the very real public interest considerations at stake. The fairly sweeping protection accorded to individual rights (even where these were used maliciously) exhibited in *Pickles* is perhaps indicative of the level of discomfort felt by the judiciary on the implications of applying a new broader concept of the public interest where to do so would interfere with established personal freedoms attached to property.

In *St Helen's v Tipping* itself, the plaintiff was eventually successful in nuisance (the case being finally determined by the House of Lords) and was awarded damages and an injunction.[24] The defendant's activities, in causing physical damage to the property, were found to constitute an unreasonable interference with the plaintiff's use and enjoyment of his land. This was the case even where the offending plant was carrying out its operations 'in as good a manner as possible.'[25] The outcome of this case, then, delivered a degree of legal protection for the environment from pollution under the law of nuisance, insofar as the contamination that resulted from the defendant's industrial activities in causing physical damage was deemed an unreasonable interference with the landowner's property rights. The whole approach in *St Helen's* suggests that the courts took the view that there is an incidental rather than a necessary connec-

---

[22] This point is further discussed in JE Penner 'Nuisance, Neighbourliness, and Environmental Protection' in J Lowry and R Edmunds above n 12 p 33.

[23] [1895] AC 857.

[24] *Tipping v St Helen's Smelting Company* (1865) LR 1 Ch App 66.

[25] An interesting counterpart to the soon to become common 'best practicable means' test in statute law as employed in the Alkali Act 1863 employed in *St Helen's v Tipping* [1865] 11 HLC 642 in a supplementary question put by the defendant to the jury.

tion (as Locke had supposed)[26] between human wellbeing and environmental protection.

Where physical damage is concerned, the law of nuisance finds itself on relatively familiar ground. But *St Helen's v Tipping* also raised the less straightforward issue of intangible interference with the use and enjoyment of land. In cases without physical damage the courts were much more reluctant to grant relief, and what amounts to an unreasonable interference with interests in land is dependent on circumstances. Lord Westbury LC stated *obiter* that:

> If a man lives in a town, it is necessary that he should subject himself to the consequences of those operations of trade which may be carried out in his immediate locality . . . If a man lives in a street where there are numerous shops, and a shop is opened next door to him, which is carried out in a fair and reasonable way, he has no grounds for complaint . . .[27]

Thus the nature of the locality in which the nuisance occurred became the key to determining whether or not relief would be granted in cases involving intangible damage. Differential standards thus became applicable under common law to this class of pollution problem. Industrial areas, where nuisance was at its worst, obtained a lower degree of protection than rural environments where problems were fewer. This particular issue was further upon expanded in *Sturges v Bridgeman* (1879).[28] The defendant, a confectioner, had used a mechanical pestle and mortar on his premises for more than 20 years. His neighbour, a doctor, then built a consulting room in an adjoining property and found that the operation of the machinery caused him disturbance. In arriving at the conclusion that a nuisance did exist Thesiger J made the following oft quoted *obiter* comment:

> . . . whether anything is a nuisance or not is a question to be determined, not merely by an abstract consideration of the thing itself, but in reference to its circumstances, what would be a nuisance in Belgrave Square would not necessarily be so in Bermondsey.[29]

Utilitarian considerations abound in such reasoning; but implicit in this line of argument is the notion that the calculus of interests is subject to environmental context: such contextual factors determine, at least in part, the way in which the utilitarian considerations are to be applied (the way the various interests are to be weighed). This approach did not, however, mean that protection from environmental pollution was non-existent in urban areas. Even in highly industrialised areas the courts would occasionally intervene if new interferences exceeded those which normally prevailed in a given locale. In *Rushmer v Polsue*

---

[26] See above ch 2.
[27] P 650.
[28] (1879) 11 Ch D 852.
[29] The quotation compares an elegant residential district with what was, at the time, the centre of the notoriously polluting tanning industry.

& Alfieri [1907],[30] for example, the plaintiff lived in Fleet Street, at that time the highly industrialised centre of the newspaper printing industry. His neighbours installed a new 24 hour printing press on their premises, which kept the plaintiff and his family awake. Cozens-Hardy LJ commented:

> A resident in such a neighbourhood must put up with a certain amount of noise. The standard of comfort differs according to the situation of the property . . . but if a substantial addition is found as a fact in a particular case, it is no answer to say that the neighbourhood is noisy, and that the defendant's machinery is of first class character.[31]

The application of the law of nuisance to relatively commonplace instances of interference with property rights by way of environmental pollution thus created geographically differential protection for property interests in industrial and non-industrial locales. Resort was made to the concept of reasonableness, both in terms of the plaintiff's expectations and the defendant's activities as a rationale for legal interference. The result was a body of decisions not as starkly utilitarian as might be supposed. The resort to environmental context displayed *both* a willingness to see the environment as subject to the calculus of interests *and* the recognition that such interests are themselves shaped and limited by the environmental context in which they arise. The resulting position represents a line of thought of surprising sophistication when compared with modern environmental thinking.

Nonetheless, the breakdown in the social homogeneity that was one of the by-products of the Industrial Revolution brought new tensions to bear on the law of nuisance. In earlier nuisance cases, the courts were being called upon to adjudicate in disputes that essentially pitted like interests against like, one private landowner against another. Even this type of case became more complicated as rival industrial interests came before the courts, as in the riparian rights case of *Pennington v Brinsop Hall Coal Company*.[32] In this case, waste water from the defendant's mine polluted the stream from which the plaintiff drew water for his cotton factory. The plaintiff argued that the chemicals contained in the water eroded his boilers, necessitating extra expense in cleaning and maintenance. The defendant characterised the plaintiff's loss at about £100 a year but argued that if granted the injunction that he sought, they would be unable to comply with it, and would have to close their colliery resulting in losses of £190,000 and 500 jobs. The defendant was prepared to pay damages to the plaintiff but argued that an injunction would have an effect disproportionate to the damage complained of. The conflicting interests were presented to the court, in particular by the defendant, in stark socio-economic terms. The Court's response was very interesting. Fry J *did* grant an injunction to Pennington, upholding his riparian rights with respect to continuing pollution and not being

---

[30] [1907] AC 121.
[31] [1906] 1 Ch 234, at 250–51.
[32] (1877) 5 Ch D 769.

sufficiently persuaded by the defendant's arguments to deny the conventional remedy. Fry J also, however, showed a degree of understanding for the defendants' plight in suspending the injunction for three months in order to facilitate compliance and to allow some latitude in seeking a solution that would allow their business to survive. Thus the plaintiff's property rights were vindicated, but a small degree of latitude was allowed to the defendant in order to try to accommodate conflicting uses of the water resource. Although the plaintiff's property rights were ultimately to be protected, there was some attempt to achieve a balance between the interests at stake.

In the new generation of nuisance cases, however, more complex conflicts emerged between individual, commercial and collective interests. These arose in the context of disputes between landowners and factory owners, as in *St Helens v Tipping*, above; between landowners and those providing public utilities, as in *Shelfer v City of London Electric Lighting Company*;[33] and between landowners and local authorities with regard to broader public interest issues, such as sanitation, as in the cases of *Goldsmid v Tunbridge Wells Improvement Commissioners*[34] and *The Earl of Harrington v Corporation of Derby*.[35] These cases provide useful exemplars of the difficult position that the courts increasingly found themselves in when determining nuisance claims, where argument focused on remedies: the question being whether an injunction should be awarded as was traditionally presumed,[36] or whether, given the circumstances, damages should be awarded instead.[37]

In *Shelfer*, the plaintiffs were the lessee and reversioner of a public house that was adversely affected by noise and vibration from the operation of the defendant's electricity substation, resulting in structural damage and interference with use and enjoyment of the property. The defendant was a private company but carried out their operations under statutory authority, sanctioning the provision of a public utility. At first instance, Kekewich J, swayed by the defendant's arguments pertaining to the public interest in continuing to use the substation to supply electricity, put to controversial use the powers under section 2 of Lord Cairn's Act 1858,[38] which conferred a discretion on the Court of Equity to award damages in lieu of an injunction.[39] Both sets of plaintiffs appealed successfully and were awarded the injunctions that they sought. The case is interesting in a number of ways, not least in showing the tensions faced by the

---

[33] [1895] 1 Ch 287.

[34] [1865] LR 1 Ch App 349.

[35] [1905] 1 Ch 205.

[36] See the House of Lords decision in *Imperial Gas Light and Coke Company v Broadbent* (1859) 7 HLC 600 '. . . when he has established his right at law, I apprehend that unless there be something special in the case, he is entitled as of course to an injunction to prevent the recurrence of that violation.', per Lord Kingsdown p 612.

[37] This issue is thoroughly examined by S Tromans 'Nuisance–Prevention or Payment?' (1982) 41 *Cambridge Law Journal* 87.

[38] (21& 22 Vict c. 27).

[39] Although the injunction is in principle a discretionary remedy, it tended historically to be awarded as of right in nuisance cases, see above n 29.

courts in giving primacy to traditional conceptions of property rights in a rapidly changing social context. In this case the property interests of the lessee and reversioner had to be set against not only the commercial interests of the defendant but also against the social interests of the public in light of their increasing reliance, even at this relatively early stage, upon electricity. The judges, while ultimately vindicating property rights, did not do so lightly and the difference in opinion between the lower and higher courts (evident from the unusually exhaustive judgments in the case) reveal a great deal of uneasiness in according primacy to individual property rights in the complex modern context. AL Smith LJ famously used the opportunity provided in *Shelfer* to lay down a working rule for the award of damages in lieu of an injunction in the context of nuisance. Four requirements had to be met: [40]

1. the injury to the plaintiff's rights had to be small;
2. they must be capable of being estimated in monetary terms;
3. they must be adequately compensated by a small payment; and
4. in the circumstances it would be 'oppressive to the defendant' to award an injunction.

The test reveals elements of cost/benefit analysis beginning to make inroads on what had hithertofore been an altogether more cut and dried consideration. The case marked the beginning of judicial sensitivity to the small revolution of Lord Cairn's Act by identifying considerations justifying an award of damages in lieu of an injunction. This represented a move away from an absolutist approach to the protection of interests in property to a more relativist and contextual approach towards the grant of relief. Smith's formulation effectively removed minor cases from the realm of the virtually automatic injunction, making the damages award (on a small scale) the appropriate redress. In so doing, the protection given to private property interests became less a question of principle and more a matter for a pragmatic response, and the commercial interests of the defendant also became an issue worthy of explicit consideration in the fourth of Smith's considerations. Other broader considerations, such as the public interest were also implicitly accorded significance under this head, where, as in this case, commercial interests were (at least in part) of broader public, and even parliamentary concern. While these developments were undoubtedly important in principle, they were to be relevant only in cases where minor interference was in question, and three out of four of Smith's considerations focused on the plaintiff's interests in any event. Nonetheless, by addressing the relevance of features other than the plaintiff's property interests as relevant to the matter of relief, *Shelfer* represented an important new departure in the law.

In *Shelfer*, issues pertaining to the public interest occupied a prominent position in the defendants' argument. They further contended that their statutory authorisation[41] placed them under a duty to supply electricity in a populous

[40] *Shelfer v City of London Electric Lighting Company*, 322.
[41] Electric Lighting Acts 1882 and 1888.

area, and provided for compensation to be paid where nuisance arose. They also argued that since the area in which they operated was a residential one and full to capacity, granting an injunction would prevent them from carrying out their business. Lord Halsbury cited as one of his reasons for granting the plaintiffs an injunction that of preventing a company from continuing a nuisance and forcing their neighbour to sell, simply because they could afford to pay compensation. Lord Lindley was particularly explicit in his examination of public interest arguments. He took the view that, although they were statutory undertakers, the defendants were ultimately engaged in a commercial undertaking, and in any event the fact that they were, in some sense, public benefactors was not sufficient to justify refusing an injunction to an individual whose rights were being persistently infringed. The rationale behind this lay in the rule that the expropriation of private property, even for compensation, could only be justified by Parliament, and that the courts were not engaged in the type of balancing of public and private interests that informed the legislative process in this context.

The various strands of reasoning adopted by the Court of Appeal combined traditional protection of individual property rights to trump claims based on the public interest with the idea that (Lord Cairn's Act notwithstanding) damages would only be awarded in lieu of an injunction in highly exceptional circumstances. The conception of property in play remained that of Blackstone: property was viewed as a right that Parliament, and the courts, should not interfere with outside a narrow range of exceptional circumstances. But decisions such as *Shelfer* represented a broadening of the kind of interests to be considered and weighed, even if the circumstances in which damages are appropriate remained elusive.

Shifting judicial attitudes towards the sanctity of private property rights can be seen in the changing approach of the courts to the award of damages in lieu of an injunction during the nineteenth century. The contrast in approach is nicely illustrated by the cases of *Goldsmid* and *Harrington*. The facts of the two cases are broadly similar, though the impact of the pollution was greater in the latter case. In *Goldsmid*, the plaintiff held a tenancy in a country estate featuring a stream and a lake that were used to water cattle and provide ice for domestic use. Both were adversely affected by increasing quantities of sewage discharged from Tunbridge Wells, for which the defendant commissioners bore the statutory responsibility to control. The plaintiff sought an injunction to restrain the commissioners from causing sewage to enter the stream and cause a nuisance on his property. The Court found for the plaintiff, Romilly MR signalling his unwillingness to countenance the defendant's arguments founded on the public interest in securing sanitary provision for Tunbridge Wells:

> . . .it has been suggested to me in argument, as a matter that ought to be regarded, that private interests must give way to public interests, that the Court ought to regard what the advantage to the public is, and that some little sacrifice ought to be made by private individuals. . . . But my firm conviction is, that in this . . . the interests of individuals are not only compatible with but identical with the interests of the public

. . . I believe that the injury to the public may be extremely great by polluting a stream . . .[42]

While it is a truism to say that the general public are adversely affected by pollution, the attempt to identify the public and private as one and the same is less than convincing (indeed, the plaintiff's relief was delayed in order to allow the defendants to address the problem, with the court stating that no action would be taken at a later point if the defendants were taking steps to prevent the nuisance). The *Goldsmid* case thus represents an uneasy compromise between the traditional supremacy of property rights, on the one hand, and the recognition of the need to protect public sanitation on the other. It was, nevertheless, an uneasy and rather unconvincing compromise.

In *Harrington,* the plaintiff owned a castle and country estate about five and a half miles downstream from Derby, which came to be adversely affected by the increased volume of sewage generated by the growing conurbation. The sewage was emitted, untreated, into the River Derwent. Derby Corporation had statutory powers pertaining to sewerage provision but had taken very little action to address the problem before obtaining new statutory powers to construct sewage works in 1901 (which were to be operational by 1906). The river had served to feed a lake on the plaintiff's land, to supply fish, to provide power for a waterwheel and potable water for humans and livestock. Increased siltation and decreased water quality, however, brought these uses to an end by 1902, and the plaintiff sued for nuisance. The court found that the Corporation was not responsible for the whole of the nuisance, since many householders in Derby had established prescriptive rights to emit sewage to the river predating the Corporation's role in public health law. The plaintiff sought an injunction to restrain the Corporation from polluting the river so as to cause a nuisance, and a further mandatory injunction requiring the Corporation to do certain works and damages. He failed in his quest for injunctions, which the court regarded as inappropriate under the circumstances, and was only partially successful in his claim for damages, which were awarded for having to find new water and power supplies, and for damage to property and fishing, totalling £500. The plaintiff was not entitled to damages in respect of the siltation problem or for amenity damage, because both he and his predecessor in title had failed to act to solve the problem when it initially became apparent decades earlier. Buckley J was satisfied that the new sewage works would serve to protect the plaintiff's property interests, and made much of the role of statute in determining the interests of the defendants and the rights of the plaintiff in this context. By this stage, then, in the context of sewerage provision, the balance between private rights and the public interest had begun to change, at least in the context of activities imposed upon local authorities by legislation. The ruling in *Harrington* demonstrates change emerging in the legislative approach to property rights, allowing them to be effectively curtailed by the public interest,

---

[42] *Goldsmid v Tunbridge Wells Improvement Commissioners*, 169–70.

in limited circumstances, on the basis of state-defined public utility rather than on natural rights.

Successful actions in nuisance, while useful to the individual in protecting his property from damage, and having a wider incidental benefit in protecting the environment, were of limited significance in practice. There are several reasons behind the relative lack of impact.[43] First, the remedy was available only to those having an interest in land, not generally the more numerous groups of those worst affected by the environmental and health impacts of industrial pollution. Most particularly, this latter group included the working class city dwellers who lived cheek by jowl with the polluting factories, and who often relied on them for their livelihood.[44] Secondly, proceedings in nuisance were extremely expensive. Until the Judicature Act 1873, two separate actions had to be undertaken: one in law for damages in respect of past interference, and a second in equity pursuing an injunction to protect against future interference. By its very nature, litigation at common law is generally somewhat erratic, *both* depending upon a host of social and economic factors extraneous to law *and* being somewhat uncertain as to its outcome. The law of nuisance in particular, with its focus on particular factual contexts and the individual interests raised in them, unsurprisingly proved ill-suited to dealing with the broad spread of industrial pollution in its myriad forms, and to the larger issues of the public interest, both positive and negative, inevitably raised by its impact.[45] Among the problems experienced in this regard was the fact that the adversarial character of litigation is ill-suited to examining the larger social and economic consequences at issue. In any event, the courts were (and still are), for the most part, decidedly uncomfortable when attempting to adjudicate between the conflicting interests of property and industry which, although they interfered with the property interests of a few, were also the source of national prosperity.

In addition to putting the general law of nuisance to work in dealing with the social challenges posed by the adverse impacts of otherwise beneficial industrial activity, the common law developed a specific response to acute pollution problems under the rule in *Rylands v Fletcher* (1868).[46] The original rule in *Rylands v Fletcher* was quite broad, invoking a general principle of strict liability for dangerous activities. This rule was subsequently contracted to operate in effect as a specialised type of nuisance. It was formulated to deal with isolated occurrences, which nuisance, concerning itself with ongoing states of affairs, did not necessarily cover. In the case of *Rylands v Fletcher* itself, Fletcher, a mine owner, brought an action against his neighbours, Rylands & Son, in respect of damage caused to land that he occupied by an escape of water from a reservoir that

---

[43] This is discussed in detail in A Ogus and G Richardson, 'Economics and the Environment: A Study of Private Nuisance' (1977) 36 *Cambridge Law Journal* 284.

[44] See McLaren, above n 12.

[45] See M Lobban's treatment of nineteenth century legal reasoning for a contextual explanation of the particular challenges facing judges at this time: M Lobban, *The Common Law and English Jurisprudence* (Oxford, OUP, 1991).

[46] [1868] LR 3 HL 330.

Rylands had had built on its land. The reservoir had been constructed for Rylands by independent contractors to facilitate an expansion of its operation of a mill on the site. When the reservoir was filled, water escaped into a disused mineshaft on Rylands's land that the contractors had failed to fill in. The offending shaft was connected to Fletcher's workings, which subsequently flooded and had to be pumped out. The initial damage was repaired, but a second escape meant that Fletcher's mine had to be abandoned. Fletcher originally brought an action in negligence for damages, though this was later changed to a claim based on strict liability, as the defendants had not themselves been negligent.[47] Blackburn J originally formulated the test for liability under these circumstances as follows:

> the true rule of law is that the person who, for his own purposes, brings on his land and keeps there anything likely to do mischief if it escapes, must do so at his peril, and, if he does not do so, he is prima facie answerable for all damage which is the natural consequence of its escape.[48]

This rule was affirmed, with a slight gloss, by Lord Cairns in the House of Lords:

> [I]f the Defendants, not stopping at the natural use of their close, had desired to use it for any purpose which I may term a 'non-natural' use, for the purpose of introducing into the close that which in its natural condition was not in it or upon it . . . and, if in consequence of their doing so . . . the water came to escape . . . it appears to me that which the Defendants were doing, they were doing at their own peril.[49]

Lord Cairns distinguished 'natural' that is, ordinary or expected or justifiable uses, with which the law would not intervene, from 'non-natural' uses, which were deemed by their particular nature to require special control. This device allowed the courts a certain amount of latitude in deciding what activities would fall under the rule and gave them the opportunity to temper the application of the rule in order to ensure that a satisfactory accommodation could be arrived at between conflicting individual and societal interests.

Initially the rule in *Rylands v Fletcher* was employed with alacrity in numerous cases involving what can be broadly categorised as 'pollution contexts.'[50] As might perhaps have been expected however, given the importance attached to qualifying the rule in *Rylands v Fletcher* from its inception by the higher courts, the non-natural user proviso was enthusiastically pressed into service to keep liability under this head in check. This element of the rule in *Rylands v Fletcher* soon became the main qualifier on liability, and is particularly interesting from

---

[47] For a detailed discussion of the somewhat unusual provenance of this case, see Cocks, above n 12 pp 9–10.

[48] *Fletcher v Rylands* (1865–66) LR 1 Ex 265 at 279.

[49] *Rylands v Fletcher*, 339.

[50] See eg *West v Bristol Tramways Co* [1908] 2 KB 14 (concerning creosote); *AG v Cory Brothers & Co* [1921] AC 521 (slag heaps); *Halsey v ESSO Petroleum* [1961] 2 All ER 145 (noxious fumes). This even extended to escapes of electricity: see *National Telephone Co v Baker* [1892] 2 Ch 186.

the point of view of controlling the impacts of industrial activity. The concept was discussed in the (Australian) Privy Council case of *Rickards v Lothian*.[51] The plaintiff's stock was damaged by an overflow of water from a hand-basin from the property above the one that he leased. The basin had been blocked by a malicious third party who then turned on the taps. The plaintiff tried to claim under the rule in *Rylands v Fletcher*, Lord Moulton responded:

> It is not every use to which land is put that brings into play that principle. It must be some special use bringing with it increased danger to others, and must not merely be the ordinary use of land or such use as is proper for the general benefit of the Community.[52]

In this case, the existence of a domestic water supply was held not to amount to a non-natural user. While this seems entirely justifiable, the same cannot be said for the conclusion reached on the user issue in *Read v J Lyons & Co Ltd* [1947],[53] in which, taking all the circumstances of time and place into account, running a munitions factory in wartime was held not to be a non-natural use. This decision was extremely damaging to the rule in *Rylands v Fletcher*, since it renders almost any imaginable use 'natural' in the context of modern societal conditions.

In the modern law, the restrictive non-natural user approach was taken to its logical conclusion, with respect to industrial activities, by Kennedy J at first instance in *Cambridge Water Company v Eastern Counties Leather* [1994].[54] This case involved the chemical contamination of groundwater by neighbouring tanneries over many years. The plaintiffs extracted the water and supplied it for human consumption until it was found, by reason of the contamination, to be unfit for human consumption under EC law. This necessitated the plaintiffs finding an alternative source of water to fulfil their supply contracts. The action under the rule in *Rylands v Fletcher* failed at first instance on the non-natural use issue. Kennedy J stated:

> [the area] is properly described as an industrial village and the creation of employment is clearly a benefit for the community . . . I hold that the storage of these chemicals did not amount to a non-natural user of land. In reaching this decision, I reflect on the innumerable small works that one sees up and down the country with drums stored in their yards. . . . Inevitably that storage presents some hazard, but in a manufacturing, and outside a primitive and pastoral society such hazards are part of the life of every citizen.[55]

This approach renders the whole concept of liability under the rule in *Rylands v Fletcher* effectively null and void since it makes it extremely difficult

---

[51] [1913] AC 263.
[52] at 280.
[53] [1947] AC 156.
[54] [1994] 1 All ER 53.
[55] at 139.

to construe any industrial activity as a non-natural use. The House of Lords however took a very different view of this issue. Lord Goff stated, obiter:

> The mere fact that the use is common in the tanning industry cannot be enough to bring it within the exception, nor does the fact that that [the village] contains a small industrial community worthy of encouragement or support. . . . Indeed I feel bound to say that the storage of substantial quantities of chemicals on industrial premises should be regarded as an almost classic case of non natural use.[56]

This approach potentially revives the rule in *Rylands v Fletcher*, though the rule faces other equally grave problems as a result of the House of Lords ruling in *Cambridge Water*: in particular the treatment of the rule as a mere variant on nuisance and the new enhanced role for foreseeability in both. The aforementioned cases are interesting because they reveal shifting attitudes as to what counts as a 'natural' use of property. Here, we seem to be rather far removed from a starkly utilitarian assessment of property rights. The idea that there might be inherent limitations on property rights is probably not a part of the juridical conception of rights, since questions of the extent of an owner's rights to engage in certain actions will only arise where the affected party raises an action in nuisance. But the body of decisions considered above do articulate a position in which property rights are inherently subject to considerations of social welfare, not on the basis of a straightforward weighing of conflicting interests, but in relation to what counts as a natural incident of ownership. This suggests that property rights have their basis in conceptions of value other than mere utility: since what counts as a 'natural' consequence of ownership varies according to the wider environmental or social context, it is reasonably clear that the notion of natural user, though clearly linked to questions of social welfare, does not reduce straightforwardly to a utilitarian calculus of interests.

While the common law could (and continues to) respond to relatively small-scale individual disputes at the interstices of increasingly pervasive statutory regimes, it does not represent the optimum strategy to solve large-scale environmental pollution problems. Actions in the law of nuisance are motivated primarily by self-interest and rationed by the availability of resources for litigation. These characteristics, together with the geographically specific and therefore spatially limited nature of the cases, inevitably make the progress of the law somewhat uneven. In reading these developments, one is powerfully reminded of Peter Stein's observation, quoted in the previous chapter, that nuisance is environmentally of enormous significance, but *local*. Yet it is equally apparent that broader issues of principle were both present in many nuisance cases *and* recognised as determining factors in decision. The undeniable unevenness of the approach of the law of nuisance to environmental problems should therefore not be mistaken for the absence of general principles or values.

---

[56] at 78–79.

Public Nuisance

Not all incidents of pollution will impact directly upon individuals. Even where individuals are affected, there is no guarantee that they will have the necessary legal or financial status to bring an action. These issues are addressed in part by the criminal law, or tort hybrid,[57] of public nuisance, which, in one of its main forms, deals with adverse environmental impacts on a broader scale than private nuisance. Public nuisance is defined in *Archbold's Criminal Pleading* as an offence at common law committed by a person:

> [w]ho does an act, not warranted by law, or omits to discharge a legal duty, if the effect of the act or omission is to endanger the life, health, property, morals or comfort of the public or to obstruct the public in the exercise or enjoyment of rights common to all her Majesty's subjects.[58]

Historically, in criminal law, proceedings could be brought by the Attorney General acting in his official capacity as the representative of the public interest. The right to bring proceedings in criminal law for public nuisance was later extended to Local Authorities by (the much-used) section 222 Local Government Act 1972. An individual may also bring criminal proceedings in respect of public nuisance, but only though a relator action, with the cloak of the Attorney General's authority, through the discretionary granting of his *fiat* to initiate litigation. The first two types of criminal action present an interesting bridge between the concepts of public and private interest by providing, in some circumstances, the potential to secure relief for those who fail to satisfy the legal technicalities to bring an action at common law, or lack the funds to do so. Individual *rights* do not receive redress in such proceedings, but the mischief complained of will, if the action succeeds, be addressed.

Individual rights can, however, be vindicated in public nuisance in its tortious incarnation. The definition of public nuisance in torts is neatly summed up by Romer LJ in *AG v PYA Quarries Ltd* [1957]:[59] '. . . any nuisance is "public" which materially affects the reasonable comfort and convenience of life of a class of Her Majesty's subjects.'[60] Here again, the blurring of the line between the purity of private nuisance and broader notions of the public interest in environmental matters is apparent. The question of what constitutes a 'class of Her Majesty's subjects' is one of fact to be determined on a case-by-case basis, though Lord Denning's view, in the same case, that public nuisance should be 'widespread in its range' is of some help in determining what mischief the law was seeking to remedy in this area. In the *PYA Quarries* case, the interference

---

[57] Public nuisance is essentially a crime that takes on a tortious nature in certain limited circumstances.

[58] JF Archibold, *Criminal Pleading, Evidence and Practice* (London, Sweet & Maxwell, 2003) para 31.40 p 2550.

[59] [1957] 2 QB 169.

[60] at 184.

complained of consisted of disruption caused to life in a small village by noise, dust and vibration resultant upon neighbouring quarrying operations. This state of affairs was found to constitute a public nuisance. Once a public nuisance has been established, proceedings may be brought in torts by an individual who has special or particular damage. This requires that the plaintiff has suffered interference over and above that experienced by the public at large. A good example is provided by *Halsey v Esso Petroleum Co Ltd* [1961].[61] Here, nuisance was raised under multiple guises, concerning the operation of an oil transfer station situated adjacent to a residential area. One of the heads of nuisance complained of involved noise nuisance caused by tankers turning in the highway. This caused interference to everyone who lived on the street, but especially to Halsey, whose house was situated opposite the entrance to the ESSO depot, where the tankers made most noise. Therefore the noise represented a widespread and thus public nuisance and Halsey, as someone suffering interference over and above that affecting his peers, was able to bring an action in tort in respect of it.

The most commonly recognised categories of special or particular damage, in the context of public nuisance, are physical injury or damage to property; depreciation in the value of land; loss of custom or business; and delay, inconvenience or expense. These overlap to some extent with the property damage or devaluation that is recoverable in private nuisance, but are considerably broader in their coverage. It is arguable that, although deriving much of its content from private nuisance, public nuisance is at least as much a creature of public law and is infused with its values and objectives, controlling socially undesirable behaviour by curtailing the rights of landowners, in the public interest. The rationale for the limitations imposed by public nuisance therefore goes beyond that invoked in private nuisance in the name of protecting the private property interests and therefore the breadth of interference brooked with private property rights in public nuisance is greater than that in private nuisance. This is not surprising: it is possible systematically to articulate and delineate public interests with much greater accuracy in legislation than at common law, and thus the utilitarian rationale underlying such efforts is much more apparent in the statutory context.

This type of cross-fertilisation between private and public law is further demonstrated in statutory nuisance, which builds upon the common law, but is invoked in the public interest and is, in all other respects, a creature of public law proper. The concept of statutory nuisance was prominent from the inception of modern public health law: it appeared in a number of guises in the Public Health Act 1875, which remains in large part the template for the modern law in this area. Statutory nuisance effectively reworks common law nuisance, taking some of its more practical features for remedying interference with property and separating them from the more onerous procedural and

[61] [1961] 2 All ER 145.

standing requirements. This relatively streamlined procedure came at a cost in terms of its relatively narrow coverage, and the fact that the remedies on offer (bar ending the nuisance) did not operate primarily for the vindication of individual interests in property. This approach seems to vindicate the role of nuisance in curtailing socially undesirable states of affairs pertaining to land, while divorcing the desirable practical result of ending a nuisance from the more principled but also confining specific property protection rationale. In taking this approach, statutory nuisance, like public nuisance imports limitations on property rights in the broader public interest.

The penalties in statutory nuisance, for the most part[62] hinge upon not the carrying on of a nuisance as such, but upon ignoring abatement notices issued by local authorities.[63] Follow-up nuisance orders[64] issued by the court are criminal and punitive in nature and therefore differ substantially from the consequences of infringing the common law.[65] Local authorities were given a proactive role, being placed under a duty both to inspect[66] their areas for nuisances and to act to secure their abatement. The powers given to local authorities under the statutory regime also extended to powers of entry to premises to inspect the performance of abatement measures. The legislation also allowed individuals, as persons affected by a nuisance, or simply as inhabitants[67] of the area to bring nuisances to the attention of the local authority for action. In an interesting example, individuals were given recourse to proceedings in statutory nuisance as 'persons aggrieved' or inhabitants of the affected area[68] by the occurrence of public health-based nuisances. Thus, statutory nuisance can be viewed as an interesting hybrid, taking what were viewed as effective elements from the common law of nuisance and grafting it on to a rudimentary public law framework, and its significance has not been limited to a mere transitional stage between the historic common law of nuisance and modern environmental pollution and public health law. Statutory nuisance remains on the statute books, and despite its (perhaps) anomalous characteristics, continues to play an important role at the margins of public health and pollution control.

The current provisions governing statutory nuisance are in most respects very similar to those found in the Public Health Act 1875, and are to be found in Part

---

[62] S 92 of the Public Health Act 1936 made provision for acute or chronic statutory nuisances to be dealt with summarily; including premises or accumulations or deposits that are 'prejudicial to health or a nuisance' (s 92(1)(a) and (c) respectively); though most will fall under the main procedure.

[63] S 94 of the Public Health Act (hereafter PHA) 1875.

[64] Ss 95 and 96 PHA 1875.

[65] Most infringements attracted initial fines with additional charges incurred at a daily rate until the nuisance was abated, as for example under s 98, though some of the broader public health provisions of the Act attracted more extreme sanctions, as for example under s 26 where buildings built in such a way as to interfere with sewers could be altered or even demolished by the local authority which could then recover the costs of doing so from the owner.

[66] S 92 PHA 1875.

[67] S 93 PHA 1875.

[68] S 105 PHA 1875.

III of the Environmental Protection Act 1990. These provisions place public authorities under statutory duties in respect of a limited class of public health-based nuisances. The regime continues to offer a more accessible, cheaper, but less versatile protection than the common law from which it is derived. Section 79 of the EPA delineates certain states of affairs which are prohibited if they are prejudicial to health,[69] or constitute a nuisance.[70] This formulation for invoking statutory nuisance remains the same as in 1875, and is a relatively unsophisticated receptor standard[71] (defined as a standard applied to a polluter administering liability for perceptible environmental harm). This form of words may appear at first glance to be a rather vague means of imposing liability, but the courts fairly quickly supplied it with a more defined content based on their experience of private nuisance. In any event, it proved quite well-suited to addressing a relatively simple environmental issue; hence its continued, if residual, utility.

Nonetheless, statutory nuisance has developed in its own distinctive manner. The courts have tended, for example, towards the view that the interference complained of must be such as to affect personal comfort, which is narrower than common law, and perhaps overly restrictive. The rationale for this limitation does, however, serve in part to ensure that the nuisances complained of are of a sufficient magnitude to justify invoking the criminal law and its sanctions, thus ensuring that there is substantial cause for bringing defendants before the court and potentially bringing fines into play and ultimately curtailing what would otherwise be lawful activities incident to and ownership.

Local authorities continue to be under a dual duty to inspect their area for such nuisances and to respond to complaints made by members of the public. If they are satisfied that such a nuisance exists or is likely to occur or to recur, they are obliged to serve an abatement notice. Appeals may be made to the Magistrates' Court[72] on carefully limited grounds.[73] It is an offence to fail to comply with an abatement notice.[74] If such a failure occurs, the local authority has a number of options: it can abate[75] the nuisance itself and bring an action to recover the costs of doing so; or it may bring summary proceedings in the Magistrates' Court. If neither of these courses of action is deemed sufficient, it can bring proceedings in the High Court. Thus, statutory nuisance offers a

---

[69] That is, are injurious or likely to cause injury.

[70] This must involve a public or private nuisance at common law, see, *National Coal Board v Neath Borough Council* [1976] 2 All ER 478.

[71] This useful term is employed by K Grundy in 'Legislative and Regulatory Trends' in RD Ross (ed), *Air Pollution and Industry* (New York, London, Nostrand Reinhold, 1972) at 121, cited by A Ogus, 'The Regulation of Pollution' in G Richardson, A Ogus and P Burrows, *Policing Pollution: A Study of Regulation and Enforcement* (Oxford, Clarendon Press, 1982) 37.

[72] S 80(3) of the Environmental Protection Act (hereafter EPA).

[73] These are laid out in the Statutory Nuisance (Appeals) Regulations 1995.

[74] S 80(4) of the EPA.

[75] This situation is in marked contrast with that in private nuisance where, for it has not been favoured as a remedy for the best part of a century, see the House of Lords decision in *Lagan Navigation Co v Lambeg Bleaching Dyeing & Finishing Co Ltd* [1927] AC 226.

relatively swift and comparatively cheap mechanism whereby local authorities can tackle the effects of nuisance, either by compelling those responsible for creating a nuisance to act to bring it to an end, or by taking concrete action themselves to tackle the problem. This development is obviously rooted in the historic law of nuisance, but goes further by offering a practical (if limited) means of dealing with some of the adverse environmental effects experienced by the public at large, and by individuals who cannot, for one reason or another, make recourse to the common law.

Part III of the EPA also continues to allow individuals affected by certain public health-based classes of nuisance to bring an action under the guise of 'persons aggrieved'.[76] This formulation, despite the absence of a statutory right to initiate proceedings as an inhabitant of the area affected, as in the Public Health Act 1875, still potentially allows for wider access to the courts than does private nuisance in that there is no requirement that a person aggrieved have a proprietary interest in the property affected. Litigation in statutory nuisance does not provide access to the same range of relief as would be available at common law. Even if successful, a plaintiff will only achieve the end of the nuisance as the defendant is forced to abate: there is no mechanism to award damages for prior interference with property interests, and no injunction to prevent future interference, although recourse can be had to further statutory proceedings. The law of statutory nuisance, then, although primarily the preserve of local government, retains a residual role for the individual in litigating, though their role and what they can ultimately gain from the proceedings is more limited than at common law. In retaining this role for the individual, primarily as a default position if a recalcitrant local authority refuses to act, statutory nuisance upholds the widest possible view of the public interest while at the same time paying lip service to the nuisance values that provide much of its heritage.

Despite subsequent developments which recognise the utility of the nuisance action as a means of protecting public interests in basic environmental quality, the law has had to evolve a considerable distance from its common law roots to be thus employed. Even where it forms the basis for a statutory regime, it is still somewhat limited in its scope. A realistic assessment of the strengths and weaknesses of nuisance, in its several forms, as a tool for dealing with the impacts of pollution makes readily apparent the need for legislative intervention on a larger scale.[77] While common lawyers such as Blackstone endorsed the republican thesis that ownership of property provided, in and of itself, sufficient motivation for the owner to conserve it as a resource, this proved an inadequate safeguard for broader environmental values in the majority of cases. The short-term gains to be made from industrial exploitation for many owners outweighed the claims of tradition and of passing on the hereditament to succeeding generations. This problem was compounded when wedded to that arising from the physical

---

[76] S 82.
[77] See, for example J Brenner, 'Nuisance Law and the Industrial Revolution' (1974) 3 *Journal of Legal Studies* 403.

effects produced by industrial usages, and the need for more coercive, state-based pollution control regimes to replace an approach based on self-interest and private law became apparent. There is no general common law *right* to pollute, in the absence of a special entitlement to behave in a particular way (where, for example, an easement or a prescriptive right has been acquired). Furthermore, the law of nuisance shows that one landowner's polluting activities can produce an actionable interference with the rights of neighbouring landowners. Thus it is arguable that, at common law, pollution is regarded at least to some extent as a socially undesirable phenomenon. As such, it is a short step to recognise the need for regulation of polluting activities in the wider public interest, if only on the pragmatic grounds of forestalling the need for numerous expensive individual legal actions.

From Remedies to Rights

The common law had started out with a consideration of *remedies*, and thence moved on to *principles* dealing with the extent of *rights* and *interests*. As has been argued, the principles determining judicial assessments of when a remedy was available are not readily understandable as bare utilitarian assessments of competing interests. Utilitarian principles, of course, played an important part in such assessments, but the contextual approach to 'natural' vs 'non-natural' user suggested the recognition of a deeper set of concerns relating to the nature of property rights themselves. Implicit in this approach is a view of property rights as *inherently*, rather than merely *instrumentally*, subject to wider social interests of a broadly environmental kind. Such a view is rather far removed from the utilitarian view of 'absolute' property rights inevitably colliding with collective goals and interests. Where property rights are seen as related to collective interests intrinsically rather than instrumentally, they do not *conflict* with the wider interests but derive their shape from them.

   Ideas of this kind are very difficult to articulate within the forms and structures of judicial reasoning. Moreover, where the underlying assumptions of juridical scholarship are positivist in outlook, the extraction of broad principles from an array of individual decisions will be viewed as the activity of the censor, and not the expositor. One is reminded, once again, of Stein's remark that the common law can offer no *general* response to environmental problems: common lawyers were aware of the problems, and could formulate ingenious solutions to them, but judicial language remained resistant to the articulation of fully general principles by which those problems (and their attendant solutions) could be rationalised. Where the common law ceases to be regarded as embodying a system of natural rights and duties based on rational principles, the development of systematic responses to generic social problems comes to be seen as the preserve of statute law.

STATUTORY RESPONSES TO ENVIRONMENTAL PROBLEMS

The Victorian age saw the Industrial Revolution reach its zenith, but it also experienced the full force of its adverse consequences. Hence, the need to deal with those negative impacts became pressing. The need first to facilitate, and later to control, industrial development and the social and environmental conditions required to promote it, played a key role in the expansion of both the role of the state and legislation. A typical pattern emerged for intervention with individual activities in order to ameliorate their wider undesirable impacts, by curtailing former freedoms where the impact of common law was minimal. Private legislation, used to such prominent effect in facilitating industrial development, increasingly came to be employed in tackling its by-products (as, for example, in the manipulation of local environments to secure a healthier workforce). Subsequently, state-sponsored legislative schemes and new regulatory machinery emerged, establishing (among other things) rudimentary pollution control. Legal intervention gradually changed in character as well as format, from piecemeal and permissive to comprehensive and mandatory.

In the nineteenth century, private legislation was used extensively to promote infrastructure projects,[78] which interfered with private property interests on a scale hitherto unprecedented in peacetime. For this reason alone, the role of the state vis-à-vis the development of communications provides an instructive example of the tensions in the social, cultural and legal spheres which emerged as modern priorities came increasingly into conflict with traditional interests. The use of private bills in the development of the railway system made the committee rooms at Westminster the focus for the battle between old and new property. Major landowners used political influence, lobbying, legal representation and the threat of drawing out the complex and costly adversarial bill-making process to wring the greatest sums of compensation possible from the railway companies desperate to build across their land. After a flurry of private acts facilitating individual rail projects, public legislation was developed to streamline the railway building process, in effect giving private enterprise the blessing of the state in recognition of its social utility. The pattern of first private and then public legislation would, as we shall see, be replicated in public health law and pollution control. In particular, the Land Clauses Consolidation Act 1845 (characterised as a compromise between landed and railway interests) proved advantageous for the landowners; for while simplifying purchase procedures for the railways and overriding much of the common law protection of interests in land, it also contained sweeping arbitration provisions which served further to bolster compensation paid to landowners whose property interests were

---

[78] It was a particular feature of the railway booms, see RW Kostal, *Law and English Railway Capitalism, 1825–1875* (Oxford, OUP, 1994) though similar strategies had been adopted on a smaller scale in earlier initiatives: see, for example, VTH Delaney & DR Delaney *The Canals of the South of Ireland* (Newton Abbot, David & Charles, 1966).

infringed. Intervention at the legislative stage was therefore only one weapon in the landowners' armoury. Arbitration and court proceedings to contest unsatisfactory compensation offers gave them further leverage. Nonetheless, the railway booms and the legislation that perpetuated them emphasised the economic value of land as a commodity that can be bought and sold like any other.

It is highly significant that this widespread legislative interference with private property was justified by appeals to the public interest, based on a clearly articulated (if rather unsophisticated) utilitarian theory of property which had come to the fore in light of prevailing perceptions of societal priorities.[79] According to this conception, property rights collide with collective interests (as well as with group-interests and with each other) and require resolution according to a purely instrumental matrix centring on harm and well-being. Such a view was to supply the pattern for assessments of legislation which interfered with property rights on the basis of social, and especially environmental, concerns.

Public Health

Despite the tensions and problems experienced in the use of private acts in the context of the railway booms, the mercantile classes quickly grasped the utility of such legislation to advance other areas of less overtly commercial development. In effect, it allowed them to 'wield . . . the power of the state'.[80] Private legislation was employed to radical effect as industrial capitalists in the major conurbations increasingly took hold of the reins of local political power, playing dominant roles in town councils and corporations.[81] They sought powers to introduce sanitary improvements in order to safeguard the health of their cities and thus maintain the well-being of their workforce. Local authorities in the second quarter of the nineteenth century began to petition Parliament in earnest, seeking private bills to authorise local public health initiatives. This was an expensive process, and although not as conspicuously contested as in the case of railway legislation, it still involved paying lawyers to argue the case before Parliament and financing an investigation of matters raised by the Commissioners of Her Majesty's Woods, Forests, Land Revenues, Works and Buildings.[82] Petitions had to be supported by detailed argument, and often concerned themselves with securing clean and safe water supplies for public and private use, and providing improved drainage, sewerage and cleansing.

---

[79] Kostal, above n 78 p 179.
[80] *Ibid*, p 152.
[81] In Belfast, a leading example of the new class of industrial metropolis, for example, in 1847 the ten aldermen of the city were either merchants or industrialists and 24 of the 30 city councillors were involved in industry, commerce or the professions.
[82] This could cost up to £10,000.

The Belfast Improvement Bill 1847[83] and the official reports upon it[84] provide a typical example of the type of legislation that emerged, and of the debate that informed it. Parliament was required to hear those opposed to schemes as well as their proposers, and the resultant reports reveal significant disquiet concerning the grant of legal empowerment to interfere with private property rights in the public interest.[85] Nonetheless, the effects of such schemes were, on the whole, positive, if necessarily somewhat uneven, depending as they did upon local initiative. In addition, the approach adopted was hardly systematic, and often the cleanup of one problem area, such as the replacement of privies and cesspools with sanitary sewerage systems, improved the streets but generated problems elsewhere as waste was flushed into watercourses.

The impact of private Acts of Parliament upon public health was, in the long term, rather broader than first appeared, and this type of intervention was at least as decisive in shaping nascent public health law as the more widely acknowledged contribution of Edwin Chadwick, the architect of the Victorian statutory public health regime. Central government quickly came to realise that local initiatives generated not only obvious improvements in public health, but also a range of social and economic benefits. Political concern formed the impetus for a plethora of inquiries and reports. Notable among these were the *Report of the Royal Commission on Noxious Vapours*,[86] the *Reports of the Commissioners on the State of Large Towns*,[87] and the *Report on the Sanitary Condition of the Labouring Population* (the Chadwick Report)[88] which tackled many of the most pressing public health concerns of the day. Such reports did a great deal to reveal the scale and the complexity of the problems to be addressed.

As a result of these developments, the appeal of applying public health initiatives on a nation-wide scale became obvious, though in the context of the relatively rudimentary nineteenth-century state, the idea of mandatory intervention was too extreme to gain initial support. Instead, the Government initially adopted a permissive approach, introducing a 'special act' procedure under the Town Improvement Clauses Act 1847. This was intended as a more streamlined alternative to the cumbersome private bill route, the hope being that this would encourage more local authorities to take up the public health challenge. Building on this model, the Public Health Act 1848 took a similar tack. These

[83] 8&9 Vict c142 1845 & 1846. Belfast was a typical Victorian city, its population rising from 24,000 in 1800 to 387,000 in 1911, taking it from the 22nd largest city in the British Isles to 9th largest, an annual mean population growth of 2.6%, the highest rate in the UK for this period–[D Campbell, Victorian Belfast in Belfast Civic Trust Tenth Anniversary Conference, Georgian Dublin–Victorian Belfast: Challenges and Opportunities 1992].

[84] 1847 BPP xxxiii 11.

[85] For example, the report on the Belfast Improvement Act 1847, *ibid*, reveals the objections of Messrs Joy, owners of a paper mill, whose water supply stood to be adversely affected by proposals to culvert the Blackstaff river, cls 29–43.

[86] 1878, c 2159.

[87] 1844–45.

[88] 1848.

Acts provided a range of tools for local authorities to tackle environmental problems that could be accessed by employing local regulations. The commitment to voluntarism was, however, relatively short-lived and, in the context of the burgeoning role of the late Victorian state, the protection of public health became a mandatory concern for local government under the codifying and rationalising provisions of the Public Health Act 1875. What had begun as a peripheral concern among a few forward-thinking local authorities had, in a very short period of time, become a mainstream state concern. The Public Health Act 1875 took state involvement in manipulating the environment to a new level. Sanitary provision had swiftly come to be regarded as essential to the public interest and was pursued as a social priority, even when it conflicted with the interests of individual property owners.

Pollution Control

The creation of new regulatory regimes, regulatory authorities and professions to prevent and manage adverse consequences of industrialisation gave the system of environmental regulation a self-perpetuating constituency, actively seeking the further development and reform of environmental legislation. Industrial pollution was deemed a threat both to human health and to the environment, but it was of course produced by powerful and profitable industries that were the source of Britain's prosperity. Such was the cumulative impact of pollution that, despite this economic fact, it was thought necessary to regulate it in the public interest, as public health came to be increasingly equated with public wealth.[89] The pattern of legal intervention that emerged was the same as that exhibited in public health law, with provisions first being applied to particularly affected localities as, for example, in the Smoke Nuisance Abatement (Metropolis) Act 1853. For the most part, though, industrial pollution problems were left to be tackled under the law of nuisance. This strategy very quickly proved inadequate, particularly in the context of industrial air pollution. Very often, no individual property interests were actually infringed by the pollution, which was, in economic terms, characterised as a straightforward externality. Thus, although depleted air quality affected the health and comfort of the population at large, the common law was usually powerless to intervene.

Where no legal sanction attaches to an activity that adversely affects others, there is no incentive for the author of the interference to ameliorate the socially undesirable consequences of his actions. The need for an alternative mechanism to the common law that would be effective to tackle externalities was, therefore, required; and so the scene was set for large-scale state intervention and the introduction of a more comprehensive regulatory regime. The policy objectives

---

[89] A Ogus, 'The Regulation of Pollution' in G Richardson, A Ogus and P Burrows, above n 71 p 30.

of such interventions were aimed at providing outcomes that, as far as possible, achieved a socially optimum balance between economically desirable activities, on the one hand, and their socially undesirable and environmentally damaging consequences, on the other. The first steps in this direction are clearly utilitarian; yet later developments would outstrip the basic utilitarian framework in important ways.

The first public act of Parliament dealing with industrial pollution as such was the Alkali Act 1863.[90] The Alkali Act represented a new approach to regulating the environment, making responsibility for addressing pollution the concern of the state, and introducing the idea of technocratic enforcement by creating the world's first 'professional' environmental agency, the Alkali Inspectorate.[91] Industrial pollution was therefore tackled, from a relatively early date, by scientifically proficient professional pollution control agencies. In contrast, 'simple' public health problems were the province of local government and, at least initially, addressed in a rather more casual fashion.[92] The central/local divide remains in place in modern practice, ostensibly allowing local input on matters affecting communities and their immediate environment, in the sphere of basic public health, while ensuring that large scale or complex problems are dealt with by informed specialist repeat players, especially where matters of broader import are concerned. Once the Alkali Act was in force, it was necessary for scheduled works to be registered with the Inspectorate in order for them to operate lawfully.[93] The legislation initially focused on the soap, glass and textile sectors though coverage was subsequently extended to other industries including the cement industry, smelting works and most aspects of the chemical industry.

In its initial guise, the Alkali Inspectorate was a specialised, if somewhat rudimentary, monitoring and enforcement unit,[94] charged with ensuring that a minimum of 95 per cent of the muriatic acid gas produced by alkali works had been condensed[95] in order to curtail emissions. The main offence under the Act lay in contravention of the 95 per cent condensation standard, resulting in a fine of up to £50 for a first offence and of up to £100 for subsequent offences.[96] While the regime may, on first appearances, seem to be quite draconian, a number of factors militated against it being particularly onerous in practice. First, the Alkali

[90] There was of course earlier legislation directed at controlling aspects of industrial activity, such as the Act for giving Facility in the Prosecution and Abatement of Nuisances Arising from Furnaces Used and in the working of Steam Engines 1821, though these were limited in intent and application.
[91] S 7 of the Alkali Act 1863 provided for appointment of a Chief Inspector, assisted by a staff of Sub-Inspectors.
[92] Modern environmental health officers of course operate in a much broader and at the same time more technical sphere than their historic counterparts and are trained and educated to a high degree of professional competence.
[93] Alkali Act 1863 s 6.
[94] *Ibid* s 9.
[95] *Ibid* s 4.
[96] *Ibid*.

Inspectorate itself was initially appointed by the Board of Trade,[97] rather than the (perhaps more obvious) Board of Public Health, an important indication of its place in the overall scheme of things. In addition, the basis of liability in the Act was comparatively narrow, in that a defence was available to owners of alkali works if they could show that they had exercised due diligence in attempting to comply with the legislation, and that the offence was committed by a named agent, servant or workman without owner's knowledge or consent or connivance,[98] who would then be pursued in respect of the offence. There was thus to be no liability in the absence of culpability, a much more lenient approach than that applied in the law of nuisance in general, and under the rule in *Rylands v Fletcher* for environmental interference at common law.

Although the Alkali Act was reasonably simple in both its scope and structure, in many ways it has acted as a template for central state regulation of pollution in the United Kingdom ever since. The whole ethos of the Alkali Act was one of technological optimism. Throughout, the Act exhibited total confidence that scientific and industrial solutions could be applied to pollution problems, if not to eliminate them, then to render them unproblematic. This type of approach continues to prevail in many ways today. The Alkali Act established an approach to legislative intervention that was triggered not by environmental pollution per se, but by the damaging *effects* of that pollution. It thus adopted an instrumental conception of environmental harm.

The next significant development, building upon the technological optimism of the Alkali Act, was the Alkali Act (1863) Amendment 1874, which aimed to clarify the scope of the regulatory regime. The 1874 Act also introduced an additional regulatory standard, on top of the condensation requirements under the 1863 Act, for emissions into the atmosphere. This was set at a maximum of one-fifth part of a grain of muriatic acid per cubic foot of air, smoke or chimney gases emitted[99]—an early example of an 'end of pipe' emission standard. This type of standard was adopted in respect of emissions that were assumed to cause damage (in contrast with receptor standards where interference is easily established) and which were realised through scientific deduction and measurement rather than by simple physical observation.[100] The significance of the emissions standards approach, however, lies just as much in theory as in practice, in that it marks a move away from a subjective approach to gauging pollution and towards an objective and overtly scientific one. This approach, regardless of its practical justification, does have potentially significant ramifications, arguably dissociating the causes of environmental problems from their effects, and shifting the focus of regulation away from the activities of the individual and

---

[97] Alkali Act 1863 s 7.
[98] *Ibid* s 5.
[99] Alkali Act 1863 (Amendment) 1874, s 4.
[100] There is some overlap between the two approaches, for example, beginning with the Smoke Abatement (Metropolis) Act 1853 and continuing through to the current Clean Air Act 1993, dark smoke emissions are 'measured' through observation employing a Ringlemann chart.

concentrating on collective harm. The methodology employed in the Alkali Act has dominated most aspects of environmental regulation ever since, arguably to the detriment of legal development in the UK in some respects, not least in the dogged insistence on clinging to the emissions standards approach when the receptor standards approach prevails elsewhere in the European Union.[101]

The 1874 Act was also highly influential in requiring that manufacturers employ the best practicable means[102] (BPM) to abatement technologies in order to prevent, or at least minimise and render harmless, all noxious gases produced in the production process.[103] Failure to employ the best practicable means to prevent or minimise discharges incurred a fine of up to £20 for a first offence, up to £50 for a second offence, along with a daily payment of £2 for the duration of the misdemeanour, this rising to £20 per day for third and subsequent infringements.[104] The 1874 Act further required that the Inspectorate serve notice on the owner of works offending under this provision, stating both the substance of the compliance failure and the means that would suffice to rectify it.[105] The regulatory regime under the Alkali Acts was designed to ensure that the need to secure an environment that was conducive to public health was not to be allowed to throttle the industry that, while responsible for creating pollution in the first place, also formed the economic backbone of the nation. In this regard the Alkali Acts shaped the UK approach to environmental law for almost a century and influenced law throughout the world.

Despite its apparently severe penalty mechanism, the BPM approach was in fact quite flexible, in that it adopted an implicit cost/benefit analysis approach to environmental protection. The BPM remained a central feature of UK industrial air pollution control law until superseded by the best available techniques not entailing excessive costs test (BATNEEC), introduced by the Environmental Protection Act 1990.[106] What was required by the BPM formulation was not an absolute standard, but rather, through the practicability requirement, one related to the specific circumstances of the companies to whom it was applied. In some respects the room to manoeuvre that the regime gave to the regulatory process was beneficial, in that it made that process less confrontational and arguably more efficient. On the other hand, the inherent flexibility of the system,

---

[101] See, K Morrow 'Nuisance and Environmental Protection' in J Lowry and R Edmunds (eds) above n 12.

[102] This term had also been employed in s 3 of the Smoke Abatement (Metropolis) Act 1853.

[103] *Ibid* s 5.

[104] *Ibid.*

[105] *Ibid.*

[106] S 7. This test has had a rather shorter shelf life and is in the process of being replaced by the Best Available Techniques (BAT) test courtesy of Dir 96/61/EC Concerning Integrated Prevention of Environmental Pollution OJ No. L 257, under the Pollution Prevention and Control Act 1999. Despite the absence of an explicit economic component, the BAT formulation also involves an element of cost/benefit analysis in that art 2(1) and Annex IV of the Directive defines 'available' broadly as: 'Techniques that are developed on a scale which allows implementation in the relevant industrial sector, under economically and technically viable conditions, taking into consideration the costs and advantages, whether or not the techniques are used or produced inside the Member States, as long as they are reasonably accessible to the operator'.

and the latitude given to the Alkali Inspectorate to employ the BPM to tailor the general provisions of the law to the specific works regulated, also proved problematic.[107]

The closed nature of the regulatory process also rendered this flexibility problematic. As public awareness of the environment grew, so too did distrust of the Alkali Inspectorate's close working relationship with the industries that it regulated and the fear of 'agency capture'.[108] Such fears were perhaps justified by the fact that the public tended, quite wrongly, to equate the role of the Inspectorate with that of the police force. This comparison was, to say the least, unhappy: although criminal sanctions are employed in pollution control law, there is in fact little congruence between the role of pollution control agencies and that of the police force in mainstream criminal law. In this area there is an ongoing relationship between the agency and the industrial actors whose activities it controls. Thus, while criminal proceedings may be justified according to the letter of the law in a particular case, it may prove counterproductive to take such action if it would result in the withdrawal of future co-operation in the regulatory process by the company in question, thus rendering the future of the regulatory process problematic. Agencies therefore very often prefer to take a conciliatory or educative approach to minor incidents, rather than resorting to criminal proceedings as a matter of course. The Royal Commission on Environmental Pollution, in addition to recognising the problems of such an approach, observed its advantages:

> The present system of control has achieved . . . the reduction of emissions and we are satisfied that much of this progress may be attributed to the policy of persuasion and co-operation that the Inspectorate have adopted. An aggressive policy of confrontation, involving prosecution for every lapse, would destroy this . . . it would harden attitudes and dispose industry to resist [pollution abatement] . . . [S]uch a policy would be counter-productive.[109]

As if a co-operation-based regulatory strategy were not enough to discourage litigation, it simply may not make economic sense for an agency to take criminal proceedings in cases where victory is uncertain: costs may be awarded against them if the case fails, and even if the case is won, any fines awarded go into the public purse and not back to the agency itself, or even to wider environmental spending programmes. Such factors serve to make prosecution a last resort. For example, towards the end of its existence, the Alkali Inspectorate was reporting between 50 and 70 infractions of the legislation per year, but prosecuting only between two and five of these.[110] Such features ultimately

---

[107] See, for example, Royal Commission on Environmental Pollution in its Fifth Report Air Pollution Control: An Integrated Approach Cmnd. 6371 (1976) Cmnd, 6371, paras 121–30.

[108] This is the process whereby agencies come to be regarded as facilitating the activities of those they are charged to regulate rather than controlling them.

[109] Above, n 107 para 227.

[110] Figures quoted in Richardson, *et al*, above n 71 p 62. But see J McLoughlin, *The Law and Practice Relating to Pollution Control in the United Kingdom* (London, Graham & Trotman, for the Commission of the European Communities, 1976) 65.

combined to create the perception of a significant gap between the law as it appeared on the statute book, and the law as it operated in practice.

The fears generated by the perceived ineffectiveness of the Alkali Inspectorate were aggravated by a number of practical problems that had become manifest in the operation of command and control in a pollution-control context. The Alkali Inspectorate was, as the first body of its kind, the first to display not only the strengths, but also the weaknesses of state-based pollution control authorities. Regulatory bodies tend to be relatively small in size relative to the industrial sectors that they regulate, and this problem grows as regulatory competences and responsibilities expand. In addition, it is often difficult for pollution control authorities to recruit and retain qualified staff, who stood to earn much more in industry than in the public sector.[111]

The Alkali Act regime was overhauled and expanded in the Alkali &c. Works Regulation Act 1881, which, significantly, placed responsibility for the system into the hands of the Local Government Board.[112] This made the context in which this facet of pollution control operated more explicitly public health based in its orientation. The overlap between pollution control and public health was unambiguously recognised by the new provision allowing sanitary authorities to raise nuisances occasioned by infringement of the Alkali Act regime with the Alkali Inspectorate.[113] Other significant features of the 1881 Act included the adoption of new standards for sulphur and nitrogen emissions,[114] the extension of regulatory coverage to controlling the waste stream[115] and the adoption of a standardised mechanism for calculating emissions.[116] In addition, the registration system applicable to regulated works was amplified,[117] both by the introduction of a new requirement that such works be registered annually, and in more elaborate provisions relating to notices served under the regime.[118]

The whole regulatory process was gradually becoming more complex and more formal. For example, the 1881 Act placed the Chief Inspector under an obligation to make an annual report to the Local Government Board, which was in turn obliged to lay this before Parliament, detailing both the running of the regulatory system and details of escapes in contravention of the controls. This development notionally rendered the operation of the Inspectorate and the regulatory regime more open to scrutiny, in that an important source of information on the activities of the one, and the efficacy (or otherwise) of the other, was now available in the public realm.

---

[111] The fact that the Alkali Acts excluded a number of classes of potential candidates, including (sensibly enough) those who worked in the regulated industries, and, less immediately explicably, land agents, did not improve the recruitment process.

[112] Alkali &c. Works Regulation Act 1881, s 14.

[113] *Ibid* s 27.

[114] *Ibid* s 3(b).

[115] *Ibid* ss 5–7.

[116] *Ibid* s 21.

[117] *Ibid* s 11–13.

[118] *Ibid* s 26.

The next development with reference to industrial air pollution was the consolidation of provisions relating to the regulation of industrial pollution in the Alkali &C. Works Regulation Act 1906. This act retained the BPM test and the basic format that had emerged steadily from 1863 onwards, and also further articulated and expanded the links between pollution control and nuisance.[119] Industry, of course, did not limit its polluting effects to the atmosphere. Pollution also expanded into water and land, and although the latter received comparatively little attention until the Control of Pollution Act 1974, the former was tackled fairly early on and provides an interesting example of another approach to pollution control. This involved a complete statutory prohibition being placed on pollution, rendering the release of emissions an offence unless they were the subject of, and in compliance with, a consent issued by pollution regulating authorities.

This regulatory strategy remains central in modern law. It was initially applied to trade effluent in the Public Health (Drainage of Trade Premises) Act 1937, and was later extended to all direct discharges into water by the Rivers (Prevention of Pollution) Act 1951.[120] This approach allowed consents to be tailored to both individual plants and their waste streams, *and* to the specific environmental conditions in which they operated. This was particularly significant in so far as emissions to the aquatic environment were concerned, because this environmental medium is subject to significant variation in terms of flow and natural composition in addition to the presence of pollutants. The current provisions are to be found in the Water Resources Act 1991, which prohibits the discharge of substances into controlled waters in the absence of either a discharge consent[121] or an authorisation permitting emissions to water issued pursuant to the integrated pollution control regime under Part I of the Environmental Protection Act 1990.[122] The main consent procedure is laid out in detail in Schedule 10 to the WRA, as replaced by the Environment Act 1995, and includes provision for consultation and publicity.

Burrows identifies the necessary characteristics of a regulatory regime to deal with externalities as: setting policy targets to decrease social cost; identifying a form of regulation; creating enforcement mechanisms; and providing just compensation for those adversely affected by the externality that is being subjected to control. [123] The basic Victorian prescription for regulating industrial pollution sits reasonably well with aspects of this theoretical approach. The policy objective of eliminating or minimising, and rendering emissions harmless, is

[119] For example in s 5 of the Alkali, &c. Works Regulation Act 1906, specific provision is made for the prevention of nuisance by the deposit of alkali waste.

[120] The same approach carried through the Control of Pollution Act 1974, the Water Act 1989, into the current regime under the Water Resources Act 1991, as amended by the Environment Act 1995.

[121] S 88.

[122] This class of authorisation is in the process of being replaced by the provisions of the Pollution Prevention and Control Act 1999.

[123] *Ibid,* 11 et seq.

clearly articulated. Less clear is the rationale for applying a command and control strategy to the regulation of that pollution, which may be an accident of history, coinciding as large-scale pollution problems did with other societal problems, such as the need to address public health issues, that were addressed primarily through the state rather than the courts. However, using the mechanism of statutory offences and the courts to enforce the regime is a logical step dictated by the choice of regulatory mechanism even if the effectiveness of this approach in relation to industrial air pollution is open to question, at least in terms of the minute number of prosecutions brought under the Alkali Acts. It is, however, arguable that a lack of prosecutions does not necessarily indicate a failure in a command and control regime if compliance is achieved in other ways, for example by education rather than coercion.

There is considerable debate as to whether criminal sanctions are appropriate in relation to environmental offences. Historically, it was certainly arguable that such offences lacked the moral opprobrium of more established forms of criminal behaviour.[124] This was demonstrated in a host of ways, not least in the creation of special agencies such as the Alkali Inspectorate to regulate pollution.[125] It is arguable that, in a modern context, the wrongdoing element of environmental offences is more pronounced, at least in so far as major pollution issues in terms of either scale or toxicity are concerned.[126] This argument is supported by the fact that prosecutions under modern pollution control law, notably the Water Act 1989 and the Environmental Protection Act 1990, have already far outstripped those under their antecedents. Certainly, attitudes towards the moral blameworthiness or otherwise of certain types of behaviour can change over time, and criminalisation can help achieve this. Sutherland, in a seminal piece on white-collar crime, stated that:

> . . . the relationship between law and mores tends to be circular. The mores are crystallized in the law, and each act of enforcement of the laws tends to reinforce the mores. The laws regarding white-collar crime, which conceal the criminality of the behaviour, have been less effective than other laws in re-enforcement of the mores.[127]

This observation seems to be peculiarly apposite in relation to past approaches to environmental offences. It is also arguable that criminalising certain actions can accelerate their transformation from acceptable to unacceptable, as in the case of drink driving. In any event, the penalties set under a command and control regime must outweigh the costs of compliance if they are to act as an effective deterrent to breaching the law. While the penalties as initially set in the 1863 legislation were reasonably substantial by the standards of the time, they failed to keep pace with economic development: they were fairly

---

[124] Richardson, et al, above n 71, ch. 2.

[125] S 13 Alkali Act 1863.

[126] See, for example, *R v Hertfordshire County Council, ex parte Green Environmental Industries Ltd* [2000] 1 All ER 773.

[127] EH Sutherland, 'White-Collar Crime and Social Structure' (1945) 10 *American Sociological Review* 132, 139.

derisory by the beginning of the twentieth century and had become ridiculous by the latter years of the century, when the Alkali Act was eventually replaced.[128] While there was nothing in the way of compensation for those adversely affected by the pollution provided for in the legislation, fines incurred were paid into the public purse. At this level, at least, notional redress for the public interest was a feature of the system. In any event, the common law route to redress partly addresses the issue of individual compensation, at least in terms of damage to or interference with property.

This 'moral' dimension to pollution issues is significant; for it does not sit strictly within a utilitarian framework. Such reasoning does not *directly* relate to the way in which respective interests are balanced, but attempts to reach substantive conclusions on the basis of principle. The conclusion of wrongdoing may, of course, remain an instrumental one rather than basing itself upon perceived intrinsic values relating to environmental protection. But the shift away from a starkly utilitarian perspective is, as will be seen, a significant step towards the latter (intrinsic) perspective.

Planning Law

The bodies of law dealing with pollution and public health saw the beginnings of a conception of property rights as limited by wider interests on the basis of *principle* rather than straightforward utilitarian calculation. Perhaps naturally, the 'moral' aspect of reasoning is less pronounced in relation to planning law. Planning law emerged subsequently to the appearance of public health law and pollution control regimes. The development of planning as a discipline, and of the legal regime promoting it, can be seen as employing a proactive approach to regulation, and therefore as representing a logical progression in the attempt to use law to control the activities of individuals in the interests of manipulating the environment to promote the common weal. The concept of town planning first appeared in embryonic form as an adjunct to public health law, in the Public Health Act 1875. This wide-ranging Act introduced rudimentary controls on building standards, prohibiting the occupation of premises with inadequate water supply and sewerage provision,[129] as a means of securing the improved physical well-being of the urban populace. It soon became apparent that, while such developments were helpful to an extent, they were not of themselves adequate to secure the desired goal, and more systematic and broad ranging intervention was required to ensure better urban quality management. Thus the need for a proactive regime of town planning was eventually recognised, though rendering such a regime a workable reality was to take rather longer to realise.

---

[128] The last remnants of the Alkali, &c. Works Regulation Act 1906 were only finally repealed by the Environmental Protection Act 1990.

[129] Part III of the Public Health Act 1875.

The term 'town planning' was first employed in legislation in the Housing, Town Planning, etc Act 1909. The 1909 Act attempted in part to address problems such as the need to separate incompatible land uses, and to facilitate the provision of amenity lands for the public good. But its main focus was (unsurprisingly, given its antecedents) the provision of public housing and slum clearance. The Act also gave local authorities rudimentary planning powers[130] allowing them to prepare 'schemes' covering land ripe for development '. . . with the general object of securing proper sanitary conditions, amenity, and convenience in connection with the laying out and use of the land . . .' This task proved extremely onerous in practice, and was made more arduous by the requirements of public and central government approval for planning schemes. As a result, the powers were not widely employed.

While the public health influences on planning were clearly visible in the 1909 Act, other, broader considerations were already coming into play which would prove influential in the longer term. The development of planning legislation followed the pattern that we have already observed in respect of both public health law and pollution control law, with permissive nationally applicable legislation following up on local initiatives. Compulsory action on planning at a local level was eventually imposed under the Housing, Town Planning, etc Act 1919 which required local authorities whose areas had a population of 20,000 and above to prepare planning schemes. The process of developing planning schemes proved to be more complex than the government had first envisaged. Progress was painfully slow, and public dissatisfaction with the planning system began to grow. As a response to popular dissatisfaction, and as part of a wider climate of administrative reform, a series of government inquiries was instituted into a whole variety of land-use issues. One achievement of the resulting reports was to inform debate and set the scene for a fuller development of planning law in the context of a new and further expanded role for the state following World War II, under the Town and Country Planning Act 1947.[131] The most influential of the inquiries resulted in the Barlow, Scott and Uthwatt Reports.[132] The Barlow Commission was charged with examining the causes of the geographical concentration of the industrial population and its adverse social and economic consequences. Its suggested solution was that the state should play a role in encouraging a more dispersed approach to industrial development. The Scott report tackled the other extreme of environmental problems, focusing on the need to control development on agricultural and coastal land. Among its recommendations was the need to concentrate new settlements to urban areas

[130] S 54 of the Housing, Town Planning etc Act 1909 (hereafter HTPA).
[131] The Town and Country Planning Act 1947 was one part of a raft of legislation that impacted upon the managing the environment including the New Towns Act 1946, and the National Parks and Access to the Countryside Act 1949.
[132] The Report of the Royal Commission on the Distribution of the Industrial Population (the Barlow Report) 1940, Cmnd 6153; The Report of the Committee on Land Utilisation in Rural Areas 194, Cmnd 6378; The Report of the Expert Committee on Compensation and Betterment (the Uthwatt Report) 1942, Cmnd 6386.

unless there were special reasons for allowing rural development. The Uthwatt Committee examined the particularly fraught issues of compensation and betterment, the inevitable conflict between private property interests and the public interest and the imperative need to reach an accommodation between them. Each of these reports contributed towards the shaping of the new planning system, and go some way to showing the range and complexity of the demands that would be placed upon it extending beyond even the most generous definition of land-use issues into fundamental social and economic concerns.

Planning played a particularly significant role in the new governmental arrangements, viewed as it was as a key factor in post-war reconstruction. Despite the fact that the introduction of a new planning regime had been prompted by observations of the inadequacy of the contemporary system and the reports and inquiries resulting from this, the political debate that should have underpinned and driven it became so mired in the problematic questions of land compensation and betterment that the planning regime itself became almost an afterthought. This was perhaps understandable, given the fact that the development of a new town and country planning system would introduce an unprecedented degree of state interference in private property rights as a means of remedying one of the flaws that had rendered planning law comparatively ineffectual.

The expense of compensation cases had thwarted much planning activity in the period prior to 1947,[133] and this had raised much popular and political discussion about the need to ensure that the selfish pursuit of private interests was not allowed to frustrate the public interest or to retard social progress. The whole tenor of the new system, while falling short of the Labour government's ultimate ideological objective of 'nationalising land', would be deliberately to subject private property interests to the public interest, a move quite revolutionary enough in itself to cause upset in the context of the traditional common law supremacy of the interests of private ownership. The crux of the new system lay in restricting future land-use by requiring that permission be sought from the state in order to undertake development in any location, not just in that falling under planning schemes. For all of these positive elements, however, progress in putting the new regime into practice proved painfully slow. The 1947 Act imposed a three-year time limit on local authorities for the submission of development plans for their areas. Few were able to comply.[134]

It is clear that planning has always been intimately affected by political considerations, and this is especially true in relation to environmental issues. Despite popular misconception, planning was not, at its inception, and is not at

---

[133] R Cocks, 'Enforced Creativity: Noel Hutton and the New Law for Development Control, 1945–47' (2001) 22 *Legal History* 21, 25.

[134] The early development of the planning system is briefly discussed by V Moore, *A Practical Approach to Planning Law*, 3rd edn (London, Blackstone, 1992).

present, 'environmental' in focus. The ethos of planning is perhaps best summed up by the comments of Sir Hugh Rossi:

> Planning is concerned with the orderly use of land and safeguarding amenity. To some extent this has had the effect of protecting the environment but indirectly rather than directly. The prime purpose of planning is to control use and development, not to safeguard the environment.[135]

Despite its inherent limitations as a tool of environmental protection, the development of the planning system represented a change of emphasis in the law, allowing the possibility of *proactive* rather than simply *reactive* control. With its relatively long and smooth development since 1947, the town and country planning system in the United Kingdom represents one of the best established and most settled aspects of the range of tools available to achieve environmental regulation and improvement. That said, the relationship between planning and other aspects of environmental regulation, most particularly pollution control, has still to be satisfactorily determined. While it is increasingly recognised that the environment is an indivisible whole which cannot be regulated effectively (at least in so far as pollution control is concerned) on the basis of artificial administrative divisions, it is impossible to integrate all aspects of environmental regulation under the auspices of a single regime and the complexity of a holistic regulatory system would be both phenomenal and impractical. In an imperfect world, administrative fragmentation seems inevitable, and hence the absence of clear indications on the interaction of planning and pollution control is likely to become an increasingly pressing and problematic issue as more sophisticated pollution control regimes and provisions are introduced.[136]

On the face of it, environmental factors (including pollution) fall readily within the elastic definition of 'material considerations' in modern planning law.[137] In reality, the relationship between planning and pollution control has long been problematic, perhaps even more so than might be expected for two regimes with notionally harmonious, and possibly even overlapping goals. The relationship between planning and pollution control were subjected to detailed scrutiny by the Royal Commission on Environmental Pollution in its Fifth Report *Air Pollution Control: An Integrated Approach*[138] as part of its ongoing responsibility for advising the government on environmental policy issues. The RCEP took a realistic view of planning and environmental protection: it was readily recognised that pollution was only one factor which would need to be taken into account in the planning process. The concern was expressed,

---

[135] H Rossi, 'The Consequences of the Green Issue and the European Dimension' *JPEL Occasional Papers* No. 17, 17–22 p 20.

[136] For example integrated pollution control under Part 1 of the Environmental Protection Act 1990 and integrated pollution prevention and control under Directive 96/61/EC and the Pollution Prevention and Control Act 1999.

[137] S 70(2) Town and Country Planning Act 1990.

[138] Cmnd. 6371, 1976.

however, that planning did not always achieve an adequate balance between conflicting interests and issues:

> Our concern is not that pollution is not always given top priority; it is that it is often dealt with inadequately, and sometimes forgotten altogether, in the planning process. In part this stems from lack of guidance and advice. Planning officers . . . are not pollution experts and they are necessarily dependent on advice on pollution matters. Such advice is not always available but even when it is, it is not always sought.[139]

The report went on to recommend the integration into strategic and subject-specific development plans of scientifically sound pollution policies. In addition, it recommended the involvement of pollution control authorities in the development control process, identifying the refusal of planning permission as the ultimate response for applications involving unacceptable pollution implications. The RCEP emphasised that these moves should be underpinned by more explicit central government guidance on the relationship between planning and pollution control.

The government was not minded to adopt the RCEP's approach. In the hey-day of development-led planning, its policy as laid out first in Circular 22/80[140] and Circular 1/85 was that authorities should consider whether suitable conditions could be used to overcome legitimate planning objections and allow development to proceed. The government's position has not, however, remained static, and successive policy statements appear to have moved towards a more environment-orientated approach. One example of this change in approach is contained in *This Common Inheritance*,[141] the first United Kingdom government environmental strategy, published in 1990. It states:

> Once broad land uses have been sanctioned by the planning process, it is the job of pollution control to limit the adverse effects that operations may have on the environment. But in practice there is common ground. In considering whether to grant planning permission for a particular development a local authority must consider all the effects including potential pollution . . .[142]

The government has not, however, sent out entirely clear signals in terms of the optimum relationship between planning and pollution control on a detailed level, despite having made the issue the subject of both general and specific discussion in Great Britain Planning Policy Guidance Notes 1 and 23 respectively. PPG 23 repeats previous injunctions to planning authorities to avoid duplicating controls that are the statutory responsibility of other bodies. This, of course, avoids the issue of borderline cases. The body of the PPG offers a more realistic approach, even if its implications are scarcely clearer:

> The dividing line between planning and pollution controls is not always clear-cut. Both seek to protect the environment. Matters which will be relevant to a pollution

---

[139] Para 335.
[140] Para 13.
[141] Cm 1200.
[142] Para 6.39.

control authorisation or license may also be material considerations to be taken into account in planning decisions. The weight to be attached to such matters will depend on the scope of the pollution control system in each case.[143]

It is significant that the Notes mention protection of the environment rather than protection of amenity: it suggests that the boundary between planning and the goals of environmental protection is not sharply defined. Planning law can, in this sense, be legitimately regarded as a response to environmental problems.

The question of the boundary between planning and pollution control does not, of course, exist merely in the abstract. One example of litigation on this point can be found in *Gateshead MBC v Secretary of State for the Environment and Northumbrian Water* [1994].[144] The case involved a proposal to build a chemical waste incinerator. The local planning authority refused planning permission on the ground that the pollution implications had not been adequately addressed. The council was of the opinion that, if planning permission were given, then an Integrated Pollution Control license[145] based on the BATNEEC[146] requirement would probably be granted, and the council was not convinced that this would adequately protect the local environment. In the Court of Appeal, the overlap between planning and pollution control systems was acknowledged, as was the appropriateness of considering such issues in the planning decision-making process. The Court even went so far as to say that in some cases, where it was clear that the failure to deal with pollution issues would lead to the refusal of an IPC license, it would be appropriate to refuse planning permission. However the Court also stated that, where issues were less cut and dried, the issues should be left to the expertise of the appropriate pollution control body, reasoning that, as grant of planning permission did not automatically indicate that a pollution control authorisation would inevitably be granted, then the environment could, in this case, be adequately protected by the pollution control regime. The courts, then, have finally been given the opportunity to provide some clarification, although the *Gateshead* decision sheds only limited light on a wider issue that really requires legislative attention.

NATURE CONSERVATION, LEISURE AND LANDSCAPE

At the same time as the courts and the legislature were developing bodies of juristic principle which represented shifting conceptions of property rights and interests, a new social attitude towards the environment was emerging which would provide the moral context within which those rights and interests would be played out. From this context would emerge reasons for imposing

[143] Para 1.34.
[144] (1994) 71 P & CR 350.
[145] Under Part I of the Environmental Protection Act 1990.
[146] S 7.

restrictions on property rights essentially untied to established interests, and to which utilitarian reasoning could not apply.

Prior to the Industrial Revolution, the most common attitude toward the relationship between humanity and the natural world was summed up by Hale in his analysis of the stewardship ethic:

> The end of man's creation was that he should be the viceroy of the great God of heaven and earth in this inferior world; his steward, bailiff or farmer of this goodly farm of the lower world. Only for this reason was man invested with power, authority, right, dominion, trust and care, to correct and abridge the excesses and cruelties of the fiercer animals, to give protection and defence to the mansuete and useful, to preserve the species of divers vegetables, to improve them and others, to correct the redundance of unprofitable vegetables, to preserve the face of the earth in beauty, usefulness and fruitfulness.[147]

Elements of this idea had been present in the writings of the seventeenth century natural rights theorists and their intellectual heirs. The juristic thought of the period between the publication of Grotius's *De Iure Praedae* and Bentham's *Fragment on Government* had taken a teleological view of the world, in which human wellbeing and environmental values were in complete harmony. In the period following the Industrial Revolution however, the stewardship ethic, as generally understood, had come to be employed almost exclusively to promote and justify, not sensible husbanding of natural resources, but rather the rank exploitation of the natural world. Eventually, as the impact of the Industrial Revolution became more intense and widespread, attitudes towards the exploitation of the natural world began to change. Industry came to be perceived, not as an unalloyed positive force for human development, but also as having a detrimental effect on the countryside. Perception of adverse impacts was not confined to the obvious generation of pollution but also, though not always accurately, to the consumption of valuable natural resources: for example, the iron industry was popularly blamed for stripping the nation of its woodlands. (In fact, in the interests of securing its timber supply, it encouraged sustainable forestry practices.)[148]

Such emerging concern about the state of the environment had, however, taken a rather different form to that governing attitudes in the seventeenth century. The classic natural rights theories viewed the untamed environment as an inhospitable and hostile place that constituted a threat to civilisation. The appropriate response was to tame and rework the environment according to human interests. The idea that agriculture and exploitation could *harm* the environment was not a question raised in seventeenth century philosophy. Unquestioning acceptance of the exploitation of the natural world gradually

---

[147] M Hale, *The Primitive Organisation of Mankind Considered and Examined According to the Light of Nature* (London, William Godbid for William Shrowsbery, 1677) 370.

[148] K Thomas, *Man and the Natural World: Changing Attitudes in England 1500–1800* (London, Allen Lane, 1983) 193.

began to change, however, as the Industrial Revolution progressed. This was in part due to increased feelings of 'isolation' from the natural world consequent on the urbanisation that accompanied it. The arts tapped into such feelings, amplifying and refining them. Poets, in particular, such as Wordsworth, Tennyson and Hopkins, and painters, such as Constable and Clare, made appreciation of the landscape not only an issue but also the fashion. On a more practical level, a fundamental change of attitude towards the natural world was significantly motivated by the writings of the great scientists, and the development of a plethora of scientific societies, on a scale not previously experienced.[149] As a result, Victorian society, and in particular the middle and upper classes that enjoyed the leisure and resources fully to pursue their interests, developed a sustained mania for the study of natural history.

So acquisitive was the character of much of the naturalism of the time that the species under study often ended up under threat, to the extent that a number of particularly popular rare species were driven to extinction.[150] Study, however, eventually brought enlightenment in the form of an emergent biocentric understanding of nature. The view of humanity as part of the wider 'balance of nature', rather than as master over it, began to replace the more traditional stewardship ethic. Nature study groups changed their emphasis from *collection* to *preservation* and study *in situ*. Landed enthusiasts set aside areas of their property to provide sanctuaries for a whole range of animals and birds, and those who did not enjoy substantial landholdings banded together to create the first voluntary nature reserves.

The industrial development of the nineteenth century not only placed the environment under threat, but also gave rise to the degree of affluence necessary to facilitate the conservation of the natural world. At the same time, it conferred on a broader range of people than ever before the leisure to enjoy it.[151] Nonetheless, change was slow to come. Leopold's observation, in his seminal text on conservation, *A Sand County Almanac*, though made in relation to the United States in the mid-twentieth century, is just as apposite in a United Kingdom context: 'Conservation,' he said, 'is getting nowhere because it is incompatible with our Abrahamic concept of land. We abuse land because we regard it as a commodity belonging to us.'[152]

Eventually, however, voluntary activity inspired the evolution of state-based initiatives, though state involvement in conservation took considerably longer to catch hold than did state action on public health and pollution control, or even planning. While the principle of resource conservation arguably appeals in

[149] For example, C Darwin, *The Origin of Species By Means of Natural Selection* (London, J Murray, 1884); JW Dawson, *Story of Earth and Man* (various edns, 1873) . But see L Pyenson and S Sheets-Pyenson, *Servants of Nature: A History of Scientific Institutions, Enterprises and Sensibilities* (London, Harper-Collins, 1999).
[150] C Reid, *Nature Conservation Law* (Edinburgh, W Green,/Sweet & Maxwell, 1994) 5 and 7.
[151] See L Pyenson and S Sheets-Pyenson, *Servants of Nature: A History of Scientific Institutions, Enterprises and Sensibilities* (London, Harper Collins, 1999).
[152] A Leopold, *A Sand County Almanac and Sketches Here and There* (Oxford, OUP, 1968) viii.

theory to both conservative and liberal political ideologies (though from rather different perspectives),[153] pursuing its goals in practice proved highly problematic. The heart of the problem is that 'the ultimate limits to conservation in a democratic society are the limits of its own culture . . .'[154] General societal values inevitably take longer to change than those of scientific elites, and these in turn impact on substantive law only gradually. At the same time, such values become tempered and refined in political debate and negotiation. There are a number of possible reasons for the relatively long gap between voluntary initiatives and state action in this context: for instance, the problems associated with species depletion are much less obvious than those of pollution. More significantly, dealing with them requires a high degree of interference with the property rights of individuals who, unlike those actively engaged in causing pollution or passively depleting environmental quality, are not regarded by society as doing anything wrong. In addition, the benefits of conservation are diffuse, often long-term and spread through the human and broader biotic community, but the costs tend to be concentrated very obviously on the activities and resources of individual landowners whose properties happen to play host to significant species or habitats. Not least among the factors to be considered is the fact that conservation measures entail *both* straightforward economic costs *and* more complex opportunity costs which serve to make it more politically sensitive for the state to intervene in the absence of very obvious societal disadvantages being encountered in a 'business as usual' scenario.

The tension between conservation and private property interests is at its most acute in the context of agriculture. For centuries, farmers have been presented as custodians of the countryside, a legacy of the traditional belief that a tamed landscape is the optimum state for the environment. The common law consolidated the position and importance of agriculture, as evidenced by Coke's statement that arable land held 'preeminency and precedency before meadows, pastures, woods, mines and all other grounds whatsoever.'[155] This view, however, came to be perceived as problematic as 'natural' landscapes came to be valued in addition to cultivated ones. These tensions grew more acute as increasing mechanisation greatly increased the physical impact of agriculture. The practice of enclosure in the eighteenth century, for example, had a twofold effect, both increasing the amount of land under relatively intensive production by two and a half million acres, and decreasing the ease of access for most people to those lands. The modernisation of agriculture resulted in a more productive but also more formal landscape, which came into conflict with the

---

[153] See R Beazley, 'Conservation Decision-making: A Rationalization' in C Kury (ed), *Enclosing the Environment; NEPA's Transformation of Conservation into Environmentalism*, (*Natural Resources Journal* 25th Anniversary Anthology) (Albuquerque, University of New Mexico School of Law 1985) 1.

[154] *Ibid* p 5.

[155] Sir E Coke, *Institutes of the Laws of England* (18th ed, corrected, London, J & WT Clarke, 1823) i sect 117.

demand for wild, rugged nature (which had until the early eighteenth century been regarded as unproductive waste), and which placed the countryside under ever greater and conflicting pressures.

Conservation issues provided an obvious point of conflict between specially protected property rights and new societal priorities. In modern law, a common means of circumventing the problems posed by interfering with property rights in the cause of conservation is to adopt an approach that combines voluntarism and paying landowners to act in an environmentally desirable fashion.[156] This approach has been much-used in the context of agriculture for both habitat conservation and for the prevention of particularly problematic diffuse pollution problems that do not lend themselves well to the command and control approach that pervades industrial pollution control.[157] The European Union has made copious use of such strategies under its (widely criticised) Common Agricultural Policy, initially in the form of Set Aside and Environmentally Sensitive Areas (ESA) designations,[158] and subsequently under the 'agri-environment' Regulation EEC/2078/92.[159] Under the latter, a notionally more sophisticated and holistic version of the ESA scheme is used to deliver a variety of habitat preservation initiatives, countryside access and countryside management, though in many respects this appears to work better in theory than in practice.[160] Even where landowners are willing to embrace conservation issues, there are limits to the state financial aid available, and the size of the property concerned as well as technical factors, serve to place significant constraints on the results achieved.

Engagement and Separation

If public health problems were a by-product of industrialisation and its attendant urbanisation, so too was the less tangible but increasing feeling of separation from nature experienced by the majority of the population. The extent of the change wrought on settlement patterns in the United Kingdom by the Industrial Revolution must not be underestimated. In 1800, about a quarter of the population lived in cities; by 1851 it was over half, and (with the exception of the Netherlands), Britain was the most urbanised country in Europe.[161] Thus, for the urban majority, the natural world was experienced in only a very limited way, if at all. The environment came to be idealised to such an extent that it obtained near mystic significance, though not to the extent that it in any way

---

[156] See for example, K Morrow and S Turner, 'The More Things Change, The More They Stay The Same? - Environmental Law, Policy and Funding in Northern Ireland' (1998) 10 *Journal of Environmental Law* 41.

[157] For example, water pollution caused by runoff from the use of pesticides and fertiliser.

[158] Originated in Regulation EEC/797/85, OJ 1985 L 93/1.

[159] OJ 1992 L 215/85.

[160] See Morrow and Turner, above n 156.

[161] GM Trevelyan, *English Social History,* 3rd edn (London, Longmans, 1946) 374.

halted mass migration to towns and cities. Nonetheless, conservation issues, whether linked to landscape, habitats or species issues, were and are much more fraught than those of pollution control, in that tackling them tends to interfere more obviously with traditional conceptions of property rights by restricting what individuals may legally do on their land in the broader public interest.

The countryside and urban green spaces began to be valued as an aesthetic and recreational resource. Amenity and access movements came into being, initiated by the Commons, Open Spaces and Footpaths Preservation Society in 1865, and continued by the National Trust (founded in 1895) and later the Campaign for the Protection of Rural England (founded in 1926). As transport became more readily available and cheaper, the importance of the countryside as a recreational resource came to the fore. While the ethos behind the amenity movement remained essentially anthropocentric, the benefits for the environment were more immediate in this field of endeavour than they had been in pollution control.

Legislation to protect the countryside emerged first on a fairly localised scale in new provisions on commons in the Metropolitan Commons Act 1866 and the Commons Act 1876. It was, however, to be a very long time before national legislation would be adopted to promote access to the countryside and to protect rural amenity. The first real progress was to be found in the Access to Mountains Act 1939, prompted by the famous mass trespass by the nascent Ramblers' Association on Kinder Scout in 1932. After a brief hiatus during World War II, the Labour government turned its attention to countryside and access issues as part of its broad ranging legislative platform, the Hobhouse Report.[162] This prompted the most significant development in this area to date, the National Parks and Access to the Countryside Act 1949. This legislation not only made provision for national parks, but also introduced a number of other designations combining landscape, species and habitat conservation with access provisions: Areas of Outstanding Natural Beauty (AONBs); nature reserves; and sites of special scientific interest (SSSIs).

As Reid has pointed out, national parks in England and Wales bear little resemblance to their namesakes in other countries, being much less 'natural' and more subject to human interference than the norm.[163] National Parks in the United Kingdom are subject to a dual statutory goal: the preservation and enhancement of natural beauty on the one hand, and the promotion of public enjoyment of the countryside on the other.[164] To that end, National Parks are basically run by the local authorities in whose area they are located, which enjoy a range of special planning, management and law-making powers better to

---

[162] *Footpaths and Access to the Countryside*, 1947, Cmnd 7207.

[163] As defined by the International Union for the Conservation of Nature in Resolution 1 of its 10th General Assembly, New Delhi, 1 Dec 1969. Reid, above n 150 p 177 et seq. Scotland finally introduced its first National Parks in Loch Lomond and the Trossachs in 2002 and the Cairngorms in 2003, http://www.snh.org.uk/ Lomond?). Northern Ireland has just begun consultation on setting up a National Park in the Mournes, *Planning* 4th October 2002 p 3.

[164] S 5(1) of the National Parks and access to the Countryside Act 1949.

achieve their objectives. Unfortunately, the goals of conservation and recreation are not always easy, or indeed possible, to reconcile. One can therefore profitably regard the various designations introduced under the 1949 Act as according differing levels of priority to one or other of these goals.

For example, AONBs are designated by the Countryside Agency, and confirmed by the Secretary of State following consultation, in particular with the local authorities or conservation boards[165] that will administer the area. They are not located in National Parks but are nonetheless deemed worthy, on landscape grounds, of greater protection than that available under the normal planning law regime. Nature reserves, by contrast, function to preserve and to provide opportunities to study and research flora and fauna and their habitats and geographical and physiographical features of particular interest in the protected area.[166] This is the most radical of the designations under the National Parks legislation in that it is actually geared to nature conservation as its prime goal, rather than the broader balancing act involving the interests of the landowner and recreation and amenity. Reserves are administered by means of management agreements entered into with landowners (or lessees or other occupiers), which can restrict their rights over the affected land.[167]

SSSIs were introduced to invoke a degree of protection in respect of land not forming dedicated nature reserves, which accounts for by far and away the majority of land with conservation value in the United Kingdom. In its original form, the SSSI designation merely required special consideration for designated sites under the planning system. The SSSI regime was augmented by the Wildlife and Countryside Act 1981 (WCA), and this form was based on a process of notification of owners that land has conservation value. This in turn placed the owner under an obligation to inform the conservation authorities of proposed activities that would adversely affect that value, allowing the opportunity for preventative action. This was a very weak 'control' mechanism in that, at worst, it did not prevent a landowner from ignoring the views of conservation authorities and acting to the detriment of conservation values in any event; at best, it fostered a form of legalised extortion, allowing landowners to use the threat of adverse environmental impacts as a bargaining tool in negotiating management agreements with conservation authorities (itself a long and drawn out process). The SSSI system was widely criticised by pressure groups and even English Nature itself [168] as ineffective, with insufficient weight to prevent the deterioration or even destruction of notionally protected sites. Thus the WCA failed to instil confidence in the SSSI designation, and the regime has been overhauled

---

[165] These may be appointed under s 86 of the Countryside and Rights of Way Act 2000 to take over most of the functions of local authorities in AONBs.
[166] S 15 of the National Parks and the Access to the Countryside Act 1949.
[167] Though compensation can be paid in this regard: *Ibid* s 16.
[168] The Environmental Protection Act 1990 split the Nature Conservancy Council into English, Scottish and Welsh bodies, the Countryside and Rights of Way Act 2000, gave legal recognition to the name English Nature.

once again by the Countryside and Rights of Way Act 2000[169] (CRWA). The whole tenor of the nature conservation regime was subtly changed by the CRWA, not least by the imposition of a new obligation on ministers and government departments to conserve biodiversity.[170] More substantively, the provisions of the CRWA greatly strengthened the SSSI system itself. Especially significant is the requirement that written permission be obtained from the designating authority for operations affecting SSSIs[171] and the introduction of new more comprehensive management provisions.[172]

The Countryside Act 1968 added country parks to the range of available control options. Nonetheless, both the National Parks and Countryside Acts offered only limited access to the countryside as, in practice, local authorities achieved widely differing degrees of success in using their rather cumbersome statutory powers to open up rural areas to the public. Much broader (and more controversial) access is to be introduced in the form of a statutory right of access to mountains, moorland, heaths, downs and registered commons for the purposes of open-air recreation under the Countryside and Rights of Way Act 2000.

On an institutional level, the government set up in 1949 the Nature Conservancy (which became known as the Nature Conservancy Council in 1973) as a scientific advisory body for nature conservation.[173] It has subsequently evolved into English Nature, a division of government charged with promoting nature conservation. Responsibility for giving advice on rural issues, including conservation, is shared with the Countryside Agency.[174] This body also has responsibility for social and economic concerns, a remit that it is likely to dilute its commitment to pursuing an environmental agenda, as has often been the case in the past in the context of nature conservation. The Agency also has powers to acquire reserve lands, usually by agreement,[175] but exceptionally by compulsory purchase.[176] The Agency can also make bye-laws in order to protect reserves.[177] These cannot, however, be used to interfere with property rights: the legislation only provides for this to be done by agreement.

The goals of protection and recreation often conflict with one another on some level. Yet it is possible to see in these developments a pale reflection of the seventeenth century assumption of harmony between human welfare and environmental interests. For it is possible to reformulate the stark assumption of

---

[169] This introduced a new s 28 into the Wildlife and Countryside Act 1981.
[170] S 74.
[171] S 28E.
[172] ss 28J–K.
[173] Following the White Paper Conservation of Nature in England and Wales 1947, Cm 7122.
[174] Created following a merger of the Countryside Commission and the Rural Development Commission under the Regional Development Agencies Act 1998.
[175] This can be done under general powers provided by s 132 of the Environmental Protection Act 1990.
[176] S 17 of the National Parks and Access to the Countryside Act 1949.
[177] *Ibid* s 20.

harmony as a prudential maxim governing engagement with the natural environment. Without rules for *protecting* areas of environmental significance, we risk losing those areas to urban development or exploitation; but without the access which allows for the appreciation and enjoyment of such areas, the benefits of preservation become (for many, at least) less obvious. Although in principle, access and protection conflict, *prudentially* one goal cannot realistically be advanced without according some measure of validity to the other. One should scarcely be surprised to find, therefore, that (in all its guises) the motivation for early nature conservation was clearly anthropocentric,[178] with both landscape and habitat conservation, and even species preservation, providing resources for human recreation and enjoyment. At the same time, the nineteenth century left a legacy of elements which have been progressively blended with later thinking to create modern environmentalism. Pollution control, planning, landscape, habitat and species conservation all remain key issues, and the ideological constructs which underlie them and the laws attempting to tackle them remain crucial in shaping modern environmentalism.

Despite the obvious utilitarian bearing of many of these developments, we should not be tempted to suppose that environmental concerns (even where translated into law) are invariably reducible to a concern with human interests. The natural rights theories of the seventeenth century had shown that an account of nature and of property could be anthropocentric without inevitably falling prey to considerations of utility.[179] The assumption that environmental protection conflicts with individual rights and liberties to use the environment derives not from the assumption that rights and liberties are determined by utility, but from the assumption that they are determined *instrumentally*. *Utilitarian* arguments about how to solve this tension depend upon what we might call 'identifiable public interests'. Since arguments about utility concern the collision between individual and collective interests, if we cannot *identify* the public interest involved, no utilitarian calculation, no matter how sophisticated, can take place.

Consider the following example. The argument that the natural environment should be protected against encroaching urban development because of the opportunities for leisure and aesthetic enjoyment such areas bring, is a utilitarian

---

[178] Modern law is not necessarily more biocentric than early law in this area. The Biodiversity Convention 1992 provides a good example of legislation that is basically anthropocentric in its tenor, despite playing lip-service to the intrinsic value of nature. The Convention's objectives are stated in the following terms: 'To conserve biological diversity, promote the sustainable use of its components, and encourage equitable sharing of the benefits arising out of the utilization of genetic resources. Such equitable sharing includes appropriate access to genetic resources, as well as appropriate transfer of technology, taking into account existing rights over such resources and such technology'.

[179] Those theories, as we have seen, often *did* conceive of property in utilitarian terms. But Hume's demonstration that the utilitarian conclusions of those theories were logically independent of their theological premises should alert us to the fact that those premises do not *inevitably* lead to a utilitarian view of property and nature. Anthropocentrism does not *necessarily* entail utilitarianism.

argument. The interests of developers and house-buyers in acquiring property in such areas are outweighed, on this view, by the wider public interest in the pleasure unspoilt rural areas afford. We are prepared to entertain such conclusions because we can identify the interests involved, and broadly agree that the utility of the developer and consumers is far outweighed by that of the wider public in the enjoyment of unspoilt areas. Such arguments need not appeal to *actual* feelings of pleasure, but may appeal to our longer-term or *rational* interests: we would miss such areas if they disappeared; living in a world devoid of green spaces would damage both our physical and our emotional health; we would become more culturally imporverished, and so on. Appeals of this sort to utility are intelligible because we perceive (or can be made to perceive) that one set of interests outweighs another set of interests. Now consider a second example: here, an area of wasteland the subject of a planning application is found to contain a rare species of indigenous amphibian, whose habitat would be destroyed if building were permitted. What interests are in play here? Those of the developer and prospective house-buyers are easily enough identified. But what *public* interest is served by the preservation of the indigenous amphibian population? Neither the knowledge of the existence of such creatures, nor the scientific knowledge gained by close study of them seem to offer a sufficient basis for the identification of a public interest which outweighs the narrower interests of the developer, the house-buyers and (we may suppose) business interests which would flourish if the development went ahead.

Nor are such examples confined to species preservation. We can readily imagine contexts in which local authorities protect environmentally fragile or significant areas even where no very large amount of public interest exists in their preservation. This is not the banal observation that it is always possible to formulate a wider conception of utility according to which a devil-may-care attitude gives way, on reflection, to longer-term, or more rational, interests. For in such terms, the resulting utility arguments are often too thin to provide the justification for the curtailment of property rights and interests. In such cases, the instrumental appearance of the argument disguises the fact that the reasoning and justification involved are *qualitatively* different from appeals to utility. Often, where property interests are held to conflict with environmental interests, the former give way not to public interests, but to deeper *moral* values: we protect fragile features of the environment not because it is in our considered interests to do so, but because we believe it is a *good*, or *right* thing to do. This does not betoken a naturalistic stance on property rights. By eschewing considerations of utility, we do not thereby commit ourselves to the view that moral values *shape* inherent features of property rights; rather, we can maintain the view that those moral values conflict with, and (where they prevail) *curtail* the right to property.

CONCLUSION

Deliberate legal regulation of the environment began with the common law of nuisance. Early nuisance cases reveal a body of law essentially limited in its ability to formulate and pursue general policies which promote environmental values, but of surprising sophistication in its awareness and achievement of a balance between property rights and collective interests in a healthy environment. Legislative developments beginning in the nineteenth century brought about a more general responsiveness to the impact of human actions upon the environment; but very often environmental protection was characterised as instrumentally rather than intrinsically valuable.

The modern legal order thus reflects a view of property rights as *competing* with environmental values and concerns, rather than *emerging* from moral reflection upon mankind's place in the world. Such a view is not inevitable: the natural rights theories of the seventeenth and eighteenth centuries rooted property rights in a teleological view of nature, and hence as determined and shaped by concerns which we could now aptly characterise as 'environmental'. Yet this conception of property is one no longer open to us. Our more complex way of life presents impossible challenges to the underlying assumption that human interests and environmental protection coincide. The natural rights theorists regarded human beings as possessing a *duty* to transform the environment from a barren, hostile wasteland into fruitful Eden; hence, we can see in those accounts an attempt to provide a philosophical basis for the systems of agrarian capitalism and agrarian communism which constituted the most important economic structures of the time. We no longer live in such a world: not only has our technological capacity to damage the environment increased beyond the imagination of the seventeenth century thinker; also our scientific knowledge has reached a stage at which it is capable of offering far more penetrating insights into the ways in which our actions can impact upon and harm the natural environment. The very agricultural practices which were held out as a moral necessity by the natural rights theorists can, it seems, create untold environmental damage. The ethical assumptions of the seventeenth century conception of property cannot survive in such circumstances.

The perception of any intrinsic relationship between property and the environment came to be replaced by a view of property understood overwhelmingly in terms of subjective, rather than objective, right, and a view of environmental protection as instrumentally and prudentially desirable rather than morally necessary. Yet, it has been argued, this instrumentalism need not, and does not, inevitably collapse into more or less sophisticated forms of utilitarianism. The modern lawyer is the inheritor of the utilitarian's assumption of a fundamental conflict between property rights and environmental values which curb the available uses of property; but this conflict is often more readily understandable as one between property rights and countervailing *moral* values than between individual rights and collective *interests*. That such values form part of modern environmental thought is not startling; that they also underpin legal responses to environmental welfare is less widely understood. Yet a quite general articulation of those values, when not attached to wider public interests, is unexpectedly difficult. For the modern lawyer most often conceives of law, not as the embodiment of moral values, but as an instrument for the pursuit and attainment of social goals, and for maximising overall welfare. Likewise, environmental law is regarded as a collection of measures which restrict property rights in the name of a wider social interest in healthy living conditions. Other than an obvious concern with human wellbeing, such measures are not typically regarded as requiring deeper philosophical explanation.

This view of environmental law is often associated with the belief that legal measures relating to environmental protection serve *policies*, but do not express *principles*. Principles, on this view, are the preserve of private law, understood as a realm in which various doctrinal definitions, rules and distinctions comprise a systematic and philosophically coherent whole. Legislated rules, on the other hand, are understood as exhibiting systematic qualities only in a limited way: they (ideally) comprise coherent strategies for dealing with particular aspects of social life, but they do not amount to comprehensive moral theories. Yet it is possible to find, in modern environmental legislation, the beginnings of moral ideas about property and the environment which are not wholly expressible within the conceptual framework of private rights and collective interests. The recognition of such ideas places considerable strain upon received understandings of the nature of environmental law as a political response to the problems of modern living, but also upon established conceptions of the relationship between public and private law. As will become clear, arguments about the nature of the public-private distinction are intimately bound to views about the moral function of legislated rules and private rights. Hence, the availability of a view of environmental law as underpinned by a systematic moral theory is neither inevitable nor a permanent possibility: it depends, rather, upon the availability of understandings of the public-private distinction which allow for the articulation of sophisticated moral positions. It is to this question that we must now turn.

5

The Changing Face of
Environmental Law

L EGAL REGULATION OF the environment had begun with the judicial interpretation of property rights as being limited in important ways by community-directed responsibilities. The notion that property rights are subject to intrinsic limitations (that is, limitations not directly imposed through deliberately posited rules) was not, however, articulated in terms of the competition between public and private interests, but in terms of natural versus unnatural user. Hence, while the nineteenth-century judges were able to respond to emergent 'environmental' problems by calling upon a doctrinal framework of considerable sophistication, they could provide no *general* solution to the problems of clashing interests and environmental protection. It was only with the development of statutory regimes of regulation and control that a direct concern with environmental protection could fully manifest itself in legal thought.

The early legislative regimes largely embodied attempts to consolidate and extend the protection of collective interests from exercises of private right given at common law, and hence tended to concentrate on specific issues, such as pollution control. But whereas the doctrinal elaboration of curbs on private rights allowed for no easy distinction between the *expression* of legal requirements and the conceptual framework of justifying *reasons*, the evolving statutory regimes were couched in a language in which express provisions require interpretation according to canons of construction quite separate from the justificationary arguments which might be marshalled in support of them. At the same time, the concern with specific issues allowed environmental law to take on the appearance of an assortment of measures united by no underlying principle other than a concern with the mitigation of emergent forms of social harm. By the time the growing body of regulative measures could be identified as forming a distinct branch of law, worthy of systematic study in its own right, 'environmental law' would already have adopted the appearance of a statutory system, devoid of obvious precursors, out of which a distinctive jurisprudence might grow.

ENVIRONMENTAL LAW AND THE PUBLIC/PRIVATE DISTINCTION

The account of legal history from which environmental lawyers would draw their assumptions about the nature of the subject depended, for its cogency, upon a particular view of the legal order. For those assumptions rest upon certain presuppositions about the relationship between the private realm of individual rights and the public realm of collective interests and choices.

The philosophical thinkers of the seventeenth century, and the common lawyers of the nineteenth, developed 'environmental' principles as part of an exploration of the intrinsic significance of property rights. The assumptions which drove such explorations had, in fact, already begun to recede in legal thought in the eighteenth century, partly as a result of the rise of legal positivism.[1] The emergence of statutory regimes dealing with such matters as pollution and (later) conservation, signalled a concern, not with the *delineation* of private rights, but with their *regulation*. The modern lawyer had begun to move within a conception of law in which statutory obligations enjoy no *essential* relationship with property rights other than as posited rules affecting them. Questions of the nature and scope of rights came to be seen, not as the expression of the intrinsic value of rights, but as the result of deliberate choice.

Views of this kind involve the drawing of rigid categorical divisions between public and private law. Private law, considered as a system of horizontal relationships of right and duty, forms a discrete body of thought in which relationships between individuals are worked out on the basis of doctrinal principle rather than assessments of collective utility. Deliberation on the extent of rights involves the delineation of a conception of justice, as distinct from the application of settled policies. Public law, by contrast, is thought to consist in a set of deliberate choices taken on the basis of aggregative and distributive policies: the rules and obligations imposed through legislation are hence not merely conventional, but the result of decisions which are arbitrary in a way that doctrinal principles are not. The doctrinal categories of private law were the reflection of complex and subtle political ideas about the nature of property and rights; but while the nineteenth century jurists had wrestled with such problems, the declaratory language of statute made wider philosophical speculation of that kind irrelevant to the grasp of specific provisions on environmental protection. Environmental law's modern period would thus be characterised by its technicality: the lawyer's task would be understood as consisting, not in the careful delineation of a conception of justice, but in the interpretation and application of fixed rules, definitions and distinctions, and the tracing out of the consequences of established policy. Rather than raising profound questions about the nature of property and rights, the law would be viewed as a set of deliberate choices between conflicting interests on the basis of collective welfare.

A conception of statutory controls as essentially removed from the body of doctrinal principles governing private rights can thus prevail only against a background of assumptions which treat 'public law' and 'private law' as distinct and autonomous legal categories. A view of the legal order which emphasises the public/private distinction in very rigid terms is traditionally associated with

---

[1] These developments were charted above in ch 3.

the juristic philosophy of Kantianism; but it is in many ways also a natural consequence of legal positivism: for the positivist tends to regard the law as underpinned by deliberate choice rather than coherence. For the positivist, therefore, the dichotomy between the public and private realms is explicable in terms of the dominant status of statute: the posited rules which emanate from the legislature regulate and refine the corpus of inherited doctrines and customary rules of the common law. If one is to take seriously the idea of the supremacy of parliamentary will, the interpretative conventions which govern the resort to statute as a source of legal principle cannot require judges to view statutes through the prism of traditional doctrinal ideas and categories. The existing bodies of doctrinal principle must therefore form a set of ideas and assumptions quite separate from those of the statutory rules which modify and replace them.[2]

The analytical plausibility of so rigid a distinction between the public and private realms is, however, open to question. It is, indeed, a challenge to the stark form of the public/private distinction which forms the subject of the first section of this chapter.[3] As will become clear, the existence of collective limitations on property rights is intrinsic to the possibility of rights in any complex society. In many cases, the distinct *form* that those limitations take will not be a matter resolved exclusively within the realm of doctrinal scholarship. But few of the legislative choices aimed at the regulation of property rights will be entirely comprehensible outwith the context supplied by traditional common law reasoning: for (it will emerge) it is only by teasing out the intellectual assumptions upon which traditional doctrinal scholarship is based (assumptions about property, rights and nature) that the full political significance of modern environmental law can be understood.

The second half of this chapter is accordingly given over to a consideration of environmental law's statutory character. The emergence of statutory regimes on environmental issues is essential to the existence of environmental law as a distinctive branch of law: legislation can address directly and comprehensively matters which, at common law, can develop only incrementally and slowly. Yet the environmental lawyer moves within a conception of law in which legal rules regulating property rights in the name of environmental protection are no longer understood and interpreted in the light of the political values out of which the modern idea of property rights emerged. One direct result of this is a narrowing of the interpretative context of statutory interventions in the private

---

[2] In other ways, of course, positivism is indicative of a rejection of a firm public/private distinction: for the entitlements and principles of private law are never regarded as sacrosanct or intrinsically shielded from collective interests imposed through statute.

[3] Although the terms in which that challenge proceeds centre on notions of property and ownership developed in previous chapters, the criticism of the public/private distinction itself is not new: indeed it does not differ in its essential respects from the challenge first put forward by RL Hale or MR Cohen in the first decades of the twentieth century. See RL Hale, 'Coercion and Distribution in a Supposedly Non-Coercive State' (1923) 38 *Political Science Quarterly* 470 and RL Hale, 'Value and Vested Rights' (1927) 27 *Columbia Law Review* 523; MR Cohen, 'Property and Sovereignty' 13 (1927–28) *Cornell Law Quarterly* 8.

use of property to questions of utility and clashing interests.[4] As the discussion in chapter four showed, however, the restriction of legal discussions of environmental protection to issues of utility fails to capture the distinctive importance and concerns of modern environmental legislation. Legal regulation and protection of the environment increasingly indicates a concern with justice and moral value, rather than a purely prudential concern with human interests. Such ideas permeate the legal consciousness best at the level of doctrine rather than in technical discussions of the interpretation and application of black-letter rules. When viewed as a series of technical rules, definitions and distinctions, environmental law becomes a curiously bloodless instrument: for it is very difficult, within such a framework, to articulate any moral concern with environmental harm other than a narrow concern with human well-being.

The final section of this chapter pursues these ideas in the context of sustainable development. Concepts such as sustainable development (it will be argued) bring into play ideas and obligations which go beyond a stark concern with the reconciliation of clashing interests: questions of rights, and of user, are considered not as belonging to a separate realm of juridical discourse, but as forming part of a conception of justice which includes respect for future generations. Such ideas cannot be explored within a juristic framework which emphasises competing rights, for there are profound problems with the attribution to hypothetical or not-yet-existent persons (who exist only in possible worlds) of entitlements which are supposed to have legal effects against owners of property in the actual world. Ideas relating to sustainability are best articulated in terms of *responsibilities*, rather than rights: it is possible to see, in the idea of sustainable development, clear echoes of the political thought of the seventeenth and eighteenth century natural lawyers, who emphasised the relationship of property to justice. Property rights are understood as forming part of a conception of justice in which limitations on private ownership reflect assumptions about political responsibility. Such ideas emphasise not what is prudent, but what is *right*: the concept of property, thus construed, is a deeply moral one in which the goals of environmental management and human flourishing are once again seen as interdependent and mutually reinforcing.

The conceptions and ideas implicit within modern environmental legislation can thus be seen as raising the same themes and concerns first articulated systematically by the natural rights theorists of the seventeenth century. A full appreciation of the political and philosophical significance of environmental law must therefore include an understanding of the way in which those ideas continue to shape our legal and moral thinking. This task might profitably be understood as an attempt to set out the interpretative background against which modern environmental law must be understood: a task which begins with a fuller consideration of the nature of the public/private distinction.

---

[4] See above ch 4.

FROM RIGHTS TO REGULATION

The preceding three chapters sustainedly explored the relationship between property rights and environmental thinking in law by charting their development as political, and legal, phenomena. In the present section, previous reflections on that relationship are summarised and extended. Recognition of property rights as distinctive intellectual (and historical) products, it was suggested, emerged through philosophical reflection on themes and concerns which we would now classify as, at least in part, 'environmental'. The philosophical origins of the notion of subjective *ius* in relation to property rights presented seventeenth- and eighteenth-century thinkers with particularly potent reasons for regarding property rights as *both* inherently proscribed and undergirded by community-orientated obligations *and* intrinsically limited by man's relationship with the natural world. The latter view, most fully expressed in (though by no means confined to) the writings of Locke, amounted to a philosophical thesis concerning the extent to which property rights could emerge *tout court*. The former embodied a series of political assumptions about the specific texture and scope of property rights within particular legal-political cultures. Whereas the more abstract, philosophical thesis is a theory about ownership in general, the various (often competing) political assumptions concerned the delineation and consequences of property rights much more narrowly. Notoriously and unsurprisingly, the common law tradition quickly abandoned the preoccupation with broader theories of ownership, and instead concentrated upon the precise systematic delineation of individual property rights.

The modern lawyer is the heir to these developments in political theory. The exact lineaments of property rights are regarded, by and large, as unfolding through highly technical definitions and distinctions, rules and principles rather than as deriving from broader theories of ownership. Echoing a long line of writers on the law of real property, Roger Smith noted in the opening pages of his recent textbook that '[t]he nature of ownership may be seen more as a jurisprudential question than a legal one.'[5] In expressing these sentiments, Smith does no more than voice the widely-held belief that English common law, in contrast to civil law traditions, lacks any abstract notion of ownership. More accurately, English law does not lack a conception of ownership but rather lacks any systematic expression of such a conception: the common law, in the words

---

[5] R Smith, *Property Law*, 4th edn (London, Longman, 2003) 6. (Earlier editions carry similar sentiments.) Whilst it is common for legal textbooks to begin an exposition of property law with a philosophical attempt to pin down the 'nature' of their subject-matter, such attempts are remarkably uniform in their concentration upon *rights* as the basic building blocks of understanding in distinction to conceptions of ownership. A typical example is supplied by the following remark drawn from the opening chapter of a seminal property law text: 'Real property deals with the rights and liabilities of land ownership whereas conveyancing is concerned with how rights in land may be created and transferred' Megarry and Wade, *The Law of Real Property*, 6th edn (London, Sweet & Maxwell, 2000) 2.

of JW Harris, *presupposes* but does not *employ* a concept of ownership.[6] In virtue of being channelled through the doctrine of tenures and estates, the English common lawyer's treatment of property rights can more-or-less alto-gether ignore the social, political and moral dimensions to property rights which earlier jurists perceived as central to determinations of the extent and scope of those rights. (Questions regarding the political and philosophical basis of the doctrine of estates need not trouble the practising lawyer, though they might well disturb the legal philosopher.)

As noted at the outset of chapter two, the modern lawyer's conception of property is at once technical and overwhelmingly positivist. It is technical in that property rights are delineated according to fixed rules and doctrines deriv-ing from statutes and decided cases; it is positivist in virtue of the legal practi-tioner's avoidance of direct resort to or reliance on substantive political and moral criteria as the primary means by which to resolve legal disputes over property. The evolution of property law as a body of highly technical posited rules was accompanied by the shift from a *dominium*-orientated approach to the concept of property to one rooted in subjective *ius*. For the conception of property as a complex systemic ordering of interpersonal rights and interests places questions of distribution and aggregation at the heart of political debates about property rather than philosophical questions concerning the origin of entitlements. Whereas questions of the latter sort require a sustained focus on the paths along which property rights naturally evolve and take shape, questions of the former sort emphasise property rights as entirely contingent products of social and political manipulation. The law of property, for the conventionalist, merely effects and accords protection to the particular array of rights and duties which unfold from political deliberation: the exact body of rules in terms of which a given distribution is effected are readily separable from the political jus-tifications which might be offered in favour of that particular distribution. For the natural lawyer, by contrast, property law gives rise to patterns of entitle-ment and obligation which are far from fully independent of the justificationary principles establishing those patterns: the legal rules through which those patterns are effected will, on the contrary, very often appear as the deductive consequences of those principles.

As we have already seen, the shift from a *dominium*-centred understanding of property to a *ius*-based conception radically alters the terms in which political debates about property are conceived. More importantly, the shift from a natu-ralistic to a positivistic perspective on law allows the lawyer to pursue ordinary legal practice within the confines of a juristic science largely isolated from wider political debates: legal reasoning is viewed as being concerned with the formal determination and transmission of entitlements through the operation of the doctrine of estates; questions relating to the moral value of property rights, or

---

[6] JW Harris, *'Ownership of Land in English Law'*, in N MacCormick and P Birks (eds), *The Legal Mind: Essays for Tony Honore* (Oxford, Clarendon Press, 1986) 143.

of the relationship between property and liberty (or other specific values) are seen as standing outside the scope of legal reasoning, and as instead inhabiting the domain of jurisprudential speculation. Because the subjection of property rights to political evaluation is regarded as inessential both to the determination of the lineaments of particular property rights and, more generally, to deduction and transmission of title in law, property rights come to be viewed as related to political values only instrumentally. Political values, including environmental values, are perceived as encroaching on property rights only contingently, as part of more general attempts at manipulation of the social order in the name of collective welfare. The idea that a polity is free to manipulate elements of social order (including individual rights) in diverse ways struck eighteenth- and early nineteenth-century jurists as a profound insight into the nature of legal regulation: not only is the legal order capable of being viewed as a complex system of intersecting horizontal and vertical relationships of entitlement, but the existence and scope of *both* horizontal *and* vertical entitlements are themselves purely conventional (and hence contingent).

Blackstone, as we have seen, adopted something approaching this viewpoint even if the naturalistic orientation of his philosophical outlook prevented him from fully appreciating the conclusions of the position. Property rights, for Blackstone, represented the 'sole and despotic dominion which one man claims and exercises over the external things of the world, in total exclusion to the right of any other individual in the universe.'[7] Blackstone's conceptual framework treated individual rights to property as otherwise absolute entitlements, variable and limitable only through deliberate legislation or custom. Once the *dominium*-centric ideology is removed from this picture, an understanding of property rights as the pure creatures of positive law-making easily follows. But although (on either model) *particular* restrictions on property rights are the contingent outcome of a society's political choices, the presence of at least some fundamental limitations on property rights—in all likelihood a great many limitations—is a necessary, formal feature of the institution of property. This last claim is tantamount to the assertion that Blackstone's depiction of property rights as, at least in the abstract, a 'sole and despotic dominion' over certain resources is misguided and flawed. Property rights cannot attain such a status regardless of whether that status is supposed to obtain naturally or by fiat. An individual's property rights, perforce, cannot amount to a claim of utter dominion as long as the polity which recognises and accords legal protection to such rights is either itself a sovereign state or a dependent territory of a sovereign state: for a claim of dominion, understood as a claim to total freedom of action within the boundaries of one's property coupled with complete immunity from unwanted legal interference in one's actions, amounts to the repudiation of any claims of political sovereignty by officials and citizens alike over the area within

---

[7] Blackstone II *Comm* 2. Blackstone's elision of the *dominium/ius* distinction here has already received comment: see above ch 3.

which dominion is asserted and exercised. A claim of unqualified dominion would thus consist in a claim by an owner to be completely ungoverned by a society's laws within that area. But in that case, recognition of (or more precisely, the grounds of) the owner's property rights can no longer stem from that society's institutions of property, but must instead derive from the owner's brute assertion of dominion itself. Property rights which derive their force from the laws of a polity, therefore, are formally subject to limitations of various kinds, though the substance of particular limitations on an individual's rights will be (at least for the positivist) the contingent outcome of that polity's political choices. An individual's rights to property are never formally unlimited, though the particular limitations to which those rights are subject are never, for the positivist, *intrinsic* limitations.[8]

Though the various limitations to which individual property rights might be subject affect the scope and quality of those rights contingently rather than inherently, there will be many limitations upon property rights which are fundamental to the shared values (not to say the long-term stability) of the society in which they figure. Most obviously, property rights cannot act as a shield to violent or murderous acts committed by an owner on his land: the combined rights, powers and liberties of the land-owner do not amount to, nor do they entail, immunity from prosecution for assault or murder simply because those acts happened to take place on the perpetrator's property. X's assault of Y with a baseball bat is hardly defendable on the basis of the fact that the baseball bat was X's coupled with the principle that one is free to use and dispose of one's property in one's own way. Similarly, property rights within a society are usually associated with a host of community-orientated obligations which restrict what an owner can do with the resources at his disposal: provisions concerning waste and nuisance supply obvious examples, as does the subjection of individual property rights to overarching socio-economic needs as explored in the copious literature on 'takings'.[9] In general, a complex society is likely to have in place a great many allocative and distributive mechanisms which modify and affect the extent of property rights and privileges for the sake of public goals.

Though the presence and precise lineaments of those curbs are viewed, by the modern lawyer, as contingent rather than strictly necessary features of the law, contingency in this sense should not be confused with the claim that those curbs invariably figure as deliberately created restrictions which supervene upon previously more expansive entitlements. Where they arise from the shared values

[8] Throughout the remainder of this discussion, the qualifier 'for the positivist' will be dropped. Clearly a natural-law orientated thinker would quarrel over the attribution of contingency to at least some of the features and limitations of rights discussed below. However, since the discussion is essentially a discussion about perceptions of property law within the modern legal order, such natural-law quibbles can, for the moment, safely be glossed over.

[9] For an excellent recent analysis and overview of various takings provisions see T Allen, *The Right to Property in Commonwealth Constitutions* (Cambridge, CUP, 2000) passim. A more theoretical discussion of takings can be found in SR Munzer, *A Theory of Property* (Cambridge, CUP, 1990) chs 14–15.

which form the core of a society's cultural life, such curbs might be better understood as forming part of the wider social and political framework within which individual rights to property take effect. Though not historically inevitable as political features of rights, community-related restrictions upon resource-usage can be fundamental to the treatment of property within a particular political culture. Even though restrictions of this kind are far from generic to the concept of 'right', they may be perceived by members of a given polity as inherent features of a particular range of rights, such as property rights, *within* that political culture. We can, somewhat loosely, consider such a view as forming part of the 'conception' of property rights of a given society.

When a society's conception of property rights is heavily conditioned by perspectives which emphasise the controls and limitations placed upon the scope of those rights for the benefit of collective interests, various theoretical perspectives become available to explain the formal characteristics of the institution of property in ways which stress the collective controls as the primary terms in which an understanding of property must be sought rather than the individual entitlements. In a recent essay, K and SF Gray argue that there is some judicial support for a move away from a rights-based notion of property in favour of one based on *responsibility*. 'The crucial variable,' they write,

> has now become the degree to which the courts are prepared to hold that the proprietary utilities available to a land-holder are inherently curtailed by a community-directed obligation to conserve and promote fragile features of the environment.[10]

According to this conception,

> Property becomes . . . an allocative mechanism for promoting the efficient or ecologically prudent utilisation of [scarce] resources. So analysed, this community-oriented [sic] approach to property in land plays a quite obviously pivotal role in the advancement of our environmental welfare.[11]

Here, the collective interests which affect individual rights to property are treated neither as necessary incidents of the concept of 'right' (or 'property'), nor as a mere collection of legislated restrictions which alter the scope of existing rights. Inherent curtailment, in the sense wielded above, suggests a collection of principles which affect the scope of property rights by constituting the moral/political framework within which claims of right are expressed and understood. Such a conceptual framework is neither historically inevitable nor incontestable, but it is nevertheless capable of redrawing the terms in which property rights are conceived. In stressing responsibilities and obligations as the fundamental terms within which property rights must be understood, the Grays' proposal removes some central determinants of property rights both from the

---

[10] K Gray and SF Gray, 'The Idea of Property in Land', in S Bright and J Dewar (eds), *Land Law: Themes and Perspectives* (Oxford, OUP, 1998) 49.

[11] *Ibid* 41.

capitalist system of free-market exchange and, at the same time, from unalloyed utilitarian calculations about the extent to which individual property rights collide with broader social welfare goals. Both kinds of allocative mechanism can, of course, continue to affect various aspects of property ownership; but certain, central aspects of ownership will, on this view, be isolated from and immune to manipulation through these channels.

The suggested approach therefore bears certain structural resemblances to the philosophical framework proposed in chapter four: measures affecting property rights might be viewed, not as utility-maximising measures aimed at increasing overall welfare at the expense of a narrow class of individual interests, but as elements of an overarching political and philosophical view of rights in which certain questions of entitlement and interest are settled in advance in favour of collective well-being. Such questions are understood as resolvable only by reference to wider principle, and as invulnerable to shifting social conditions or patterns of utility. The Grays' proposal might thus be read as but one instance of the general approach suggested in chapter four, which viewed property rights as subject to alteration and revision, not (exclusively) on the basis of utilitarian calculations concerning conflicts between individual and collective interests, but on the basis of political and philosophical principles aimed at resolving conflicts between property rights and competing moral values.[12] The Grays' proposal in effect suggests that those moral values be understood predominantly in communitarian terms: the approach is avowedly 'community-orientated'; but as the earlier discussion in chapter four revealed, moral conflicts involving property rights can be understood much more widely.

Such moral values can be fleshed out in a number of different ways. Curbs on property rights in the name of preservation of the natural environment may, though they need not, appeal to specifically community-related values. (As noted in chapter four, many seemingly community-orientated arguments are in fact better understood as arguments based on some conception of intrinsic value.) Legislated measures curtailing certain uses of private property might be based, not on social welfare concerns, but on religious concerns. Here, the view would be that private rights to property derive their force from, and are delineated according to, transcendent conceptions of justice reflective of God's intentions.[13] Not only might such schemes require restrictions on usage for the realisation (say) of some egalitarian distribution of resources, it is equally possible that those restrictions might arise out of monastic ideals of poverty and labour: ownership of property, it might be felt, is inconsistent with the good life except insofar as property rights are necessary for the prudent management of

---

[12] More accurately, the discussion in ch 4 was concerned to demonstrate that conflicts which seemed to concern individual and collective interests actually concerned individual interests and moral values which might have a purely coincidental relationship with collective welfare.

[13] For a classic debate along these lines see Bartlet *et al*, *Property: Its Duties and Rights*, new edn, (London, Macmillan, 1922). The essays in this collection show that religiously motivated accounts of property need not (as Bentham appeared to think) collapse into more-or-less clear cut versions of utilitarianism.

resources, the avoidance of waste, cultivation of the earth and so on. Alternatively, curbs on property rights might be understood as articulating moral limits to ownership of resources arising from an ethic of stewardship. In this case, individual rights to property must be understood primarily in terms of responsibilities: responsibilities, rather than rights, would form the basic counters in our understanding of property, though the responsibilities would not be owed primarily, or wholly, to identifiable communities. Still other environment-orientated perspectives stress restrictions on property usage as aligned with moral conceptions of worth in relation to natural resources which are not exhausted by, and are possibly independent of, their instrumental value to human communities.

The presence of such perspectives need not, of course, be present in any particular society's legal arrangements. The aim of the present discussion is not to suggest that any of the above conceptions of property are reflected in the present arrangements of the English or any other legal system. The aim was rather to show that a society's legal treatment of property is not immune from, or independent of, such thinking. A society's property laws are shaped and textured by that society's deeply held moral values. Yet the moral values which thus shape and inform our conception of property, and property rights, need not and (very probably) do not amount to any single coherent philosophical position. Not only do individual interests in the use of property compete with various moral values, those moral values compete with one another. It is the task of both political philosophy and legal reasoning to sort out which values take precedence over others: for example, are environmental values considered more important than collective interests and if so, when? Do our basic moral insights into the nature of property conform to essentially utilitarian patterns of reasoning or to some other idea of justice? That there are no easy answers to such questions might be due as much to the absence of genuine consensus over values as to the failure of scholars to agree upon how best to represent those values. Perhaps we should not expect any coherent overall picture to emerge from those investigations. More plausibly, the result of our deepest and most careful analyses may leave us with a picture of property rights both fragmentary and suggestive, in which various conceptions of property vie and compete. That competition between alternative perspectives will take place within the law as well as in political theory: we may find, in the common law and in legislation, no overall perspective from which to view property rights, but rather an ongoing attempt to systematise and render coherent various competing conceptions of property, right and moral good.

Property, Environmental Value and Legal Regulation

The foregoing reflections provide the philosophical framework within which the remainder of this book pursues its enquiries. Property rights, it has been argued, are quite often the subject of limitations and curbs arising from moral values which compete with the value of unbridled freedom to use one's goods and resources as one wishes. Whilst many of these values are aligned with community-orientated goals and projects, many others are best understood as only contingently connected with human welfare. Moreover, it has been suggested, values of both kinds may compete with one another. In chapters two and three, it was argued that property rights were overwhelmingly regarded as intrinsically limited by the nature of humanity's relationship with the external world: values which we might with some justification refer to as 'environmental' dominated conceptions of the origin and nature of the right to property. These values, according to natural law, provided a strong foundation for human interests as well as promoting protection and cultivation of the natural environment. As the eighteenth century progressed, the latter, specifically environmental, values came to be seen as only contingently connected with the former, human interests, and even as often competing with them. Property rights came to be seen as exclusively concerned with human interests, most particularly with individual freedom, and hence as capable of limitation only where restrictions would result in a net increase in social welfare or liberty.

In chapter four, it was argued that property rights at common law continued to undergo restriction where specific usages resulted in environmental harm or nuisance. Whilst the earliest cases analysed such conflicts as instances of the collision of individual rights with collective interests (for example, in a healthy environment), the courts—and later Parliament—rapidly extended the scope of environmental protection on grounds which were only partially, if at all, effected on the basis of identifiable collective interests. Forms of environmental protection emerged which seemed to place some moral value on the natural environment for its own sake. In the present chapter, this theme will be pushed further. The recognition of environmental law as a distinct and fruitful area of legal investigation at once highlights shifting patterns of thought about the importance of environmental issues and (ironically) disguises the tradition of principled thought which made such recognition a possibility. Whilst increasingly expressive of a standpoint which views property rights as essentially subject to moral limitations, modern environmental law frequently misrepresents the philosophical basis upon which such limitations are most forcefully argued. By seemingly advocating restrictive measures on the basis of policy, rather than principle, environmental regulation is portrayed as a piecemeal and unsystematic response to a social problem. Hence, legal and political censure of environment-damaging actions is frequently limited to the claim that those actions cause or store up harm for actual or future communities.

In the present chapter, such claims are explored in the context of modern environmental law, and found to be far from fully expressive of the justifying grounds upon which environmental legislation is based. Rather than relying completely upon community-orientated values and proposals, modern environmental law frequently rests upon conceptions of obligation which stress the intrinsic worth of the natural environment, ecosystems and species. Legal regulation of property rights to protect the environment is therefore much less than totally justified in instrumental terms. Yet the legal and political terms in which environmental protection is viewed render the expression of such non-instrumental claims highly difficult. For such claims require a philosophical theory of property and ownership as moral values which coexist with other, competing values. A philosophical theory of this kind must not only express and justify such ascriptions of value, but also suggest ways in which the various values should be delineated where they overlap or compete. Modern environmental law lacks such a theory: as such its articulation of conceptions of non-instrumental moral value are enormously difficult to pin down. Not only do such expressions of value resist systematic treatment, they fall short of embodying firm notions which would allow for their full interpretation in the light of existing conceptions of property rights and collective welfare. Though suggestive of certain strands of seventeenth century thought about property and the natural world, current environmental thinking must move within legal and political structures and modes of thought which are alien to the values which made the seventeenth century conceptions possible.

Before undertaking that investigation, it is worth saying a little more about environmental law's modern character. Modern lawyers are the inheritors of a conception of law which attempts to delimit, through the analysis of legal institutions, two conceptually separate realms: the private realm of individual freedom and choices, wherein an individual can formulate and pursue projects unmolested by the collective interests or policies pursued by the state; and the public realm of policies and rules which encroach upon individual autonomy in the name of the common good. The public/private distinction is thus at once an analytical thesis regarding the institutional characteristics of the legal order, and a substantive political position (most frequently associated with certain strands of liberalism) which seeks to emphasise the existence and sanctity, from the point of view of political morality, of a realm of private discretion unstructured by political decision. Liberals accordingly interpret the legal order as the embodiment of two intersecting patterns of entitlement and disentitlement: an individual's 'horizontal' legal rights, powers, and privileges vis-à-vis other individuals, as well as any immunities he may possess against exercises of powers by others, define a realm of private autonomy which is subjected to encroachment and manipulation through the imposition of 'vertical' patterns of rules specifying duties and responsibilities. Since encroachments upon an individual's horizontal entitlements necessarily reduce his autonomy (by curtailing his ability to formulate and pursue certain projects) liberal theorists have traditionally supposed that unless the private realm is generally protected against collective interference and manipulation, individual autonomy becomes fragile and illusory. The state (it is argued) should not legally interfere with individual entitlements merely because to do so would marginally increase overall levels of welfare. Curtailment of private rights, where necessary, must be premised on more substantial justifications of important, or significant social interests identified by overarching policies. Liberal theorists have tended therefore to emphasise the legislative process, rather than the common law, as the most appropriate means by which collective interference in the private realm may occur. Accordingly, lawyers have generally pursued the implications of the public/private distinction through the distinction between the body of rules and mandates collectively designated as 'public law' and the distinctive realm of doctrine and principle known as 'private law'.

It is with something like this idea in mind that many lawyers—including environmental lawyers—have characterised environmental law as little more than a collection of legislative responses to pressing social problems arising from property-use. Environmental law's supposed instrumental character is neatly explicable in terms of a view which places the highest political value on individual autonomy, coupled with a view of legislative mandates as collective intrusions on private rights. For public law incursions into the private realm are understood against a justificationary metric in terms of which individual rights both exist independently of, and in opposition to, collective interests, *and* remain at least prima facie shielded from the force of such interests. This view of environmental law's political significance (as well as that of other branches of public—and private—law), if not thoroughly dependent upon the public/private distinction, is at least significantly bolstered by that distinction.[14] Yet we can see now how the argument pursued earlier in this section casts significant doubt on the sustaining force of the public/private distinction, and hence challenges the view of environmental law as justified simply according to an overarching concern with collective wellbeing.

We saw earlier how private rights to property are inherently restricted by community-orientated concerns, and other moral concerns unconnected (or only contingently connected) with the common weal. Private rights, far from comprising a realm distinct from public value, are in fact comprehensively and pervasively shaped by the latter. The conception of dominion which lies behind the view of private property rights as naturally or originally unfettered rights which become increasingly subject to and hemmed in by public duties is unsustainable in a society of any complexity or sophistication: for it is only through the imposition of collective duties and restrictions that the private rights gain substance. Without the recognition and protection accorded to private rights through duty-imposing legal institutions, individual autonomy would reduce to the seemingly all-inclusive but in reality completely insubstantial 'liberty' possessed by the unhappy individual in the Hobbesian state of nature. Rather than comprising a realm of choice wholly separate from, and in collision with, the

---

[14] For a classic account of contract law which undermines this conception of the public/private distinction, see PS Atiyah, *Promises, Morals and Law* (Oxford, Clarendon Press, 1983). For an account of tort law which likewise raises problems for such a conception see R Mullender, 'Prima Facie Rights, Rationality and the Law of Negligence' in MH Kramer (ed), *Rights, Wrongs and Responsibilities* (Palgrave, Macmillan, 2001).

realm of collective interests, the realm of private right is wholly determined by and within a structure of collective decision. To be sure, such a conception is *compatible* with a conception in which the most appropriate metric for the analysis of property is that of right rather than, say, responsibility. For, as Matthew Kramer has observed, it might be argued that private owners, unlike public officials, can coherently and fully defend their uses of their resources by reference to their own preferences and interests rather than justifying their actions by reference to the common good. However (as Kramer goes on to note) such a point is quite incapable of generalisation in the way that defenders of the public/private distinction might have hoped: for '[a]lthough such a thesis does accurately describe numerous *instances* of private ownership, it does not cover *all* such instances (either actual or conceivable).'[15]

Indeed, not only is it not necessarily the case that individuals base their actions and justifications in relation to their resources upon exclusively selfish grounds, such justifications are *in fact* frequently excluded by the framework of rules and regulations within which private property rights take effect. Insofar as owners of resources are debarred from burning toxic substances on their land, or from exceeding allowable emissions as a by-product of industrial processes (and so on), and insofar as such actions are themselves grounds for the application of a legal sanction, an individual's actions in relation to his resources are frequently justified according to public (and perhaps moral), not private, standards. The individual 'is accountable to the public for his misdeed, and cannot excuse himself by asserting that he is free to do with his goods as he sees fit.'[16] Where such curbs are pervasive, conceptions of responsibility rather than conceptions of right provide the most appropriate metric for understanding private property. The realm of private discretion takes effect *within* the structures of moral and public obligation, and is at the same time itself structured by the values those obligations express. The fact that the exact content of those duties changes over time (and may grow more extensive with time) is not sufficient reason to assert that the private realm should be understood fundamentally in terms of rights which suffer encroachment by collective interests. Nor is private property *historically* understandable in such terms: as explored in chapter four, the judicial view of property in the eighteenth and nineteenth centuries saw property rights as in some ways intrinsically subject to community-orientated values and responsibilities.

The public/private distinction in its analytic form was the product of nineteenth century attempts to comprehend the changing face of the legal order, and the relationship between statute and individual autonomy. Yet the realm of private right described in this way by the nineteenth century jurists never truly existed. Despite the considerable influence the distinction has had on modern legal thought, the conceptual separation of two distinctive realms

---

[15] MH Kramer, 'In Praise of the Critique of the Public/Private Distinction', in MH Kramer, *In the Realm of Legal and Moral Philosophy* (London, Macmillan, 1999) 121. Emphasis added
[16] *Ibid.*

fundamentally misrepresents the structure of the legal order. As Nigel Simmonds has observed,

> It is only in the context of a political theory that distinguishes between the area of autonomy within which individual transactions may have effect according to the will of the parties, and the area of central regulation and public planning, that a distinction between public and private law can be maintained. If we view the legal order purely as a collection of norms and powers we will be unable to discover, in its formal structure, any distinction between the public and the private.[17]

It is the misleading view of the law's formal structure which, above all, accounts for modern misconceptions of the philosophical significance of environmental law. Rather than requiring explication wholly in terms of instrumental restrictions on private rights, environmental law can be understood more deeply as an expression of both community-orientated responsibilities and wider moral responsibilities towards the natural environment. As previously noted, such expressions of value both resist systematic treatment and fall short of fully interpretable conceptions of moral concern. The remainder of this chapter hence amounts to a partial exploration of those non-instrumental expressions, though falls short of suggesting any overarching theory or framework within which to understand them. Instead, the subsequent reflections on environmental regulation merely relate such conceptions suggestively to themes explored earlier in the book.

ENVIRONMENTAL LAW AS PUBLIC LAW

The twentieth century saw a rapid expansion in environmental legislation, and the development of the first truly comprehensive legislative attempts at environmental regulation in its own right. These developments were, not unnaturally, accompanied by the general impression that the environment is primarily a public law issue: though the judicial resolution of disputes concerning conflicting property uses and nuisance claims elicited a body of principle of considerable subtlety and sophistication, it is only within the public-orientated language and aggregative mechanisms of statute law that a specific focus on environmental matters could emerge. This basic insight would gradually merge with the anachronistic belief that the early environmental statutes represented the *first* attempt to articulate environment-centred concerns within the law; and this, in turn, encouraged the emergence of a curiously narrow interpretation of the political and moral significance of statutory attempts to regulate the environment. Rather than situating the emergent statutory regimes within the rich vein of juristic thinking on the significance of property rights and collective interests, environmental lawyers would come to regard legal regulation of the

---

[17] NE Simmonds, *The Decline of Juridical Reason* (Manchester, MUP, 1984) 130–31.

environment as, at once, a distinctively *modern* development, and as a collection of mechanisms essentially pragmatic in effect and significance.

It was in the context of sanitation and pollution that the courts first began to recognise the fact that statutory provisions were in place to sideline the common law.[18] The process of what could, at its most radical, be viewed as a deliberate disengagement of the common law in this area, or, less purposively, as an incidental waning of its influence, was in any event very gradual. The motivating force behind the shrinking role of the common law in respect of pollution lay in increased judicial deference to statutory controls. As Farber and Frickey put it:

> In essence, the common law courts began viewing themselves as operating in the shadow of the legislature, especially where the legislature had erected statutes having a penumbral relationship with the common law problem at hand.[19]

This attitude was particularly apparent in the long line of cases arising from non-feasance[20] by sanitary authorities, resulting in pollution affecting individual property interests. Cases of this type began to emerge in numbers from the last quarter of the nineteenth century onwards. In many ways the kind of dispute involved can be viewed as a microcosm of the larger issues at stake. Essentially the facts pitted the public interest in sanitary provision against the individual interest in protecting property from damage and interference. The conflict manifested itself in this area in a particularly acute but also widespread form.

The most notable of these decisions with regard to the relationship between the common law of nuisance and the new statutory regime was that of the Court of Appeal in *Glossop v Heston and Isleworth Local Board* (1879).[21] Glossop, like Goldsmid and Harrington,[22] owned an estate that was adversely affected by sewage being allowed to drain into a watercourse running through it. The pollution was the result of the Local Authority's failure to make adequate sanitary provision upstream of Glossop's property. The angle from which the courts addressed the issues was, however, subtly different from that in other cases in that James LJ was particularly keen to divorce the damage sustained by Glossop from the traditional law of nuisance. He took the view that the complaint centred instead upon an alleged failure by the local authority to comply with the provisions of the Public Health Act 1875 and further that the duty owed by the

---

[18] This approach was not limited to the United Kingdom, it was also a feature of US law, see DA Farber and PP Frickey, 'In the Shadow of the Legislature: The Common Law in the Age of the New Public Law', [1991] *Michigan Law Review Symposium: The New Public Law* 875, 888 et seq.

[19] *Ibid* p 888. The philosophical currents which led to this point of view are discussed above in ch 3.

[20] Misfeasance on the other hand still attracted liability in the traditional way, ie under the rule in *Geddis v Proprietors of Bann Reservoirs* (1878) 3 App Cas 430, whereby there is no liability for damage caused by doing what is authorised by statute, provided that it is not done negligently. In this context activities will be done 'negligently' where the damage caused by doing them is avoidable.

[21] (1879) 12 Ch D 102.

[22] See ch 4.

local authority under that enactment was to the whole district and not to individual property owners within it. The reasoning behind this view is succinctly stated:

> If the neglect to perform a public duty for the whole of the district is to enable anybody and everybody to . . . file a distinct claim because he has not had the advantages he otherwise would be entitled to have if the Act had been properly put into execution, it appears to me that the country would be buying its immunity from nuisances at a very dear rate indeed by the substitution of a far more formidable nuisance in the litigation and expense that would be occasioned by opening such a door to litigious persons, or to persons who might be anxious to make profit and costs out of this Act . . .[23]

Given the minor legal industry that had sprung from profitable litigation and related 'negotiations' as part and parcel of the railway booms and their interference with private property in the public interest,[24] such fears were arguably well founded. Nevertheless, *Glossop* represents a fairly bald statement of the need to sublimate claims relating to individual interests to the broader public interest. It is highly significant that it was in the context of sanitation as a public utility in the purest sense[25] that the courts thought it necessary to take an early and decisive stand on curtailing the applicability of nuisance. The ultimate course adopted was to deny landowners affected by pollution as a result of non-feasance in the context of sanitation a remedy at common law, *Attorney-General v Guardians of the Poor Union of Dorking* (1882)[26] precluding relief in nuisance unless the authorities had actively caused the problem. *Hesketh v Birmingham Corporation* [1922][27] eventually made it clear that the only remedy for damage caused by non-feasance in a sanitation context would be that provided for by the statutory regime, in this case, as very often in others, an application to the Local Government Board under section 299 of the Public Health Act 1875 and an award of compensation by agreed by arbitration under section 308 of the same. In this type of approach, with a readiness to compensate for interference with individual interests replacing a right to their absolute vindication in cases where the public interest was also at stake, arguably lay the key to making the more traditional nuisance mechanism work in like contexts. A greater willingness to award damages in lieu of an injunction in nuisance cases themselves would arguably have served to retain the relevance of the common law action, which stood to be significantly eroded by clinging to the primacy of the injunction. Damages, although regarded in principle as a less satisfactory remedy than an injunction[28] would arguably have made a more appropriate

[23] at 115.
[24] Above ch 4.
[25] In contrast railways and electrical undertakings exhibited a hybrid identity as public utility and profit making private enterprise.
[26] (1881–82) LR 20 Ch D 595.
[27] [1922] 1 KB 260.
[28] See, for example, the discussion of *Shelfer*, above ch 4.

remedy of first resort in cases where there was a legitimate public interest at stake.

While the law of nuisance was effectively sidelined in regard to sanitation-based pollution nuisances at quite an early stage, the same cannot be said for the parallel strand of cases involving nuisances generated by industrial pollution. In these cases, the courts often favoured the individual over industry, even in cases involving the utilities and raising very obvious public benefit considerations. One example of such a case is *Farnworth v Lord Mayor, Aldermen and Citizens of Manchester* [1929].[29] In this case the defendant local authority was to all intents and purposes acting as an industrial operator in providing electricity to its area under a private act. The operation of the power station that it had con-structed for this purpose caused sulphur dioxide to be emitted on to the plain-tiff's neighbouring farmland causing serious physical damage. The plaintiff failed in his nuisance action at first instance. The Court of Appeal examined a number of wider issues. The first was the nature of statutory authorisation. There was, unusually,[30] no statutory compensation regime available under the statute in question, a situation that normally predicated judicial intervention to protect private interests from such unwarranted interference. However, the case was an awkward one for the courts in that there was no authority wherein an injunction had been granted or damages awarded in a situation where a public body had been given 'onerous statutory public duties'[31] to perform, unless the authority in question had acted ultra vires or negligently. In the instant case, Scrutton LJ took the view that the statute made it clear that Parliament had known of the pollution risks when authorising the power station. On the other hand, the defendants had not shown that the interference suffered by the plaintiff was the inevitable result of the carrying out of statutorily authorised operations and therefore those activities were not immune from challenge.

On the facts before it, the court was not, in the end, convinced that the authority had acted without negligence and so damages were granted along with a modified injunction, restraining the local authority from continuing to operate the power station unless and until all reasonable steps had been taken to terminate or mitigate the nuisance. This injunction was suspended for 12 months. The House of Lords affirmed the judgment by a majority, reflecting the controversial nature of the case.[32] Thus, once again, even in the context of a public utility provided by a local authority, the courts were still at least paying lip-service to the protection of individual property interests from unwarranted invasion by pollution, though at the same time trying to arrive at a practicable compromise in terms of protecting the broader public interest from the conse-quences of such a decision if time would allow a compromise to be reached.

[29] [1929] 1 KB 533.
[30] It is a time-honoured legal principle that compensation will be provided for those whose inter-ests are impaired by the exercise of a statutory power, and in the absence of such provision reasons for its absence are normally given.
[31] Scrutton, LJ, 559.
[32] *Farnworth v Lord Mayor, Aldermen and Citizens of Manchester* [1930] AC 171.

It would seem, however, that the willingness of the courts generally to give wide latitude to public authorities in exercising their statutory powers in the public interest could, on occasion, promote abuse by the less scrupulous, as in the case of *Wood v Conway Corporation* [1914].[33] In this case the defendant local authority operated a gasworks adjacent to the plaintiff's estate. Emissions from the works adversely affected a plantation on the plaintiff's property but not his house. He had complained to the defendant about the problem and it agreed to attempt to address the matter, but instead extended the works closer to the plaintiff's property and increased the scale of its operations. The plaintiff succeeded in his claim for damages and an injunction at first instance. The defendant's appeal was in part based on the fact that it was under a statutory obligation to supply gas. The Court of Appeal was most unsympathetic to the defendant's request that the court exercise its discretion to award damages in lieu of an injunction, despite the defendant's argument that granting an injunction to the plaintiff would cause it hardship. The court characterised what the defendant sought as an attempt to sanction a solution that would enable it to 'buy the right to continue the nuisance.'[34] Buckley LJ succinctly stated the Court's position on this line of argument:

> It does not lie in their mouth to say that they will be exposed to considerable expense if after erecting these additional buildings they have to go elsewhere. If the result is an unfortunate one for them, they have brought it on themselves.[35]

While all of the judges alluded to the problems that granting an injunction would pose the defendant (Channell J in particular referring to the fact that the pecuniary costs that it would encounter would greatly exceed that of the damage sustained by the plaintiff) they regarded it necessary, in order to do justice between the parties, to grant the injunction sought. *Wood* then demonstrates that, while as a general rule the courts would, if possible, find a way to try to accommodate the public interest while ensuring a degree of vindication for adversely affected individuals in the context of activities carried on in the public interest, this did not give statutory undertakers *carte blanche* to behave as they chose and simply pay damages or compensation: the threat of the injunction remained a potent one. This was certainly true in another case involving sewage pollution of the River Derwent,[36] *Pride of Derby and Derbyshire Angling Association Ltd v British Celanese Ltd* [1952],[37] in which the plaintiff angling association obtained an injunction and damages in respect of interference with its interests in the river by untreated effluent. This case also dealt a blow to the misfeasance/non-feasance distinction in a sanitation context. The court effectively went back to basics and determined that the central question

---

[33] [1914] 2 Ch 47.
[34] Cozens-Hardy MR, at 56.
[35] at 59–60.
[36] See the *Harrington* case, above.
[37] [1953] 1 Ch 149.

regarding liability for nuisance in a statutory context lay in identifying whether the nuisance in question was both contemplated and authorised by the applicable statute.

Nuisance, of course, often arose in situations that did not involve disputes between public authorities and individuals, but ostensibly simpler conflicts of a more traditional kind between neighbouring private landowners. One example of such a dispute arose in the Privy Council decision of *Stollmeyer v Trinidad Lake Petroleum Company Ltd* [1918].[38] The case partly involved the pollution of a seasonal rainfall-fed watercourse by oil from the defendant's petrochemical operations. These activities constituted the sole industry in the area. The plaintiffs were riparian owners of land downstream from the defendants, the land being unsuitable for agriculture and so unused. Furthermore, the plaintiffs had not sustained any pecuniary damage as a result of the contamination. The courts in Trinidad had dismissed the plaintiff's actions for damages and an injunction, not least fearing the effect that such remedies would have on industry. The Privy Council however took the view that the plaintiff's rights *were* being infringed and that they were therefore entitled to relief. However, in the circumstances, the relief granted was limited and the plaintiff's injunction was suspended for a two-year period to allow the defendant to amend its operations, and the defendants were authorised to apply for a further suspension if necessary. In addition, the defendants gave an undertaking to pay damages as determined by a court of first instance to cover any pecuniary loss sustained by the plaintiff in the interim.

Halsey v Esso Petroleum Co Ltd [1961][39] also involved nuisance originating in the petrochemical industry, though in a very different context. It concerned the 24-hour operation of an ESSO oil-processing plant situated adjacently to a residential area, causing atmospheric and noise pollution. The courts found that a nuisance did exist, but the relief granted was carefully tailored to ensure that the defendant's activities could continue provided that justice was also done to the plaintiff. In this case the defendant was acting to ameliorate the nuisance and although damages were paid for nuisance, injunctive relief was delayed in order to allow them to continue to carry out works on the site.

The development of statute law relating to industrial operations, and its relationship to private property rights, was a complex one; but in contrast to the sanitation context, it was not one that automatically favoured community interests in all cases. This was certainly the situation where private acts authorising individual industrial plants were concerned, but just as significant was the impact of the more generally applicable pollution control legislation. The rationale underpinning that regime lay in minimising or preventing pollution in the interests of public health, rather than for environmental reasons as such. Improvements in environmental quality were of course sought under pollution

[38] [1918] AC 485.
[39] [1961] 2 All ER 145.

control regimes, but for their instrumental significance rather than for their own sake. This approach prevailed as late as COPA. Protection of the environment in its own right had to wait until the EPA 1990.

The development of regulatory regimes was rather uneven across the three major environmental *fora*, with the atmosphere enjoying the first and most sophisticated protective regimes. The Alkali Act 1863, despite being the first piece of legislation of its kind, represents perhaps the classic example of the application of a command-and-control approach to the regulation of industrial pollution. As noted in chapter three, the Act introduced scientifically-based control, carried out on a nationwide basis by a professional inspectorate, and its central approach remains the basis of modern pollution control regimes. In principle, statutory regulation of polluting enterprises and activities offered manifold advantages over the earlier, and inevitably more particularised, common law approach. The most significant innovation that a regulatory approach offered was its proactive nature: by requiring that emissions be prevented or minimised, such regimes largely served to prevent pollution problems, including nuisances, from arising in the first place. They also offered a uniformity of approach, and were not dependent on actions based around private property rights and the lottery of litigation in delivering basic environmental quality in the public interest.

Despite its many advantages, statutory regulation was problematic in a number of respects. Not least of these was the fact that it was, at best, partial in its coverage. The Alkali Act, for example, covered acidic emissions but did not deal with the equally problematic proliferation of industrial smoke.[40] The Alkali Act regime itself was subsequently augmented, in particular by the introduction of the Best Practicable Means concept in the Alkali Act 1874, and numerous other updating provisions were consolidated in the Alkali etc. Works Regulation Act 1906. This Act remained in place for the better part of a century until it was replaced by the ultimately short-lived integrated pollution control and local authority air pollution control regimes under Part I of the Environmental Protection Act 1990.[41] Thus, even emissions which affected a single environmental medium were and are subject to a number of different regulatory regimes and to a mixture of centralised[42] and local authority[43] control based, at least in part, on the complexity of the emissions in question.

A rather more ambitious but ultimately unworkable approach was taken to water pollution, in the form of an absolute prohibition contained in the Rivers

---

[40] This class of emission was covered, by separate regimes, including the Smoke Nuisance Abatement (Metropolis) Act 1853. National controls for smoke emissions were not introduced until the Clean Air Act 1956.

[41] These regimes are under the process of being replaced by the Pollution Prevention and Control Act 1999 and the Pollution Prevention and Control (England and Wales) Regulations 2000 SI 2000/1973, giving effect to the Directive Concerning Integrated Prevention of Environmental Pollution (the IPPC Directive) 96/61/EC OJ No. L 257.

[42] For industrial emissions.

[43] For emissions of smoke.

Prevention of Pollution Act 1876. A more feasible regime governing aquatic pollution was eventually introduced in the Rivers (Prevention of Pollution) Act 1951. The new law was more akin to that governing emissions to the atmosphere, and applied to both industrial releases and sewage. Even then, the control regime was incomplete. Tidal waters, estuaries and groundwater were only subjected to regulatory intervention in 1960[44] and 1963[45] respectively. While the Control of Pollution Act 1974 seemed on paper to offer much-needed rationalisation for this aspect of environmental regulation, it was implemented only slowly and partially, and this area of law remained problematic in many respects. Privatisation of the water industry in the Water Act 1989 provided the opportunity to modernise the regulatory regime, and separation of regulatory concerns in the Water Resources Act 1991 ultimately put in place a consolidated and coherent system that can finally stand comparison with the more natural atmospheric pollution control regime.

If progress in establishing a national regime for regulating the aquatic environment was uninspiring, attempts to govern pollution to land on this scale were non-existent until the introduction of a rudimentary waste licensing regime under Part 1 of the Control of Pollution Act 1974. As might be expected of the first attempt to apply a traditional 'command-and-control' regulatory system to waste issues, the regime was flawed in many respects.[46] Gaps in the COPA regime included the pre-disposal control over production, storage, carriage, transport, and treatment of waste, and failure to ensure environmental safeguards for landfill sites. On a more profound level, COPA caused problems by placing core regulatory responsibility in the hands of local authorities. Given the dispersed nature of the sector to be regulated and the comparatively limited understanding, at the time, of the scale and complexity of the problems to be addressed, and the fact that local authorities had long been relied on as environmental regulators in the context of basic air pollution, this approach was perhaps understandable but it nonetheless proved to be disastrous. The situation was exacerbated by a lack of central government guidance to local authorities. The fatal flaw however lay in the fact that, in the distinctive waste context, local authorities were placed in an impossible position by their operational responsibilities for waste disposal, on the one hand, and their regulatory role on the other. This created what has become known as the 'poacher/gamekeeper' dichotomy, which points to the huge difficulties inherent in a split regulated/regulator status. As a result of these major problems, the COPA regime soon proved insufficient as increased understanding of waste issues emerged.

A new regime was eventually introduced in response to the inadequacies of COPA, under Part II of the Environmental Protection Act 1990. Significant developments included: a new, wider, waste management licence; the

---

[44] Clean Rivers (Estuaries and Tidal Waters) Act 1960.
[45] Water Resources Act 1963.
[46] For a full discussion of the problems of Control of Pollution Act in this regard see the House of Commons Environment Committee Second Report, Toxic Waste (1988–98 Session).

imposition of new technical and financial qualifications for licence holders; new controls on landfill sites, both during their active life and following closure; new controls for contaminated land;[47] and new regulatory arrangements aimed at tackling the poacher/gamekeeper problems which had existed under COPA.[48] Also included was the imposition of a new duty of care incumbent upon all involved in the waste chain, as well as increased priority and support for recycling.

Whilst the development of statutory regimes undoubtedly extended both the range and depth of legal responses to environmental problems which are difficult to tackle at common law, it has not been an unalloyed success. Waste disposal and other (especially industrial) land uses often leave behind a legacy of soil contamination. The problems of soil contamination are manifold and particularly difficult to remedy. They also raise particularly acute problems at the nexus between environmental law and property law. The intractability of such problems is illustrated by the problematic and brief life of section 61 of the EPA 1990 relating to closed landfill sites. The provision ostensibly allowed regulatory authorities to inspect and clean up closed landfill sites, a recognition of the continuing ability of such sites to pose a serious pollution threat. To this end, section 61 contained the strongest powers in modern UK environmental law—but it was never brought into force and was finally repealed by the Environment Act 1995 in response to prolonged and widespread pressure by the property sector. Broader contaminated land concerns have scarcely fared better. Admittedly, the issue does pose peculiar regulatory problems, not least in the fact that land is usually in private ownership and is a major economic resource.

Notwithstanding such difficulties, it is often (correctly) believed that regulatory regimes can articulate and pursue policies and welfare-orientated strategies which are incapable of expression within the dispute-orientated confines of the common law. Such observations contribute considerably to the view that environmental protection can only emerge as a distinctive concern within the sphere of a statutory regime. Yet even within the context of such a regime, the common law is not redundant as an instrument of environmental regulation. Take the example of emissions: though environmental regulation of emissions and polluting activities certainly serves to curtail the conduct of industry, it does not, on the whole, interfere with the traditional property rights of industrialists as such. Instead the law has been used at least partially to internalise the undesirable externalities of pollution by imposing the costs of addressing the problem on those creating it. The operation of regulated industrial processes does, however, often interfere with the interests of neighbouring landowners. On the whole, statutory pollution control schemes do not address, or do so only minimally, the

---

[47] The proposed regime proved abortive and, despite a number of attempts to revive it, a new approach was deemed necessary and included in the Environment Act 1995.

[48] These measures did not go far enough to ensure a convincing regulatory regime and the Environment Act 1995 made significant changes to the regulatory landscape by giving the Environment Agency a clear role in governing waste regulation, taking over from local authorities.

issue of compensating individuals for such interference. This is one important consequence of the public interest focus of regulatory systems. For this reason there were and indeed are plenty of opportunities for common law litigation.

Innovative litigation has also been generated by the potential of state-sanctioned pollution interference with the interests of individuals in public law proceedings. A clear example of this can be found in *R v The Environment Agency and Redland Aggregates Ltd, ex p Gibson*,[49] where a judicial review was raised in respect of the Environment Agency's decision to grant variations on IPC authorisations under section 11 of the EPA. Gibson lived near the site and wished to challenge the Agency's decision to allow Redland to use Substitute Liquid Fuels (SLF) instead of petcoke. The change actually represented an environmental improvement on the petcoke originally employed, and the application failed as the Agency was within its statutory powers in granting the variation.

The Public-Private Dichotomy Reconsidered

A picture of environmental law emerges from these developments which is of some interest to the scholar who wishes to make sense of the changing face of legal attempts to regulate the environment. Private rights had always been underpinned by public interests (for private rights could not emerge except through a collective concern with stability and mutual forbearance);[50] but a systematic expression of underpinning public interests was difficult to articulate within the dispute-centred language of the common law. The development of statutory regimes made it much easier to state clearly the interests involved, yet a full expression of those interests, and of the relationship between private rights and collective welfare, required the interpretation of statutory provisions against the background of established ideas about the nature of private rights and justice implicit in doctrinal principle. The legal historian who regards the emergence of statutory controls as signifying a wholesale *replacement* of ideas about the limits of proprietary interests, and the social control of those interests, with fixed rules aimed at the regulation of specific consequences of property use, misunderstands the significance of the developments in legal and political thinking which made the emergence of those controls a possibility. Yet it is such a history that is implicit in the majority of environmental law textbooks and scholarly discussions.

The sustained juristic speculation upon the nature of property rights and justice, which began in its modern form in the eighteenth century, and continued in the nineteenth, provides the intellectual context within which the significance of the early environmental statutes must be understood. While in many ways altering received views about entitlements and the extent of collective interests,

---

[49] 8 May 1998.
[50] See the earlier discussion in the first section of this chapter.

environmental law continues to move within the concepts and categories established by the doctrinal structures of private law. Those doctrinal categories were *themselves* a response to the very complex ideas, first explored systematically by writers such as Locke, on the meaning and relationship between property, rights and nature. The juristic language of the common law, as well as its dispute-focused character, made it particularly suited to exploring those issues in the context of disputes between *private* owners, but less well-suited to a full reflective consideration of the boundaries between private rights and public interests: such matters hence received their most sophisticated discussion, at common law, in the context of tort rather than property law.

The doctrinal structures of private law made a consideration of the relative boundaries of private entitlement and collective interests at once inevitable and pressing. As noted earlier, the juristic category of 'private right' requires explication in the context of underpinning collective interests in stable social structures of mutual forbearance, toleration and respect. Only against the background of stable social interests and expectations can the realm of private right have genuine meaning. The dispute-focused language and structure of the common law encouraged a view of private entitlement as fundamentally in collision with collective interests, although the basic juristic concepts with which the private lawyer worked continued to reflect the political assumptions of writers such as Hobbes and Locke, for whom the public and private realms were mutually dependent and mutually explicable. Statutory engagement with private entitlement and collective welfare, in the shape of environmental regulations, is an heir to these political questions. If the doctrinal categories of the common law are a reflection of a society's political form, then a statutory framework represents its deliberate political choices. Just as statutory provisions set specific limits to private property rights, property rights cannot emerge except through sustained deliberation on the form of social life and the articulation of collective interests through law. Regulatory regimes thus reflect, even if they do not overtly express, profound conceptions against which are made the deliberate moral and political choices that define and determine the nature of the polity. The environmental lawyer must be understood as moving within, rather than separately from, these fundamental questions, and hence as invoking profound ideas about the extent and nature of rights, ownership and responsibility.

The modern environmental lawyer nevertheless interprets the significance of statutory provisions very narrowly. Environmental law is perceived, on one level, as a series of attempts to resolve clashes between public and private interests as they arise. Such measures are hence viewed as constituting an essentially piecemeal response to social problems, politically significant only insofar as they are connected with individual freedom and principles of harm, and not requiring systematic explanation according to deeper moral values. The narrowing of the explanatory context of environmental legislation has thus, in turn, led to a position in which the deeper political commitments of environmental law are almost wholly submerged beneath the utilitarian language and patterns of thought which are readily associated with aggregative legislation.[51] This dimension to environmental thinking in law is particularly evident in the background to the House of Lords decision in *Cambridge Water*.

Cambridge Water presents a good example of the way in which complex and subtle doctrinal questions raised by the legal regulation of the environment have largely become questions about the delineation and application of distinct policies. Doctrinal exposition tends to require the elaboration of bodies of juristic principle in the context of underlying moral values and ideas; whereas the application of policies is most often a matter of the clarification and delineation of technical rules, distinctions and definitions.[52] For the first half of the twentieth century and beyond, the courts employed the law of nuisance with flexibility and vision in order to try to do justice to extremely complex claims relating to environmental pollution and conflicting individual and public interests. Unfortunately, more recent case law shows that the law of nuisance is in danger of becoming a dead letter as the courts become increasingly unwilling to allow it its place alongside negligence and statutory provision in the mosaic of legal techniques available to address such issues. Arguably no case has ever given greater cause for concern in this regard than that of *Cambridge Water Company v Eastern Counties Leather* [1994][53] which represents possibly the most profound crisis that the law of nuisance has ever faced, threatening not only its viability, but even its very identity as an independent tort. This crisis had been a long time coming: as negligence came to dominate the whole of the law of torts during the twentieth century, its endless flexibility enabled it effectively to colonise others areas of law; and it was perhaps inevitable that the law of nuisance would eventually face the same fate.

At one time it was possible to treat negligence and nuisance as entirely separate from one another: the focus in negligence lying in how a defendant acted, the focus in nuisance on the result of a defendant's actions in relation to the plaintiff's protected interests. It remains true that negligence as such is not relevant in nuisance, in that even the defendant's best efforts to avoid damage to the plaintiff will not allow him to escape liability if unreasonable interference with the plaintiff's interests occurs. However, given the all-prevailing nature of the tort of negligence, and the fact that nuisance and negligence can also, on occasion, subsist on the same facts, it was perhaps inevitable that the ideas underpinning negligence should cross the boundary into nuisance, as had happened with regard to the notions of fault and foreseeability. The law in this area was the cause of some confusion for many years, as evidenced by the words of Lord

---

[51] See above ch 3.

[52] The lack of any rigid distinction between legal principle and moral values does not, in this context, presuppose a rejection of legal positivism: the positivist does not necessarily deny that a legal system's criteria of recognition involve reference to moral criteria; only that it necessarily involves such reference.

[53] [1994] 1 All ER 53.

Reid in *Overseas Tankship (UK) v Miller Steamship Co The Wagon Mound (No 2)* [1967]:[54]

> It is quite true that negligence is not an essential element in nuisance. Nuisance is a term used to cover a wide variety of tortious acts , and in many negligence in the narrow sense is not essential . . . fault of some kind is almost always necessary, and generally involves foreseeability.

Cambridge Water involved the chemical contamination of an aquifer by neighbouring tanneries over many years. The plaintiff's business comprised the extraction of this water and its supply for human consumption, until it was found to be contaminated and unfit for drinking under EC law. As a result the plaintiff had to find an alternative source of supply in order to fulfil its contractual obligations. The plaintiff brought an action under several heads, including nuisance and under the rule in *Rylands v Fletcher*. In disposing of the nuisance claim, the House of Lords brought the issue of foreseeability in nuisance centre stage. Lord Goff commented on this specific point:

> . . . it is still the law [as far as nuisance is concerned] that the fact that the defendant has taken all reasonable care will not itself exonerate him from liability . . . But it by no means follows the defendant should be held liable for damage of a type which he could not reasonable foresee; and the development of the law of negligence . . . points towards a requirement that such foreseeability should be a prerequisite of liability for nuisance, as it is for liability in negligence.

The common law in this area was left in poor shape by the *Cambridge Water* ruling, as the line between nuisance and negligence was eroded to the point of non-existence. This became very apparent in the extremely complex case of *Yorkshire Water Services Ltd v Sun Alliance London Insurance Plc* [1997],[55] a case that was also of great interest in explicitly raising the link between statutory pollution control and liability at common law and insurance. The case involved the collapse of the Yorkshire Water's sewage sludge tip, blocking a nearby river, and causing water pollution necessitating action by the National Rivers Authority, damaging the defendant's sewage works and interfering with the activities of a number of neighbouring businesses. Several of the latter took precautions to prevent flooding to their properties. The case centred on contested liability under Yorkshire Water's insurance policy with Sun Alliance and a number of technical arguments based on exclusion clauses. The facts on the ground however concerned nuisance and negligence. No liability was found on most of the claims in nuisance since expenses undertaken for the purposes of preventative action are not recoverable in that tort.[56] These expenses were not recoverable in negligence either, as only special circumstances will justify the imposition of liability for pure economic loss. No claim for statutory compen-

---

[54] [1967] 1 AC 617.
[55] [1997] 2 Lloyd's Rep 21.
[56] *Midland Bank v Bardgrove* (1992) 60 BLR 1.

sation under section 180 of the Water Resources Act was viable on the facts, as Yorkshire Water had made alternative arrangements for dealing with the effluent produced by the neighbouring businesses. The case creates a damaging precedent in a number of ways, not least in acting as a disincentive to mitigate. The NRA's claims too concerned preventative works and based in nuisance and negligence and failed for the reasons already discussed and due to a lack of proprietary interest in respect of the former.[57] One result of the *Yorkshire Water* case is that it is clear that regulators can only recover in respect of expenses undertaken to protect the environment through statutory provisions[58] and in this case Yorkshire Water's insurance policy excluded liability in respect of claims based on statutory duties or requirements. On the whole, the approach adopted by the court in *Yorkshire Water* is decidedly limiting in respect of using either nuisance or negligence to tackle environmental pollution-related problems.

The approach in *Cambridge Water* and subsequent cases served to blur further the dividing line, such as it was, between nuisance and negligence to the detriment of the former. This view is borne out by the difficulty encountered by plaintiffs attempting to sue in nuisance in subsequent case law. The issue proved central in *Savage v Fairclough* [1999][59] in which the plaintiffs sustained contamination to their water supply as a result of the defendants' spreading of organic and chemical fertilisers on their neighbouring farm.[60] The plaintiffs failed at first instance because, having regard to good agricultural practice and applying the test of the 'hypothetical good farmer', the defendants could not have foreseen that their activities would give rise to a real risk of contaminating the plaintiffs' water supply. The Court of Appeal upheld this ruling, Mummery J concluding that the evidence did not, in spite of a less than blameless record of behaviour on the part of the defendants, establish fault on their part. The view adopted towards the foreseeability question was that it was necessary to ascertain, first, whether the defendants were aware that contamination was being caused and, second, whether, if they were aware, they could have carried on with their activities regardless. The reasoning adopted in the case is less than robust in this respect and also in failing adequately to distinguish between foreseeability and causation issues when determining liability.

The picture of nuisance cases in the nineteenth and early twentieth centuries shows the courts very often dealing with hugely complex issues of public and private interest and the nexus between statute and common law in a nuanced and highly sophisticated way. Although it became increasingly clear as the nineteenth century progressed that statute law was moving centre stage in the battle

---

[57] *Hunter v Canary Wharf Ltd London Docklands Development Corporation* [1997] 2 All ER 426.

[58] In this case under s 161 of the Water Resources Act 1991.

[59] Transcript (Smith Bernal) 30 July 1999.

[60] For the sake of argument, agriculture is included within the definition of industry in this case, a view that is certainly borne out by the impact of intensive farming practices which have increasingly come to be regulated in a fashion much more akin to that of other polluting activities.

against pollution, the attitude of the courts allowed the common law to remain a vibrant and viable option in suitable fact situations. In the latter part of the twentieth century the courts have not adopted the same robust approach, with the law of negligence and, to an even greater degree, statute law gaining ever greater precedence, and the law of nuisance effectively being squeezed out. This gives cause for concern on a number of levels, not least with the often insurmountable difficulties encountered in establishing causation in nuisance in environmental pollution cases.[61] Statutory regimes do not necessarily engage with the needs of the individual in respect of environmental pollution, geared as they are to protecting the public interest. The instruments in question are often narrower in their focus than the law of nuisance, as for example in the case of *Nash v Parkinson Cowan* (1961)[62] and the case ultimately turns on whether the statute in question is open to an interpretation that favours the individual, inevitably a comparatively rare occurrence as demonstrated by *Belfast City Council v Irish Football Association* [1988].[63]

The Return of the Common Law

All in all a rather gloomy picture of the future of the common law in respect of nuisances involving environmental pollution had emerged by the latter part of the twentieth century, and there appeared to be little cause for optimism. However the common law, as is its wont, is currently enjoying a somewhat unexpected resurgence, though the reasons for this revival lie in the changing statutory context, rather than in the common law itself: this has heralded, to some extent, the return of the common law as an interpretative background to statute law. The impetus for the resurrection of liability in nuisance in particular comes from the impact of two major constitutional changes in the legal landscape. First privatisation, the legacy of Thatcherism, changed the shape of public service delivery in the UK almost beyond recognition and this has in turn reopened questions about the nature of the relationship between the public interest and individual interest, and the role of the law in adjudicating between them. From the nineteenth century onwards, the courts had taken the view that public authorities, in carrying out statutory duties, would not be liable for damage caused to individuals by environmental pollution in nuisance without negligence on their part. This approach was first used in highway cases in the eighteenth century, *Russell v The Men of Devon* (1788)[64] which proceeded on the principle that the highway was a public resource and the public was responsible for it, but that no action lay against the public for damage sustained by an

---

[61] See K Morrow, 'Nuisance and Environmental Protection', in J Lowry and R Edmunds (eds), *Environmental Protection and the Common Law* (Oxford, Hart Publishing, 2000) 139–59.

[62] (1961) 105 SJ 323.

[63] (1988) 11 NIJB 85.

[64] (1788) 2 TR 667.

individual due to its disrepair. In the nineteenth century, the courts adapted the *Russell* approach to a variety of areas involving purely public utilities such as water and sewerage services, and mixed commercial and public services such as gas and electricity supply, as discussed in chapter three. The line of authorities beginning with *Glossop v Heston and Isleworth Local Board* (1879)[65] and culminating in the ruling in *Robinson v Mayor and Corporation of the Borough of Workington* [1897][66] determined that the only route to address pollution due to non-feasance by a public authority in providing sewerage services was through statutory mechanisms, and this approach was assumed to have conclusively dealt with the matter.

In retrospect, privatisation should have provided ample opportunity, and perhaps the necessity, for a reassessment of the relationship between the public and private interest in the context of sanitation issues. In *British Waterways v Severn Trent Water* [2002][67] the Court of Appeal seemed to be getting to grips with the notion that privatised utilities should be exposed to more intense scrutiny than the public authorities which had previously carried out similar tasks. The case involved Severn Trent's insistence that it could continue to discharge through its pipes into a British Waterways watercourse without permission and without paying compensation. Severn Trent succeeded at first instance but in the Court of Appeal the judges refused to imply a power to discharge water into a watercourse without compensating persons who suffered loss or damage under section 159 of the Water Resources Act 1991. The reasoning implicit in this seems to be that the privatised utilities act primarily for commercial gain rather than solely in the public interest, even if, in carrying out their functions, they do provide great benefit to the public. Nonetheless, privatisation had shifted the focus of discussion in this area from situations in which affected individuals are pitting themselves against the public interest when they act to tackle damage to their property caused by a sanitation based nuisance, to one where two conflicting private interests are at stake (though there are of course more complex communal interests at play behind the scenes).

It is interesting that the Court of Appeal in the *British Waterways* case took a very narrow view of what powers it would be appropriate to imply in circumstances involving a commercialised utility context. This stands in fairly stark contrast to the much more generous approach towards public authorities carrying out similar functions adopted in nineteenth century case law such as *Durrant v Branksome Union District Council* [1897][68] (which was regarded as decisive by Arden J at first instance in *British Waterways* itself). The Court of Appeal, having had thorough regard to the context of the 1991 Act and in particular the absence of a compensation provision under section 159 allowed British Waterways's appeal against the first instance decision allowing Severn Trent to

[65] (1879) 12 Ch D 102.
[66] [1897] 1 QB 619.
[67] [2002] Ch 25.
[68] [1897] 2 Ch 291.

discharge into its watercourse without permission. The first instance decision sat plumb with nineteenth century case law but the Court of Appeal made serious adjustments to the traditional approach. The crux of the matter was succinctly dealt with by Chadwick LJ: he took the view that it was highly unlikely that Parliament would have intended to allow sewerage undertakers to discharge without paying for the facility. Once again, in the context of sanitation nuisances, even where broader communal interests are at stake, the courts will protect individual property interests, at least by the provision of compensation for interference endured as a result. This approach chimes with that adopted by the European Court of Human Rights in *S v France* (1990).[69]

Further evidence of a newly revitalised role for the law of nuisance, extending beyond the utilities sector, is to be found in the Court of Appeal decision in *Bybrook Barn Centre Ltd v Kent County Council* [2001].[70] This case involved flooding to the claimant's garden centre caused by the respondent's failure to widen a culvert for which it was responsible as highway authority. The clearance capacity of the culvert had become inadequate due to increased water volumes caused by development pressure upstream. The evidence suggested that the respondent had known of the problem for a number of years, knew of the cost of rectifying the situation (substantial but not prohibitive for a public authority) but had elected to do nothing about it. Bybrook's nuisance claim was dismissed at first instance[71] but was allowed by the Court of Appeal. The basis upon which liability was imposed was founded on the line of authority begun by *Sedleigh-Denfield v O'Callaghan* [1940][72] and developed in *Goldman v Hargrave* [1967][73] and *Leakey v National Trust* [1980].[74] The respondent's attempt to rely on the lines of authority exemplified by the ruling in *Glossop v Heston and Isleworth Local Board* (1879)[75] and *Stovin v Wise* [1996],[76] in order to avoid liability, proved unavailing. The court took the view that there was nothing in the existing law that protected statutory authorities from liability in nuisance in situations where a private individual would be liable. In addition in this particular fact situation there was nothing in the applicable statutes to prevent the imposition of liability. Applying *Sedleigh-Denfield, Goldman* and *Leakey*, Waller LJ, giving the judgment for the court, stated:

> A defendant is not entitled simply to say that something was not causing a nuisance when it came on his land or when it was constructed and thus no liability can be

---

[69] (1990) 65 DR 250. See below.
[70] [2001] LGR 239.
[71] Although the claim in this case was framed in nuisance, on the facts there was considerable overlap with negligence.
[72] [1940] AC 880.
[73] [1967] 1 AC 645 PC.
[74] [1980] QB 485.
[75] (1879) 12 Ch D 102.
[76] [1996] AC 923. This judgment of Browne–Wilkinson LJ in this case states the rules for liability of public authorities in negligence.

imposed on him. A defendant's duty is to do that which it is reasonable for him to do.[77]

Here the court gave considerable weight to the fact that the case involved an adverse impact on a private landowner and that the local authority could have dealt with the problem at some cost but without much difficulty. The approach adopted in *Bybrook* showed a positive willingness on the part of the court to rejuvenate the law of nuisance by looking in a new way at older authorities and drawing out aspects of them.

Encouraging though these developments are, they would not necessarily have served to revive the law of nuisance without the Human Rights Act 1998 providing an additional impetus for change. On the face of it, it would have appeared that the potential of the Human Rights Act to affect the mainstream nuisance law was quite limited, in that the Act limits the imposition of obligations to public authorities. However, through a somewhat indirect route the Human Rights Act is proving to be more influential in the sphere of nuisance than a surface reading of the legislation would suggest. The law is developing in this fashion due to the fact that the courts themselves, as public authorities, are under an obligation imposed by section 6(1) of the Act to fulfil its purposes. The effect of this obligation came to the fore in *Douglas v Hello* [2001],[78] a case involving much more obvious human rights issues of alleged interference with privacy and breach of confidence. In the *Douglas* case Keene LJ took the view that the courts' obligations under the Human Rights Act include 'interpreting and developing the common law.'[79] But, he went on to say, this approach prevailed 'even where no public authority is a party to the litigation.'[80] While this approach appears to sit ill with the Human Rights Act on its face, and even with the European Convention for the Protection of Human Rights and Fundamental Freedoms (ECHR)[81] itself, which is ostensibly geared at placing obligations on states parties, it is actually very much in harmony with Convention jurisprudence, which is also to be given effect under sections 2 and 6 the Act. The ramifications of this are considered by Brooke LJ,[82] discussing the ruling of the European Court of Human Rights in *A v UK* (1998),[83] a case brought under Article 3 of the Convention[84] by a child who had been beaten by his stepfather with a garden cane. On the face of it, this case simply involved an action between two individuals, but the European Court of Human Rights was of the opinion that the obligation placed on signatory states by Article 1 of the Convention, to secure convention rights and freedoms for all inhabitants of

---

[77] Para 42.
[78] [2001] 2 All ER 289.
[79] Para 166.
[80] *Ibid.*
[81] 4 November 1950; TS 71 (1953); Cmd 8969.
[82] Para 81 et seq.
[83] (1998) 5 BHRC 137.
[84] Right to freedom from torture, inhuman and degrading treatment.

their jurisdictions, extended to taking the necessary measures to ensure these in practice. In addition, in *A v UK* it was specifically what Brooke referred to as 'the deficiencies of the common law'[85] that were deemed to put the UK in violation of its Convention obligations.

The Court in *Douglas* went on to refer to some of the jurisprudence involving Article 8.1,[86] in particular *X v The Netherlands* (1985)[87] and *Lopez Ostra v Spain* (1994)[88] and these cases in particular are of great potential relevance to the future development of the law of nuisance. In *X v The Netherlands* the European Court of Human Rights stated:

> The Court recalls that although the object of Article 8 is essentially that of protecting the individual against arbitrary interference by the public authorities, it does not merely compel the State to abstain from such interference: in addition to this primarily negative obligation, there may be positive obligations inherent in an effective respect for private or family life. These obligations may involve the adoption of measures designed to respect for private life even in the sphere of the relations of individuals between themselves.[89]

It would seem therefore that the approach adopted in Convention jurisprudence, and the receptive and even expansive attitude of the UK courts towards it exhibited in *Douglas*, has the potential to be very far reaching indeed, not least in respect of nuisance. The *Douglas* case is also significant in that it shows the potential of human rights based litigation to re-open issues of law previously regarded as settled at common law,[90] and this approach has proved highly influential in subsequent cases. This would seem to be borne out in the case of *McKenna v British Aluminium Ltd* [2002].[91] The *McKenna* case involved an attempt by a number of claimants to bring a claim in nuisance against the respondent in respect of noise, emissions and invasions of privacy to their property caused by their neighbouring factory. The claimants were children and lacked proprietary interests in the affected property. The claimants accepted that, on the basis of the ruling in *Hunter v Canary Wharf* [1997],[92] they could not have a claim in nuisance, but they brought their action instead under the Human Rights Act with reference to 'a common law tort analogous to nuisance'[93] to protect their rights under Article 8.1 of the ECHR, which are not dependent on any proprietary interest in land. The respondent applied to have

---

[85] *Douglas v Hello* [2001] 2 All ER 289, para 86.
[86] Right to respect for private and family life.
[87] (1985) 8 EHRR 235.
[88] (1994) 20 EHRR 277.
[89] Para 23.
[90] For example, in *Kaye v Robertson* [1991] FSR 62 it was held that there was no right to privacy in UK law, Brooke and Keene LJJ stated obiter in Douglas that the case would have been unlikely to have been decided in the same was following the passing of the Human Rights Act at paras 61 and 167 respectively.
[91] [2002] Env LR 30.
[92] [1997] 2 All ER 426.
[93] Quoted from the claimant's pleading p 17 of the case transcript.

the claim struck, but Neuberger J refused to do so on the basis that the law in this area is currently in a state of development and that it was 'a matter of speculation and uncertainty'[94] whether the courts would choose to effect that development through nuisance, strict liability, negligence or human rights law. He referred to *Douglas v Hello* and the obligation of the court to develop the common law in harmony with the ECHR and went on to cite *Aston Cantlow PCC v Wallbank* [2001][95] as an example of this approach in action. Neuberger J went on to point out the inherent limitations of the *Hunter* and *Cambridge Water* cases, rightly pointing out that these identify claims in nuisance and under the rule in *Rylands v Fletcher* as property claims, rather than claims for personal injury or personal damage. However, the judge went on to add the following telling comment:

> . . . there is a real possibility of the court concluding that in light of the different landscape, namely Article 8.1 now being effectively part of our law, it is necessary to extend or change the law, even though, in circumstances where the Convention was no part of English law, the majority of the House of Lords thought otherwise.[96]

Such comments certainly underline the profound potential impact of the Human Rights Act and the ECHR in this area. They also point to a possible mutation of nuisance from a straightforward device to protect interests in property law to a hybrid concept based on occupation interests and the rights attached to them, which is closely related to the approach adopted by Lord Cooke in his innovative and challenging minority speech in *Hunter*. Lord Cooke, in arriving at his conclusion that the law of nuisance should serve to protect the interests of those resident in affected property, based on a 'right of occupation', in the absence of a proprietary interest, drew on the Canadian authority of *Motherwell v Motherwell* (1976)[97] and the Court of Appeal decision in *Khorasandjian v Bush* [1993].[98] Significantly, Lord Cooke also took into account broader legal developments, such as the UN Convention on the Rights of the Child[99] (in particular Article 16[100]), the Universal Declaration of Human Rights[101] (in particular Article 12) and the ECHR (in particular Article 8). He saw such instruments as offering protection to the home that could extend to nuisances[102] and that such protection was not limited to the protection of property rights. He ultimately concluded that where the line was drawn in terms of identifying the necessary interest upon which to base a right to sue in nuisance

---

[94] *Ibid.*
[95] [2001] 3 WLR 1323.
[96] [2002] Env LR 30, para 52.
[97] (1976) 73 DLR (3d) 62.
[98] [1993] QB 727.
[99] New York, 20 November 1989; TS 44 (1992) ; Cmd 1976.
[100] No child shall be subjected to unlawful interference with his or her home and that child has the right to the protection of law against such interference.
[101] 10 December 1948; UN TS 2 (1949) ; Cmd 7226.
[102] As in *Arrondelle v UK* (Application No 7889/77) (1882) 26 DR 5 with respect to aircraft noise and *Lopez Ostra v Spain* (1994) 20 EHRR 277 with respect to fumes and smell from a waste treatment plant.

was a matter of policy and not an issue that could be determined by analysis alone.

The Human Rights Act has provided the necessary impetus to initiate a change in policy and a change in the character of nuisance, divorcing it from proprietary interests in land *simpliciter* and recognising that nuisance can evolve to take into account more modern ways of looking at interests in land, based on rights to enjoy it securely. Lord Cooke's speech in *Hunter* can thus be viewed as a precursor for cases raising nuisance and related issues under the Human Rights Act. This is, perhaps, unsurprising given the propensity of human rights questions to throw up the sorts of deeper issues left untouched by the highly technical arguments encountered in the context of public law. In human rights contexts, the political commitments of legal rules are brought very close to the surface indeed.[103] Human rights cases however, like nuisance cases, must often tackle the problem of arriving at a workable balance between the individual interest and the wider public interest, as in the cases of *Clingham v Kensington & Chelsea London Borough Council* and *R v Manchester Crown Court, ex p McCann* [2002].[104] Both cases involved attempts to challenge the imposition of Anti-Social Behaviour Orders (ASBO)[105] under the Human Rights Act[106] for alleged infringements of Article 6[107] of the ECHR. The House of Lords dealt with a number of issues including whether ASBOs could be issued on the basis of hearsay evidence. Their Lordships decided that they could, specifically because

> striking a fair balance between the general interests of the community and the protection of the defendants' rights required that the scales come down in favour of community protection.[108]

However, while the balancing of public and private interests is an issue in a number of human rights based contexts, it will not always be determined in the same way. In nuisance cases, for instance, the claimant will, in contrast with *Clingham* and *McCann*, usually not be at fault in any way, and in such cases arriving at a fair balance will be a much more complex issue. This is illustrated by the Court of Appeal decision in *Marcic v Thames Water Utilities Ltd* [2002].[109] Mr Marcic owned a house that had, since 1992, been periodically affected by sewage flooding from sewers that had become inadequate to deal with the sewage and surface water that drained into it. The sewers were the responsibility of TWU, which had inherited them from its predecessors in title. The problem worsened over time and Mr Marcic had been forced to take action

---

[103] See J Morgan, 'Law's British Empire' (2002) 22 *Oxford Journal of Legal Studies* 729–46.
[104] [2002] 3 WLR 1313.
[105] Issued under s 1 of the Crime and Disorder Act 1998.
[106] Neither case fell directly under the Human Rights Act but the parties invited their Lordships to treat them as if it did apply.
[107] Right to a fair trial.
[108] at 1314.
[109] [2002] QB 929.

to prevent foul water from invading his home. His garden continued to be very badly affected by periodic flooding.

The defendants were under a statutory duty courtesy of section 94(1) of the Water Resources Act 1991 to provide and improve the public sewer system and ensure effectual drainage. As a large company, covering a considerable geographical area,[110] TWU typically experienced a considerable range of demands on its resources for tackling sewerage problems. It used a points system to determine priority, which accorded greatest weight to those problem areas where houses were being flooded internally by sewage. Under the points system there was no realistic prospect of any action being taken regarding the flooding that affected Marcic.[111] Rather than complaining to the Director General of Water Services under section 18 of the Water Resources Act, Marcic instituted civil proceedings seeking damages at common law (in negligence, nuisance, and under the rule in *Rylands v Fletcher*) damages for breach of statutory duty and arguing that there had been a breach of section 6(1) of the Human Rights Act. The High Court found for Marcic on the Human Rights Act on the basis of breach of Article 8 of the ECHR and Article 1 of the First Protocol of the ECHR,[112] allowing for a fair accommodation between the individual and the public interest to be arrived at. Most Convention rights are qualified and the High Court looked to the European Court of Human Rights' ruling in *Powell & Rayner v UK* [1990][113] for guidance:

> . . . regard must be had to the fair balance that has to be struck between the competing interests of the individual and the community as a whole; and in both contexts the state enjoys a certain margin of appreciation in determining the steps to be taken to ensure compliance with the Convention.[114]

The High Court further found that there was no problem in imposing liability for an omission to act under the ECHR thanks to the ruling in *Guerra v Italy* [1998].[115]

Marcic's claims in negligence, nuisance and under the rule in *Rylands v Fletcher* were dismissed under *Glossop v Heston and Isleworth Local Board* [1879][116] and his claim in respect of negligent failure to carry out a statutory duty was dismissed under *Stovin v Wise* [1996].[117] The result of this ruling was that Mr Marcic was entitled to damages—but only for the period from 2nd October 2000, when the Human Rights Act entered into force. On appeal, Phillips MR agreed with the first instance decision that the Human Rights Act

---

[110] Thames Water Utilities (hereafter TWU) is responsible for 80,000km of public sewers serving 5. 4 million properties and a population of 12 million.

[111] There were 18,000 properties subject to internal flooding which were accorded the highest priority by TWU.

[112] Right to peaceful enjoyment of possessions.

[113] [1990] 12 EHRR 355.

[114] at 368.

[115] [1998] 26 EHRR 357.

[116] [1879] 12 Ch D 102.

[117] [1996] AC 923.

had been infringed.[118] Having said this, the court took the view that Marcic's entitlement to damages at common law displaced his claim for damages under the Human Rights Act, which acted to his advantage as he would be entitled to damages for the whole duration of the nuisance. The court further took the view that the mechanism provided by section 18 of the Water Resources Act did not in fact address Mr Marcic's situation as it was geared to complaints by those affected by the failure of a public utility to deliver those services which it was charged to do by statute. The claim for breach of statutory duty was denied as a matter of construction.[119] In any event, the claim was also characterised as being based on interference with human rights as an incident to the performance of TWU's statutory duty.

The way that the Court addressed the common law claims was rather less cut and dried. The claim under the rule in *Rylands v Fletcher* was dismissed, applying the approach taken by Lord Denning in *Pride of Derby and Derby Angling Association v British Celanese* [1953][120] that supplying sewerage services is a 'use proper for the general benefit of the community.'[121] The Court, found, however that there was a valid claim in nuisance, applying the authorities on adoption and continuance of a nuisance begun in *Sedleigh-Denfield v O'Callaghan* [1940][122] and developed in *Goldman v Hargrave* [1967][123] and *Leakey v National Trust* [1980][124] in much the same way as in *Bybrook Barn Centre Ltd v Kent County Council* [2001].[125] The court took the view that since TWU was acting in a commercial capacity, and since the company was aware of Marcic's problems, it owed him a duty to take reasonable steps to prevent the offending discharge. Relevant considerations in identifying what would constitute 'reasonable steps' in these circumstances included TWU's interest in the land where the problem originated,[126] its resources[127] and, given the nature of its role, its statutory powers.[128] However, the court took a restrictive view of the capacity of statutory powers to enable the defendants to escape liability. It found that TWU could not use the defence of statutory authority because the nuisance was not an inevitable consequence of it exercising its statutory powers. In addition, in this case the responsibility to abate was found to exist independent of TWU's statutory obligations.[129]

[118] TWU appealed and Marcic cross-appealed The Court of Appeal dismissed TWU's appeal and allowed Mr Marcic's cross-appeal.
[119] at 988.
[120] [1953] 1 Ch 149.
[121] at 189.
[122] [1940] AC 880.
[123] [1967] 1 AC 645.
[124] [1980] QB 485.
[125] [2001] BLR 55.
[126] TWU did not own the land by they did have powers of compulsory purchase under the Water Resources Act 1991 pursuant to effectively carrying out its statutory role.
[127] *Marcic v TWU* [2002] QB 1000.
[128] [2002] QB 996–97.
[129] The Court contrasted this situation to that in *Stovin v Wise* [1996] AC 923, where there was no duty to act independent of the applicable statute.

Central to the case was the vexed issue of arriving at a fair balance between the rights of the individual and the public interest. The court raised the issue of the potential role of compensation in this regard as a means of arriving at a 'fair balance' between the interests of the individual and the community, regardless of whether means existed which should reasonably have been taken to prevent the interference. Phillips MR summed up the court's view of the situation up as follows:

> The flooding is a consequence of the benefit that is provided to those making use of the system. It seems to us at least arguable that to strike a fair balance between the individual and the general community, those who pay to make use of a sewerage system should be charged sufficient to cover the cost of paying compensation to the minority who suffer damage as a consequence of the operation of the system.[130]

Phillips MR pointed out that, had the rule in *Rylands v Fletcher* been applicable to sewage, then this result would have been achieved, but that this would have required a 'modification of legal principle,' though he added that '[s]uch modification may, however, be necessary if our common law is to march in step with the requirements of the Convention.'[131] Citing the decision of the European Commission of Human Rights in *S v France* (1990),[132] Phillips MR concluded:

> . . . where an authority carries on an undertaking in the interest of the community as a whole it may have to pay compensation to individuals whose rights are infringed by that undertaking in order to achieve a fair balance between the interests of the individual and the community.[133]

This conclusion echoes the pragmatic approach of earlier common law authority dealing with nuisance caused by activities carried out in the public interest, where the courts awarded damages in lieu of an injunction and suspended injunctions to allow time for adjustment in the attempt to arrive at a workable accommodation between the rights of the individual and the needs of the community.

The whole area of nuisance, in which the rights of the individual are pitted against the interests of the broader community, is now something of a litigation hotspot throughout the common law world. For example, in *Hamilton v Papakura District Council* [2002][134] (a Privy Council decision originating in New Zealand), involved a claim in contract, negligence and nuisance or *Rylands v Fletcher* against a local council that supplied water to the claimants who subsequently claimed that it had caused damage to their hydroponically grown tomatoes.[135] A majority of their Lordships found that the claim failed across the

---

[130] *Marcic v TWU* [2002] QB 1001.
[131] *Ibid.*
[132] (1990) DR 250.
[133] *Marcic v TWU* [2002] 1002.
[134] Times Law Reports 5 March QB 2002.
[135] Due to the presence of hormone herbicides in the water.

board, and in particular emphasised the fact that the defendant could not have foreseen the damage and this effectively caused their claim to fail.

The potential reach of so much legal activity in this area is revealed by the decision in *Dennis v Ministry of Defence* [2003].[136] In this case the claimants owned an estate near a RAF base and claimed damages and a declaration in respect of severe nuisance caused to them by noise from Harrier Jump-jets. At first instance Buckley J held that the noise constituted a serious nuisance and was aggravated by its persistence and unpredictability. He further held that the noise from the jets did not constitute an ordinary use of land, even in the context of twenty-first century society. The main issue here was whether the public interest could justify the interference experienced by the claimants. Buckley J applied *Marcic,* taking the view that only reasonably necessary interference would be covered. At the same time he pointed out that a public interest defence would only be allowed to stand in a nuisance context if it would also succeed in a human rights claim on the same facts. In this case, the public interest *did* require that the RAF continue to fly but that the claimants should not be expected to carry the cost of the public benefit. Buckley decided that justice would be served by refusing the declaration sought but by granting damages to cover the loss of capital value and past and future loss of use and amenity. In conclusion the newly revitalised law of nuisance was deemed sufficient to dispose of the case, though the judge added obiter that, had this not been the case, the application of Article 8 of the ECHR and Article 1 of the First Protocol would have achieved the same result.

As leave has been given for the *Marcic* case to proceed to the House of Lords, and the *Dennis* case will surely also be appealed, the whole issue of the relationship between the law of nuisance and the Human Rights Act awaits a definitive answer. Yet it is undeniable that the human rights dimension brings with it a renewal of interest in the traditional doctrinal issues long neglected by the evolution of complex statutory regimes. As Scott LJ stated *obiter* in *Haseldine v C A Daw & Son Ltd* [1941]:

> The common law of England has throughout its long history developed as an organic growth, at first slowly under the hampering restrictions of legal forms of process, more quickly in the time of Lord Mansfield, and in the last 100 years at an ever-increasing rate of progress, as new cases, arising under new conditions of society, of applied science, and of public opinion, have presented themselves for solution by the courts.[137]

Sedley LJ took much the same tack more than half a century later in *Douglas v Hello* [2001]:[138]

> The common law . . . grows by slow and uneven degrees. It develops reactively, both in terms in the immediate sense that it is only ever expounded in response to events

---

[136] [2003] EWHC 793.
[137] [1941] 3 All ER 156, 174.
[138] [2001] 2 All ER 289.

and in the longer-term sense that it may be consciously shaped by the perceived needs of legal policy.[139]

These sentiments reflect a resurgence of interest in the doctrinal categories and principles of the common law as an interpretative basis for a statutory system of environmental regulation. This resurgence is in no small part due to the judiciary-orientated focus of the Human Rights Act. The operational context of that Act demands the explication of statute as part of a deeper system of moral and political values, in a way that is particularly suited to the doctrinal structure of the common law. For the Act embodies an implicit rejection of the public/private distinction explored earlier: the lawyer is encouraged to think of private rights and obligations as taking effect within a context of collective interests and responsibilities; and those interests and responsibilities are conceived, in turn, as reflective not only of deliberate *choice*, exercised through legislation, but also of shared values and assumptions indicative of a wider conception of justice. By requiring the interpretation of legal rules and provisions against a background of shared values, the Human Rights Act has the effect of bringing the political significance of the rules much closer to the surface of legal argumentation.

A Brief Summary

The prevalent conception of environmental law is one of a body of statutory provisions directed at the regulation of a particular social problem. Whilst it is possible to study those provisions collectively and systematically, (it is thought), the body of rules which make up 'environmental law' must be understood as forming a distinct area for legal study only in the minimal sense that they possess a common *purpose*: though the rules aim to regulate damage to the environment (wrought mainly through the exercise of property rights) in the name of public welfare, they do not require understanding through the prism of a deeper theory of justice. This conception relies for its plausibility upon a version of the public/private distinction which is analytically unsustainable, if nevertheless widely accepted. For it is only in terms of that distinction that the image of property rights as a category of interests subjected to collective impositions only contingently, can make any sense. But (as was made clear in an earlier section) the category of property rights is itself possible only within a juristic context in which private entitlements are *inherently* subjected to collective restraint. The systematic control of property rights on the basis of social welfare thus demands to be understood in the context of ideas of justice, obligation and responsibility which transcend the boundaries of 'public' and 'private.' Environmental statutes, as much as any regulatory measures, must be understood as forming part of the systematic *delineation* of rights according to a complex theory of justice which has its philosophical roots in the doctrinal categories of the common law.

[139] Para 109.

Environmental law can be understood as the attempt to trace out the relationships which hold between concepts such as property, right, and responsibility in the context of environmental management. The relevant interpretative context within which those relationships are worked out is not one in which the jurist, faced with the problems of clashing interests, attempts a reasonable reconciliation on the basis of desirable policy, but one involving competition between various moral values, assumptions and interests. Attempts to articulate a wider framework of moral responsibilities towards the natural environment however resists straightforward systematic treatment and, as noted earlier, falls short of establishing fully interpretable conceptions of moral concern. The environmental lawyer is left with a series of partial, often overlapping, conceptions of justice and moral value within which the limits to individual property rights are explored. One prominent attempt to give expression to these ideas can be found in the concept of sustainable development. It is in the context of ideas relating to sustainability and future generations that the linkages between modern environmental law and the philosophical ideas explored in the foregoing chapters are most clearly seen: for the concept of sustainable development may be viewed as part of an attempt to give expression to a conception of humankind's relationship with the natural world which is at once structured overwhelmingly in terms of subjective right *and* deeply moral in its preoccupations and outlook. It is to an exploration of this concept that we now turn.

SUSTAINABLE DEVELOPMENT (AND BEYOND)

A society's statute law represents its deliberate political choices. Those choices are therefore at once a product of, and a reflection (perhaps a distorted reflection) of, the society which makes them. The integration of new environmental thinking into mainstream environmental legislation and governance provides one example of this; and by far the most significant development to have emerged in recent years is the inclusion of the concept of sustainable development in the Environment Act 1995. On the face of it, the rise to prominence of the concept of sustainable development offers perhaps the most serious, and certainly most high-profile, political attempt to date to alter the way in which humanity views its relationship with the world of which it forms part. Sustainable development has been presented as providing 'a framework for the integration of environment policies and development strategies,'[140] but whether the concept is in fact as far-reaching as this is far from self-evident. Sustainable development remains, ultimately a product of the global society that has defined it.[141]

---

[140] World Commission on Environment and Development (hereafter WCED), *Our Common Future* (Oxford, OUP, 1987) 40.

[141] A Escobar has described the concept as 'the last attempt to articulate modernity and capitalism...' See A Escobar, *Encountering Development: The Making and Unmaking of the Third World* (Princeton, NJ, Princeton University Press, 1995) 202.

The entry of sustainable development into UK law is ultimately a product of the UN Conference on Environment and Development in 1992, filtered through the lens of EU environmental policy. Sustainable development was the major theme of the EC's Fifth Environmental Action Programme, *'Towards Sustainability*1993–2000.'[142] The Commission's 'Progress Report and Action Plan on the Fifth Programme of Policy and Action in Relation to the Environment and Sustainable Development'[143] concluded that, although progress had been made towards sustainable development, much remains to be done. The EU's view on sustainable development at all institutional levels is reinforced in many official documents, and in particular Decision No 2179/98/EC of the European Parliament and Council on the Review of the EC Programme of Policy and Action in Relation to the Environment and Sustainable Development.[144] This states:

> **Para 17**: Whereas the objectives, targets, actions and time-frames indicated in the Programme constitute a useful start in moving towards sustainable development; . . . action needs to be stepped up . . . sustainability of activity and development will not be attained during the life-span of this programme and, consequently, further and still more progressive priority objectives and measures will be necessary beyond the year 2000 to maintain the momentum of Community Action.

Given the sustained level of commitment, and its prominent role in the 6th Environmental Action Programme, it seems certain that sustainable development will be the key value underpinning future EU environmental policy and EC law.

It is against this background that the UK's attempt to assimilate sustainable development into domestic policy should be understood. The first such attempt is to be found in the 1994 document *'Sustainable Development—a UK Strategy.'*[145] The current government has revised its approach to sustainability, following wide consultation and producing a series of documents, culminating in its strategy for sustainable development, entitled *'A Better Quality of Life.'*[146] The Environment Act takes the process a stage further by enshrining sustainable development in domestic environmental law and governance. Section 4 of the Act lays out the principal aim of the newly-instituted Environment Agency in the following terms:

> (1) . . . (subject to and in accordance with the provisions of this Act or any other enactment and taking into account any likely costs) in discharging its functions so to protect or enhance the environment, taken as a whole, as to make the contribution towards attaining the objective of achieving sustainable development mentioned in subsection (3) below

---

[142] OJ C138, 17 May 1993.
[143] Com(95) 647 (final), 24 January 1996.
[144] OJL 275, 10 October 1998, http://europa.eu.int/eur-lex/en/lif/dat/en–398D2179.html
[145] 1994 CM 2426.
[146] 1999 CM 4345 at http://www.environment.detr.gov.uk//sustainable/quality/life.htm

(3) (Ministerial) . . . guidance . . . must include guidance with respect to the contribution which, having regard to the Agency's responsibilities and resources, the Ministers consider it appropriate for the Agency to make, by the discharge of its functions, towards attaining the objective of achieving sustainable development.

While being neither an example of elegant drafting nor an unqualified endorsement of sustainable development,[147] the inclusion of this section is, in principle, highly significant and shows domestic legislation attempting to give legal shape to broader political ideas in a more visible form than any yet seen in the development of environmental law.

Sustainable Development and Moral Values

The concept of sustainable development is rooted in the scientific discoveries and discussion of the nineteen-sixties and -seventies, which saw the emergence of new ways of thinking about the relationship between humankind and the environment. One of the first and most influential developments is to be found in what has become known as the Club of Rome report, *'The Limits to Growth'* issued in 1972.[148] The report recognised the complexity and inter-related nature of the global system, and highlighted the impacts of industrialisation, population growth, resource depletion and environmental deterioration. The report demonstrated that social and economic considerations were inextricably intermingled in each of these areas and in this way laid the foundation for subsequent attempts to tackle the myriad of problems faced by humanity as a result of environmental stress in all its many guises. The Club of Rome attempted to construct a computer model that would inform decision-makers in their future activities. The report concluded that, despite technological progress, there were absolute limits to unchecked economic growth imposed by environmental constraints, which would be almost certainly reached within a century if contemporary trends continued. The report did, however, suggest that it would be possible to alter these trends and 'establish a condition of ecological stability that is sustainable far into the future' by developing a state of equilibrium meeting human needs within the global limits. The Club of Rome model turned out to have been flawed in many ways, but it served at least to generate both concern and discussion and initiated debate about what has become known as sustainable development.

---

[147] It is very clear that the Agency's role with respect to sustainable development is to be curtailed not only by its remit, but also by financial considerations See, for example, T Jewell and J Steele, 'UK Regulatory Reform and the Pursuit of "Sustainable Development": the Environment Act 1995' (1996) 8 *JEL* 283. The Agency has however attempted to pursue its responsibilities in this regard in a number of ways, notably by publishing An Environmental Vision–The Environment Agency's Contribution to Sustainable Development. This can be found at: http://www.environment-agency.gov.uk/aboutus/vision/index.htm

[148] DH Meadows, *et al*, *The Limits to Growth* (New York, NY, Universe Books, 1972).

One of the key products of international activity on the environment has been the 1987 World Commission on Environment and Development Report *Our Common Future*[149] also known as the Brundtland Report.[150] The 400 page report, commissioned by the UN, attempted to marry scientific debate to social, political and economic realities. The Report had three objectives: to re-examine environment and development issues and formulate realistic policies to deal with problems; to propose new forms of international co-operation on these issues in order to bring about change; and to improve understanding of environmental and development issues at every level from citizen to state.[151] The Report also reflects contemporary environmental thinking by recognising that environmental issues cannot be approached in isolation: it touches upon every other area of human activity, not least upon the way in which we organise our societies, political institutions, economies and our use of science and technology.

The crux of the Report lay in identifying sustainable development (as opposed to a 'business as usual' scenario) as the basis for future human activities with environmental impacts. But while the value of sustainable development may be almost universally acknowledged as the accepted orthodoxy,[152] its exact meaning is rather more controversial. The definition of sustainable development is almost infinitely variable: the 'key elements' of the social, the economic and the environmental are notoriously open to manipulation to suit the ends of whoever is trying to call the concept in aid. The Brundtland report itself offers a definition of sustainable development that has gained wide publicity and offers a reasonable starting point for examining the modern approach to environmental issues:

> Sustainable development is development that meets the needs of the present without compromising the ability of future generations to meet their own needs.[153]

Sustainable development as defined by Brundtland synthesises social, economic and environmental concerns in a way that is essentially anthropocentric in its orientation, employing a dual focus in looking at human priorities and human interaction with the environment. Sustainable development as espoused by Brundtland represents a 'light-green' perspective on environmental issues, focusing on linear progress towards a more evenly developed world. The concept is deeply imbued with technological optimism, proceeding on the assumption that science and technology can enable us to 'enhance the carrying capacity of the resource base.' Sustainable development essentially concerns itself with meeting human needs, and encapsulates *both* a conception of intergenerational

---

[149] (Oxford, OUP, 1987).

[150] Called after the chair of the WCED, Gro Harlem Brundtland.

[151] *Ibid* p 3.

[152] Sustainable development is not without its critics: see, for example, M McCloskey 'The Emperor has no Clothes: The Conundrum of Sustainable Development' (1999) 9 *Duke Environmental Law and Policy Forum* 153.

[153] Above n 140, p 43.

justice *and* a concern with inter-societal justice between North and South within the context of the present generation.

Both of these issues are ultimately problematic. The Brundtland Report clearly acknowledges the basic injustice which has resulted from historic patterns of economic development, and stresses the need to redress the balance between North and South as the key to responding to the environmental imperative posed by the planet's inability to support current, let alone future, patterns of resource-use in the face of pollution and other forms of environmental degradation.[154] While this focus is laudable in principle, it presents huge difficulties in practice, as exhibited in the enormously problematic negotiations of international treaties such as the Vienna Convention for the Protection of the Ozone Layer 1985, and its 1987 Montreal Protocol.[155] In the ozone negotiations, inter-societal justice was a key issue and funding was, in turn, thought to be the key to addressing it. The Less Economically Advanced Nations (LEANs) argued, with good reason, that they had not caused the ozone depletion problem, and that they should not have to bare the cost of tackling it by foregoing the cheap development that ozone depleting chemicals had given the More Economically Advanced Nations (MEANs). At the same time, if the LEANs refused to come on board with the ozone regulation regime, the problem would continue to escalate and the measures employed by the MEANs to address it would be rendered useless.[156] The LEANs were therefore in a position to demand an additional funding mechanism under the Protocol[157] to help pay for its implementation.

Membership of the regime was also rendered more attractive to the LEANs by provisions for accessing substitute technology on a non-commercial and non-profit-making basis. The MEANs were not anxious to meet these demands, for while they accepted the principle of differentiated burdens of responsibility for the ozone problem, they feared setting a financial precedent, given much more expensive environmental problems, such as global warming, which were appearing on the horizon. The Framework Climate Change Convention 1992[158] and subsequent developments have clearly revealed that the inter-societal justice issues raised by ozone depletion are just the tip of the iceberg. Yet if tackling inter-societal justice issues is problematic, the obstacles to addressing inter-generational justice issues

---

[154] These concerns are discussed in detail in A Dobson, *Justice and the Environment: Conceptions of Environmental Sustainability and Theories of Distributive Justice* (Oxford, OUP, 1998), in particular see ch 3.

[155] Convention and the Vienna, Montreal Protocol at http://www.uneporg/ozone/vienna.htm and http://www.uneporg/ozone/mont_t.htm respectively.

[156] A Aman, 'The Montreal Protocol on Substances that Deplete the Ozone Layer' in F Francioni and T Scovassi (eds), *International Responsibility for Environmental Harm* (London, Graham & Trotman, 1991) 185 and R Benedict, *Ozone Diplomacy: New Directions in Safeguarding the Planet* (Cambridge, Mass, Harvard University Press, 1998).

[157] That is aid in addition to existing aid packages.

[158] Climate Change Convention 1992 and Kyoto Protocol at http://www.unfccc.de/text/resource/convkphtml

verge upon the insurmountable.[159] The idea of sustainable development is, by its definition, geared to operating far into the future, representing not an end-state but an ongoing process. It is no coincidence that the Brundtland Report explains the central importance of sustainable development as lying in environmental impacts upon future conditions: '[T]he results of present profligacy,' the report states, 'are rapidly closing the options for future generations.'[160]

The thinking behind the report is thus clear: the present state of environmental damage and environment-damaging practices are conceived as generating injustice for our descendants. Yet strategies of this kind are not unproblematic.[161] One problem is that the potential scale and seriousness of environmental degradation is impossible to gauge. It is also extremely difficult to envisage the full impact of our actions for our descendants, as even issues that appear quite minor to current scientific models may generate disproportionate or even totally unforeseen consequences.[162] (One might bring to mind, in this context, the supposition of the seventeenth century writers of an intrinsic relationship between human welfare and environmental flourishing: as noted in chapter three, the appearance of harmony could subsist only within a context of relative ignorance concerning the negative impacts of farming practices which emerged in the nineteenth century.) There is of course a huge degree of difficulty in factoring future imponderables into current decision-making processes,[163] and this is aggravated by the huge timescales involved.

These difficulties are not necessarily insurmountable: we could, for example, give voice to our notional descendants in sustainability-oriented decision-making by appointing someone to act in an *amicus curiae* capacity on their behalf. Alternatively, we could (as Edith Brown Weiss suggests)[164] adopt a trust-based approach to environmental resources which recognises an obligation to act responsibly towards our environmental heritage and pass it on to our successors intact.[165] This is an interesting but flawed approach in that it conflates

[159] See, for example Agora, 'What Obligation Does Our Generation Owe to the Next? An Approach to Global Environmental Responsibility' (1990) 84 *American Journal of International Law* 190–212 (symposium).

[160] Brundtland Report p 8.

[161] For detailed discussion of this issue see, GS Kavka and V Warren, 'Political Representation for Future Generations', in R Eliot and A Gare (eds), *Environmental Philosophy: A Collection of Readings* (Milton Keynes, Open University Press, 1983).

[162] A D'Amato, 'Do We Owe a Duty to Future Generations to Preserve the Global Environment?' (1990) 84 *American Journal of International Law* 190–93.

[163] This issue is discussed by DA Farber, *Eco-Pragmatism: Making Sensible Environmental Decisions in an Uncertain World* (Chicago, Il, University of Chicago Press, 1999) ch 5, in particular p 149 et seq.

[164] E Brown Weiss, 'The Planetary Trust: Conservation and Intergenerational Equity' (1984) 11 *Ecology LQ* 495.

[165] There is considerably difficulty in translating a feeling of moral obligation to theoretical successors into practical legal constraints. Richard A Epstein, 'Justice Across the Generations' (1989) 67 *Texas Law Review* 1465, 1463 suggests that viewing the obligations as owed to actual descendants provides one way round this (and provides the maximum level of ability to identify with them). The problem with this approach is that, the further removed the descendants are for us in time, the less weight we are likely to accord to their needs.

our descendants' interests with rights and our own moral responsibility with legal duty in a way that may be difficult to justify in jurisprudential terms. The attribution of right to hypothetical persons, and the attempt to trace the consequences of that attribution within the concrete circumstances and arrangements which make up the actual world, have already been touched upon. More importantly, a focus on the establishment of duties shifts the emphasis of sustainability away from the environment as an object of moral concern, and places it instead on human beings. Responsible (and sustainable) property use, originally the essence of sustainable development, becomes a mere consequence of the delineation of duties correlating with hypothetical rights, and thus (in all probability) the subject of the narrowest possible interpretations on the basis of likely harm. The problems involved in considering future generations in this way are clearly indicated by the complications encountered in tackling global warming, where a combination of scientific uncertainty, gains and losses to be made from action or abstention (as well as timescales extending for hundreds of years) have all combined to hamper effective international action with the Climate Change Convention, and the subsequent Kyoto Protocol proving both hugely controversial and ultimately disappointing.[166]

Notwithstanding such difficulties, sustainable development at least provides an incentive to address environmental problems in collective rather than purely individualistic terms.[167] The concern with inter-societal and inter-generational justice in turn provides a useful antidote to the tendency to reduce environmental issues to questions of individual interest which, although they continue to dominate our legal system, are increasingly perceived as being outmoded and undesirably narrow in focus.[168] As Kevin Gray has rightly argued, clinging to narrow definitions of property in the context of environmental resources in which there exists a broad range of interests, is increasingly untenable in intellectual terms. Gray's analysis of 'ownership' in terms of an aggregation or bundle of powers over resources, representing a continuum of interests in them, is one that readily accommodates inter-societal and inter-generational interests but sits ill, as he acknowledges, with traditional views on resource ownership.[169] By breaking down the monolithic concept of ownership, Gray robs it of much

---

[166] There is a voluminous literature on this topic, the following are particularly recommended: R Grubb, *et al*, *The Earth Summit Agreements: A Guide and Assessment* (London, Earthscan, 1993); R Churchill, 'Controlling Emissions of Greenhouse Gases' in R Churchill and D Freestone (eds), *International Law and Global Climate Change* (London, Graham & Trotman, 1991); C Stone, 'Beyond Rio: Insuring Against Global Warming' (1992) AJIL 455; M Grubb, C Vrolijk and D Brack, *The Kyoto Protocol: A Guide and Assessment* (London, Earthscan/Royal Institute of International Affairs Energy and Environment Programme 1999); and D French, '1997 Kyoto Protocol to the 1992 Framework Convention on Climate Change' (1998) 10 *Journal of Environmental Law* 2.

[167] See M Stallworthy, *Sustainability, Land Use and Environment: A Legal Analysis* (London, Cavendish, 2002); C Redgwell, *Intergenerational Trusts and Environmental Protection* (Manchester, MUP, 1999).

[168] K Gray, 'The Ambivalence of Property', in G Prins (ed), *Threats Without Enemies: Facing Environmental Insecurity* (London, Earthscan, 1993).

[169] *Ibid* p 159.

of its totemic significance and renders it open to a more functional analysis: 'Ownership,' he says, 'breaks down, as it were, into distinct quantums of "property" in a resource, which are then distributed variously to perhaps a vast range of persons.'[170]

This type of approach recognises the potential for contiguous claims, with respect to resources, which necessarily inhibit the scope for an 'owner' to exploit those resources to their detriment, as this will interfere with other interests (including possible future interests) in those resources.[171] Property is therefore seen to be an inherently *limited* concept. In any event, as Gray points out, not all contested resources are 'owned' as such, referring to the global commons[172] and their dual owned/unowned[173] status. Gray identifies the commons as a type of 'public property', notionally to be protected in the interests of all:

> Only a relatively small part of the total field of economic facility and human capacity is at present permitted to be the subject of private property. The withholding of private property in certain crucial resources is what gives a new and invigorated content to the assertion that property jurisprudence is ultimately concerned with claims of access to natural and social good—of access to a common heritage of mankind.[174]

Clearly, this state of affairs is one that can be projected indefinitely into the future, in terms of addressing the interests of our successors in title.

The forgoing reflections point to the concept of sustainable development as consisting in a series of reflections on issues of inter-generational justice in which limitations on property rights are articulated through the metric of *responsibility*. The continued focus on rights as the distinctive means through which society gives voice to these ideals makes very difficult the understanding of our putative responsibilities in systematic terms. And yet it is possible to see, in these developments, the pale echo of a conception of property and justice essentially Lockean in its terms. For sustainable development might be viewed as a reassertion of the Lockean assumption of harmony between the goals of environmental protection and conservation, on the one hand, and that of human flourishing, on the other. The reliance on forms of inter-generational justice suggests a concern not merely with the uncontroversial idea that the welfare of future generations of human beings is dependent upon their inheritance of a healthy environment; it rather points to a deeper set of assumptions according to which questions of property, and property rights, are intrinsically tied to an account of justice and moral value.

Just as the early natural rights theorists had assumed an intimate link between human interests and sensible environmental management, the modern environmental lawyer is faced, in the context of sustainable development, with a set of ideas which explore a prudential concern with human welfare within a wider

[170] *Ibid* p 158.
[171] *Ibid* p 158.
[172] *Ibid* p 160.
[173] The atmosphere and the high seas belong at one and the same time to no one and everybody.
[174] Gray, above n 168, 161.

moral framework which emphasises the values of justice and responsibility. Though these values are seen as being fully in line with long-term self-interest, they are not reducible to a set of interests. It is therefore in the context of sustainable development that established property rights and interests most openly conflict with countervailing moral values and ideals. Sustainable development might therefore be seen as a distinctively modern reassertion of the most fundamental insight to have emerged from the natural law tradition: that it is only through the exercise of right reason and reflection upon humanity's place in the world that human interests are best served.

Sustainability and Beyond

The Brundtland report had set out to describe the consequences of a sustainability-focused approach to environmental policy in great detail. Priority areas for action identified by the WCED included the recognition of the need to improve legal mechanisms to deal with environmental problems. The specific legal priorities acknowledged included: recognising and respecting the rights and responsibilities of individuals and states in respect of sustainable development; establishing and applying new norms for state and inter-state conduct in order to achieve sustainable development; strengthening and extending the application of existing international laws and agreements which support sustainable development; and reinforcing existing methods and developing new procedures to avoid and resolve environmental disputes.[175] Thus it is very clear that Brundtland viewed the role of law in progressing sustainable development as pivotal.

While much of the Brundtland approach is controversial in itself, it does not represent by any means the most extreme option available: if anything the report has come to represent the orthodox approach to policy, which will shape and inform both environmental law and the broader relationship between humankind and the environment in this millennium. Other strategies are much more radical: 'deep green' approaches to environmental issues, as espoused for example by the Green Party[176] or the economist Herman Daly,[177] actually go so far as to make out a case *against* economic growth. These approaches argue that growth is necessarily unsustainable, and advocate instead a steady state economic policy leading to a sustainable society in which resources are recycled and a state of equilibrium, designed to echo the 'ecological equilibrium of nature', rather than linear economic development, is achieved.[178] In this type of societal ideal, the emphasis would be placed on qualitative development rather than

[175] Brundtland Report, ch 12.

[176] Green Party Manifesto 1991.

[177] H Daly, 'Towards a Stationary-State Economy' in J Harte and R Socolow, *Patient Earth* (New York, NY, Holt, Rinehart & Winston, 1971) 237; H Daly, Steady State Economics (Washington, DC, Island Press, 1991).

[178] DA Meadows, DL Meadows and J Randers, *Beyond the Limits: Global Collapse or a Sustainable Future* (London, Earthscan, 1992) ch 7.

growth as such. Laudable though this would be, it would involve a change of emphasis from current patterns of economic and political development that would be immensely difficult to realise.[179]

The UN Conference on Environment and Development at Rio in 1992, in addition to generating some rather disappointing substantive law, also introduced soft law to develop global environmental principles to underpin future law and governance in this area in the form of the Rio Declaration on the Environment and Development[180] and Agenda 21.[181] Both of these documents attempted, in different ways, to take sustainable development from the realm of theory into the real legal and political world. The Rio Declaration builds on the legacy of the Stockholm Declaration of 1972 and contains a clear commitment to integrating environmental considerations with development issues.[182] Despite these developments it is clear that, as expressed in Principle 1 of the Rio Declaration, 'sustainable development', while a revolutionary concept in some respects, remains determinedly anthropocentric:

> Human beings are at the centre of concerns for sustainable development. They are entitled to a healthy and productive life in harmony with nature.

The Declaration does not, however, give any detailed consideration to the difficulties of integrating the problematic concepts of environment and development: for this we must look to Agenda 21, the UN's action plan designed to achieve sustainable development. It is a lengthy document running to some 40 chapters and 500 pages. While not legally binding, it is a document of considerable political and practical importance.

Agenda 21 is much more detailed than the Rio Declaration, running to almost 300 pages and some 40 Chapters. It is an interesting document in many respects, not least in its emphasis on state/governmental action but also in the idea that the concept of sustainable development can only work if it also touches the individual: it is as much about a 'bottom-up' as a 'top-down' approach to societal change. Agenda 21 is, in the final analysis, a rather cumbersome document covering almost every imaginable area of human activity, including social and economic activities,[183] conservation and management of resources for

---

[179] Even more difficult to envisage is a yet more fundamental shift from dominant anthropocentric models of interaction with the environment to a ecocentric model, such as that espoused by Christopher Stone, which, taking its lead from biological sciences, views humans simply as part of the broader biotic community. See C Stone, *Earth and Other Ethics: The Case for Moral Pluralism* (Milton Keynes, Harper & Row, 1987). This type of approach goes so far as to accord rights to the non-human world, an approach which, while interesting in its contextualising of the interests of other species, is also fraught with many of the same difficulties as according rights to future generations as discussed above. For a thorough discussion of these issues see M Warren, 'The Rights of the Nonhuman World' in R Elliot and A Gare (eds), *Environmental Philosophy: A Collection of Readings* (New York, NY, Open University Press, 1983).

[180] UNCED Doc A/Conf/151/5.

[181] UNCED Doc A/Conf/151/4.

[182] Principle 4.

[183] For example, combating poverty, changing consumption patterns and promoting sustainable settlements.

development,[184] means and implementation,[185] and strengthening the role of major groups, including women, NGOs, local authorities and trade and industry. It is in this respect, in particular, that the depth and scope of Agenda 21 becomes apparent. Significantly, following Rio, the Commission on Sustainable Development (CSD) was set up to oversee the implementation of Agenda 21, and has proved itself extremely active in forwarding the sustainable development agenda, in particular in adding flesh to the bones provided at Rio.[186]

Whatever else it may be, sustainable development is certainly *not* a value-neutral concept, and has been criticised as supplying the basis for developing a global framework that, far from changing the way in which all humans relate to their environment, simply represents a new means whereby the developed world can impose its will on less developed countries. The Club of Rome, having initiated debate on sustainable development, has indeed continued to draw out important themes that continue to inform current debate.[187] King and Schneider, in the report by the Council of the Club of Rome, issued 20 years after *The Limits to Growth*,[188] get to the heart of the matter:

> . . . the interdependence of nations and the globalisation of a number of problems call for the raising of universal awareness and for a new international ethics.[189]

The problem is that meaningful change responding to environmental and social imperatives will require a true paradigm shift in how we regard our relationship with the world of which we form a part; and sustainable development, amorphous as it is, is unlikely in its current form to provide the impetus for such a transformation. This would seem to be borne out by the distinctly unbalanced approach to the three limbs of sustainable development exhibited at the World Summit on Sustainable Development in Johannesburg in 2002, where environmental considerations were pushed firmly into the background by social and economic issues.[190] The shift of focus that had taken place between Rio and Johannesburg, with environmental issues blending into the background as more strongly contested development issues came to the fore, had already become clear in the preparatory committees for the WSSD.[191] Globalisation and the escalating tensions between North and South also serve to demonstrate that

---

[184] For example, protection of the atmosphere, promoting sustainable agriculture, protection of the quality and supply of water resources and environmentally sound waste management.

[185] For example, funding, technology transfer, scientific development, education, and international cooperation.

[186] See T Bigg and F Dodds, 'The UN Commission on Sustainable Development' in F Dodds (ed), *The Way Forward: Beyond Agenda 21* (London, Earthscan, 1997).

[187] As, for example, in DA Meadows, DL Meadows and J Randers, *Beyond the Limits: Global Collapse or a Sustainable Future* (London, Earthscan 1992).

[188] In particular in A King and B Schneider, *The First Global Revolution* (London, Simon & Schuster, 1991), report by the Council of the club of Rome twenty years after The Limits to Growth.

[189] *Ibid* p 180.

[190] www.johannesburgsummit.org/html/documents/summit_docs/131302_wssd_report_reissued.pdf

[191] See, for example, UN/CSD–10 [2002] *Environmental Policy and Law* 60, and MA Buenker 'Progress at Bali—But not enough for Johannesburg' [2002] *Environmental Policy and Law* 140.

agreement on sustainability issues, as things stand, is far from being reached.[192] The WSSD, which in theory provided an opportunity to put sustainable development back on centre stage in world affairs, failed miserably to do so and merely served to reveal that a paradigm shift in the way in which we relate to the environment remains a long way from coming to fruition.

The values implicit in arguments about sustainable development are best understood as distorted reflections of seventeenth- and eighteenth-century assumptions about the relationship between property, rights and nature. Given the nature of the global political system, and the hugely complex arrangements of domestic political orders, it is increasingly unlikely that any systematic account of those values of the kind offered by the natural rights theorists can emerge from deliberation on environmental issues. The possibility of such a systematic treatment is tied to a conception of the legal order ever more out of step with the dominant tradition of legal positivism: for the modern lawyer confronts a legal order understood overwhelmingly in terms of posited rules. Private law, once looked upon as a realm of systematic thought essentially different from public law, is increasingly relegated to a residual role as the domain in which legislated rules are applied to particular cases. When conceived as a system of rules and rights, the law comes to be seen as a technical instrument for the attainment of social goals and policies, rather than a body of principles aiming at the articulation of a conception of justice and the good life. The ideals of responsibility and justice to which the principle of sustainable development appeals, are difficult to articulate within such a system. Such ideas require explication as part of a wider philosophy of property rights which resists expression outwith the juristic categories and principles of the common law.

The advent of human rights litigation provides an opportunity to revise these trends in legal thinking. Though in many ways unsuited to environmental thought, the concept of human rights as enshrined in the Human Rights Act fosters a conception of law in which black-letter rules must be understood against the background of underpinning moral and political principles and ideals. It is, paradoxically, through the exploration of environmental conservation and protection as a *human* right, that a systematic exploration of the relationship between property, rights and nature is most likely to emerge. The possibility of such an account of property depends upon a grasp of the moral, philosophical and political significance of property rights as explored in the earlier chapters of this book. A philosophical understanding of this kind, in turn, depends upon a view of the legal order which emphasises the fundamental inter-relationship between the public and private realms, and the realm of moral values: the possibility of a deeper account of environmental law is not a *permanent* possibility.

---

[192] There is a plethora of literature on this topic, for example, P Dixon, *Futurewise: Six Faces of Global Change* (London, Harper-Collins, 1999); N Klein, *No Logo* (London, Flamingo, 2000); N Klein, *Fences and Windows: Dispatches from the Front Lines of the Globalisation Debate* (London, Flamingo, 2002).

This book, and this chapter, began by offering a challenge to the prevailing view of environmental law as a collection of statutory responses to the problems of modern living. On the prevailing view, environmental law is essentially a modern development which has grown out of political and social necessity. It is a distinctive branch of law only in that the various rules, mechanisms and controls which make up the legal protection of the environment can be studied systematically as a complex and sophisticated regulatory regime, out of which a principled jurisprudence can gradually grow. Such a jurisprudence, it is thought, will centre upon questions of social harm, and the extent to which individual rights and interests should give way to collective interests in a clean and healthy environment. Environmental law, thus conceived, consists in a series of restrictions (as well as positive obligations) on owners of property, which are not typically thought of as requiring any deeper explanation in terms of fundamental moral or political values.

The argument of this book has been for a rejection of this view of environmental law. For the environmental lawyer can be regarded as raising questions of the moral and political significance of property rights of the most fundamental kind. Environmental law, viewed as a series of arguments concerning responsibility and justice, might be thought of as the product of a sustained reflection upon the relationship between property, rights and nature: a body of philosophical speculation which has its roots in the deliberations of the natural rights theorists of the seventeenth century. For the natural lawyers, property rights are imbued with a moral (and religious) significance which shapes and refines their specific characteristics on the plane of juristic thinking. Within the natural rights tradition, property was thought of as central to the nature and political fabric of the polity itself. The examination of that tradition in chapter two revealed a continuum of thought running from Grotius to Locke, which viewed the idea of property as suggesting particular truths both about relationships between human beings, and about the relationship between human beings and the external world. These two aspects of property were seen as interconnected: settled rules of property were regarded as necessary for peace and social order, and as responding to basic moral notions of justice and entitlement. A system of property which could fulfil the requirements of justice (or objective *ius*)[193] was one which operated within the natural limits ordained by the natural law. These limits turned out to be versions of an agrarian ideal which emphasised sound environmental management, and sanctioned waste.

The conception of property at work in the writings of the natural rights theorists emphasised the intrinsic importance of values which can, with some justification, be regarded as environmental. Property rights were regarded as

[193] For an explanation of the objective *ius*/subjective *ius* distinction see above ch 2.

arising from, and moving within, conceptions of social justice which were fundamentally tied to the cultivation and care of the environment. The assumption of harmony between environment-improving practices and the goal of social welfare, at work in the writings of the natural rights theorists, gave way in the eighteenth century to a conception of property which enjoyed no intrinsic relationship with environmental values (or with moral values more generally). A combination of technological insight and the emergence of radically new forms of property essentially divorced from the agrarian model suggested an idea of property conceived overwhelmingly in terms of subjective *ius*: property rights were seen as constituting legal relationships between individuals structured by posited rules, rather than underpinned by intrinsic values. Within this idea of property, the environment would come to be seen, not as a context for property rights, but as an object of ownership itself. A conception of property rights as connected with environmental values only instrumentally, rather than intrinsically, is hence as much a contingent product of intellectual and social history as is a conception overwhelmingly conceived in terms of intrinsic value: the modern lawyer possesses an idea of property which reflects central assumptions of legal positivism which have never fully penetrated the consciousness of the common law mind.

The doctrinal structures of the common law continue to embody a conception of property which links property rights to moral values through the use of justificationary argument. Yet given the nature of juridical discourse, such values very often resist expression in any *systematic* way when posed as solutions to new, and difficult social problems. The judges and juristic commentators of the nineteenth century grappled with the emerging impacts of industrialisation through a principled distinction between natural and unnatural use. Although amounting to a juristic framework of considerable subtlety and sophistication, the nineteenth century jurists could provide no general solution to the increasing problems of pollution and environmental damage. Despite the articulation of the natural/non-natural distinction, and long-established doctrines such as adverse possession, the traditional assumption that property rights are intrinsically bounded by community-orientated obligations and environmental responsibilities, began to fragment and fade away as the century progressed. The gradual emergence of large-scale statutory regimes of environmental regulation *both* focused the legal mind on the problem of environmental protection *and* further undercut the assumption, implicit within the doctrinal structure of property law, that property rights are structured by, and emerge from, moral values. Environmental law, as a distinctive body of law, came to be viewed as a series of policy-driven measures directed at the regulation of property rights in the name of collective well-being.

The burden of the final two chapters of this book has been to suggest that such a conception of environmental law is worth rejecting. On the one hand, the 'regulatory' conception (let us call it) narrows the interpretative context of environmental law to questions about the resolution of clashes of interest through deliberate policy choices. Such choices are presented as a more-or-less utilitarian working-out of welfare maximisation, with the major interest groupings being represented by property rights and a concern with public health, leisure and cultural enrichment.[194] While policies of this kind undeniably play a major part in modern environmental law, the legal regulation of the environment extends well beyond the purely instrumental approach suggested by the regulatory conception. As suggested in chapter four, very many of the regulatory measures associated with environmental law operate to the detriment of more obvious and powerful interests, and in favour of narrower and less easily defined interests. In many cases also, the interests involved are difficult to pin down at all. In the face of these observations, it seems more accurate to speak of the law subjecting property rights, not to the calculus of interests, but to a context of countervailing moral values. Environmental law, understood in this way, demands interpretation against a background of sophisticated moral and political principles, rather than straightforwardly utilitarian rules and policies.

On the other hand, the 'regulatory' conception rests on a dichotomy between public law and private law which is open to challenge on a number of grounds. By attempting to explicate environmental law as a series of legislative intrusions upon private entitlements, the environmental lawyer presupposes a conception of the legal order in which property rights are delineated according to black-letter rules rather than by reference to underpinning moral values. Such a view (it was argued) advances a conception of property in essentially Blackstonian terms: proprietary claims are regarded as unrestricted except insofar as they are limited through black-letter rules, and such restrictions on private entitlements thus represent incursions by the public interest into the realm of individual autonomy. The effect of such a view is to encourage the supposition that legislative incursions into the realm of private entitlement are justifiable only on grounds of welfare or utility. Questions of the moral and political value of property, and of rights to property, are thus viewed by the modern lawyer as falling outside the scope of legal reasoning, and as having no bearing on the exact delineation of those rights. As we have seen, however, such stark divisions between the public and private domains are analytically unsustainable: for genuine entitlements to property are possible only against a framework of values which emphasise mutual forbearance and recognition of claims. Within such a framework, essential in any complex society, it is the collective interest in social peace and stability (and, one might add, human flourishing) which ultimately underpin the private entitlements. The two realms of public and private are therefore not separate and competing domains, but interrelated and interpenetrating ones. Private rights are thus inevitably shaped by restrictions and curbs representing the polity's shared moral and political values. Those values, far from expressing extraneous philosophical theses about rights, might be said to form

---

[194] One could of course extend this indicative list: tourism interests suggest one example.

a part of a society's conception of property; values which will thus be reflected in the way those rights unfold in law.

A society's property laws are the product of deeply held moral values. Yet the moral values through which property rights are refined and textured should not be assumed to amount to any single coherent philosophical position. The notion that property rights are shaped by responsibilities towards the natural environment forms but one strand of moral thinking about property; thinking which very likely conflicts with other conceptions of the moral basis of property which might be expressed through law. For it is obvious that a theory of justice and ownership which is heavily imbued with environmental ethics will suggest a pattern of distributions quite at odds with a theory which emphasises, say, wealth-maximisation and free market conditions. It is partly the role of environmental law to suggest solutions to these problems of competing values. The environmental lawyer might then be understood as a participant in the attempt to systematise, and render coherent, the various competing conceptions of property, right and moral good which find expression within the law. The very flexibility exhibited by property rights in the face of changing social attitudes might thus act as a catalyst for the development of a new theory of property, driven as much by notions of responsibility as by right.

The concepts of sustainable development, of inter-generational justice, and of human rights are best understood as attempts to offer an account of property rights according to underpinning conceptions of justice and responsibility along the lines suggested above. The values underlying these conceptions, too, conflict and compete. And yet it is possible to see, in those developments, a faint echo of the attempt, which received its most sophisticated expression in the writings of Locke, to explore the relationship between property, rights and nature. Such a possibility is both important and fragile: for the conception of law within which the modern lawyer moves is overwhelmingly positivist in orientation. Too often, the environmental lawyer is represented as engaging in a series of technical arguments concerning the meaning, scope and inter-relationship of various policy goals as expressed in black-letter rules. Where the focus on the interpretation and application of black-letter rules dominates, it becomes exceedingly difficult for perspectives which emphasise intrinsic moral value to find a foothold in legal reasoning. The changing face of the legal order represents a movement towards technicality and positivism. If the environmental lawyer is to stand any chance of articulating a deeper conception of environmental responsibility and intrinsic value, the attempt is better undertaken sooner rather than later.

Such an attempt is worth undertaking. The argument of this book has sought to connect modern environmental law with its philosophical foundations, in the form of reflections on the relationship between property, rights and nature. Environmental law without a sense of philosophy and history is a pale and bloodless creature; environmental law imbued with a sense of intrinsic value and philosophical depth represents an intellectual achievement only provisionally available, and soon forever lost.

Select Bibliography

Books

J Alder & D Wilkinson, *Environmental Law and Ethics* (London, Macmillan, 1999)

T Allen, *The Right to Property in Commonwealth Constitutions* (Cambridge, Cambridge University Press, 2000)

PC Almond, *Adam and Eve in Seventeenth Century Thought* (Cambridge, Cambridge University Press, 1999)

JF Archbold, *Criminal Pleading, Evidence and Practice* (London, Sweet & Maxwell, 2000)

PS Atiyah, *Promises, Morals and Law* (Oxford, Clarendon Press, 1983)

Bartlet et al, *Property: Its Duties and Rights* (new ed.) (New York, Macmillan, 1922)

L Becker, *Property Rights: Philosophic Foundations* (London, Routledge & Kegan Paul, 1977)

R Benedict, *Ozone Diplomacy: New Directions in Safeguarding the Planet* (Cambridge Mass, Harvard University Press, 1991)

J Bentham, *Of Laws in General*, HLA Hart ed. (London, University of London, 1970)

——, *A Comment on the Commentaries and A Fragment on Government*, J Burns & HLA Hart eds. (London, Athlone Press, 1977)

——, *Introduction to the Principles of Morals and Legislation*, J Burns & HLA Hart eds. (London, Athlone Press, 1982)

W Blackstone, *Commentaries on the Laws of England (in four books): A Facsimile of the First Edition of 1765–1769* (Chicago, University of Chicago Press, 1979)

——, *An Analysis of the Laws of England* (1771)

D Boonin-Vail, *Thomas Hobbes and the Science of Moral Virtue* (Cambridge, Cambridge University Press, 1994)

J Bowle, *Hobbes and his Critics: a Study in Seventeenth Century Constitutionalism* (London, Frank Cass, 1951)

A Brett, *Liberty, Right and Nature* (Cambridge, Cambridge University Press, 1997)

KC Brown, (ed.) *Hobbes Studies* (Leo Strauss et al.) (Oxford, Basil Blackwell, 1965)

S Buckle, *Natural Law and the Theory of Property: Grotius to Hume* (Oxford, Clarendon, 1991)

W Cobbett, *The Parliamentary or Constitutional History of England* Vol. XVII (London, Bagshaw, 1806–20)

E Coke, *Institutes of the Laws of England* 6 ed. (London, W Rawlins, 1794–1817)

M Cranston and R Deters, (eds.) *Hobbes and Rousseau: A Collection of Critical Essays* (New York, Anchor Books, 1972)

H Daly, *Steady State Economics* (Washington DC, Island Press, 1991)

C Darwin, *The Origin of Species by Means of Natural Selection* (London, J Murray, 1884)

JW Dawson, *Story of Earth and Man* (New York, Harper & Bros, 1873)

VTH & DR Delaney, *The Canals of the South of Ireland* (Newton Abbot, David & Charles, 1966)

P DIXON, *Futurewise: Six Faces of Global Change* (London, HarperCollins, 1999)

A DOBSON, *Justice and the Environment: Conceptions of Environmental Sustainability and Theories of Distributive Justice* (Oxford, Oxford University Press, 1998)

R DWORKIN, *Taking Rights Seriously* (London, Duckworth, 1977)

A ESCOBAR, *Encountering Development: The Making and Unmaking of the Third World* (Princeton, Princeton University Press, 1995)

DA FARBER, *Eco-Pragmatism: Making Sensible Environmental Decisions in an Uncertain World* (Chicago, University of Chicago Press, 1999)

R FILMER, '*Patriarcha*' in P Laslett, *The Political Works of Sir Robert Filmer* (Oxford, Basil Blackwell, 1949)

O GIERKE, *Natural Law and the Theory of Society 1500–1800* (Cambridge, Cambridge University Press, 1950)

K GRAY & SF GRAY, *Elements of Land Law 3 ed.* (London, Butterworth, 2001).

H GROTIUS, *De Iure Praedae Commentarius,* GL Williams trans. (Oxford, Oxford University Press, 1950)

——, *De Iure Belli ac Pacis* Accompanied by an abridged translation by William Whewell with the notes of the author, Barbeyrac and others (Cambridge, Cambridge University Press, 1853)

——, *Introduction to the Jurisprudence of Holland*, translated with brief notes and a commentary by RW Lee, DCL Vol. I, Text translation and notes. (Oxford, Clarendon Press, 1926)

——, *Mare Liberum* (1609), trans. as *The Freedom of the Seas* (York, Batoche Books, 1916)

M GRUBB et al, *The Earth Summit Agreements A Guide and Assessment* (London, Earthscan 1993)

M GRUBB, C VROLIJK & D BRACK, *The Kyoto Protocol: A Guide and Assessment* (London, Earthscan/Royal Institute of International Affairs Energy and Environment Programme, 1999)

M HALE, *The Primitive Organisation of Mankind Considered and Examined According to the Light of Nature* (London, William Godbid for William Shrowsbery,1677)

——, *A History of the Common Law (5 ed)* (London, W Clarke & Son, 1794)

D HUME, *A Treatise of Human Nature*, ed. Selby-Bigge, (Oxford, Oxford University Press, 1888)

——, *Enquiry Concerning the Principles of Morals*, ed. Tom L. Beauchamp (Oxford, Oxford University Press, 1998)

T HOBBES, *Leviathan*, ed. CB MacPherson (Harmondsworth, Penguin, 1968)

——, *Dialogue Between a Philosopher and a Student of the Common Laws of England* (London, W Crooke, 1681)

I KANT, *Kant's Political Writings*, ed. H Reiss (Cambridge, Cambridge University Press, 1985)

JP KAY-SHUTTLEWORTH, *The Moral and Physical Conditions of the Working Classes Employed in the Cotton Manufacture in Manchester* (Manchester, Morten,1969)

A KING & B SCHNEIDER, *The First Global Revolution* (Simon & Schuster, London, 1991)

N KLEIN, *No Logo* (London, Flamingo, 2000)

——, *Fences and Windows: Dispatches from the Front Lines of the Globalisation Debate* (London, Flamingo, 2002)

RW KOSTAL, *Law and English Railway Capitalism, 1825–1875* (Oxford, Oxford University Press, 1994)

MH Kramer, *John Locke and the Origins of Private Property* (Cambridge, Cambridge University Press, 1997)

——, *Hobbes and the Paradoxes of Political Origins* (London, Macmillan 1997)

A Leopold, *A Sand County Almanac and Sketches Here and There* (Oxford, Oxford University Press, 1968)

D Lieberman, *The Province of Legislation Determined* (Cambridge, Cambridge University Press, 1989)

M Lobban, *The Common Law and English Jurisprudence* (Oxford, Oxford University Press, 1991)

J Locke, *Two Treatises of Government*, ed. P. Laslett (Cambridge, Cambridge University Press, 1988)

——, *Essays on the Laws of Nature*, ed. W Von Leyden (Oxford, Clarendon Press, 1954)

——, *Essay on Human Understanding*, ed. PH Nidditch (Oxford, Clarendon, 1975)

J McLoughlin, *The Law and Practice Relating to Pollution Control in the United Kingdom* (London, Graham & Trotman for the Commission of the European Communities, 1976)

CB MacPherson, *The Political Theory of Possessive Individualism: Hobbes to Locke* (Oxford, Clarendon Press, 1962)

DH Meadows, DL Meadows, JJ Randers, WW Behrens III, *The Limits to Growth* (New York, Universe Books, 1972)

DA Meadows, DL Meadows & J Randers, *Beyond the Limits: Global Collapse or a Sustainable Future* (London, Earthscan, 1992)

R Megarry & HWR Wade, *The Law of Real Property* (6 ed.) (London, Sweet & Maxwell, 2000)

V Moore, *A Practical Approach to Planning Law* 3rd ed (London, Blackstone, 1992)

SR Munzer, *A Theory of Property* (Cambridge, Cambridge University Press, 1990)

A Parel and T Flannagan, (eds.) *Theories of Property: Aristotle to the Present* (Calgary, Wilfrid Lavrier, 1979)

JGA Pocock, *Virtue, Commerce and History* (Cambridge, Cambridge University Press, 1985)

——, *The Ancient Constitution and the Feudal Law* (Cambridge, Cambridge University Press, 1957)

G Postema, *Bentham and the Common Law Tradition* (Oxford, Clarendon Press, 1986)

S Pufendorf, *The Law of Nature and of Nations* [1672] ed. Jean Barbeyrac, trans. B Kennet (London, J & J Bonwicke, 1749)

——, *On the Duty of Man and Citizen According to Natural Law*, ed. Michael Silverthorne (Cambridge, Cambridge University Press, 1991)

——, *Elementorum Jurisprudentiae Universalis*, trans. WA Oldfather (Oxford, The Clarendon Press/London, H Milford, 1931)

L Pyenson and S Sheets-Pyenson, *Servants of Nature: A History of Scientific Institutions, Enterprises and Sensibilities* (London, HarperCollins, 1999)

C Redgwell, *Intergenerational Trusts and Environmental Protection* (Manchester, Manchester University Press, 1999)

C Reid, *Nature Conservation Law* (Edinburgh, Green/Sweet & Maxwell, 1994)

AD Rosen, *Kant's Theory of Justice* (Ithaca, Cornell University Press, 1993)

J Rousseau, *The Social Contract and Other Later Political Writings*, V. Gourevitch ed. (Cambridge, Cambridge University Press, 1997)

B Russell, *The Principles of Mathematics* (London, Routledge, 1903)

A RYAN, *Property and Political Theory* (Oxford, Basil Blackwell, 1984)

R SCHLATTER, *Private Property: The History of an Idea* (London, Unwin, 1951)

NE SIMMONDS, *The Decline of Juridical Reason* (Manchester, Manchester University Press, 1984)

FB SMITH, The Nation's Health Check 1830–1910 (1979)

R SMITH, *Property Law* (4ed.) (London, Longman, 2003)

AWB SIMPSON, *Leading Cases in the Common Law* (Oxford, Oxford University Press, 1995)

M STALLWORTHY, *Sustainability, Land Use and Environment: A Legal Analysis* (London, Cavendish, 2002)

H STEINER, *An Essay on Rights* (Oxford, Blackwell, 1994)

C STONE, *Earth and Other Ethics: The Case for Moral Pluralism* (New York, Harper & Row, 1987)

K THOMAS, *Man and the Natural World: Changing Attitudes in England 1500–1800* (London, Allen Lane, 1983)

GM TREVELYAN, *English Social History*, 3 ed (London, Longmans, 1946)

R TUCK, *Natural Rights Theories: Their Origin and Development* (Cambridge, Cambridge University Press, 1979)

J TULLY, *A Discourse on Property: John Locke and his Adversaries* (Cambridge, Cambridge University Press, 1980)

J WALDRON, *The Right to Private Property* (Oxford, Clarendon, 1988)

C WALTON and P JOHNSON, (eds.) *Hobbes's Science of Natural Justice* (Dordrecht, M Nijhoff, 1987)

World Commission on Environment and Development, Our Common Future (Oxford, Oxford University Press, 1987)

Essays

A AMAN, 'The Montreal Protocol on Substances that Deplete the Ozone Layer' in F Francioni & T Scovassi (eds.), *International Responsibility for Environmental Harm* (London, Graham & Trotman, 1991)

R BEAZLEY, 'Conservation Decision-making: A Rationalization' in C Kury (ed) *Enclosing the Environment; NEPA's Transformation of Conservation into Environmentalism, Natural Resources Journal 25th Anniversary Anthology* (Albuquerque, University of New Mexico School of Law, 1985)

T BIGG & F DODDS, 'The UN Commission on Sustainable Development' in F Dodds (ed), *The Way Forward: Beyond Agenda 21* (London, Earthscan, 1997)

P BIRKS, 'Five Keys to Land Law' in S Bright & J Dewar (eds.) *Land Law: Themes and Perspectives* (Oxford, Oxford University Press, 1998)

R CHURCHILL, 'Controlling Emissions of Greenhouse Gases' in R Churchill & D Freestone (eds.), *International Law and Global Climate Change* (London, Graham & Trotman, 1991)

R COCKS, 'Victorian Foundations?' in J Lowry & R Edmunds eds. *Environmental Protection and the Common Law* (Oxford, Hart, 2000)

H DALY, 'Towards a Stationary-State Economy' in J Harte & R Socolow, *Patient Earth* (New York, Holt, Rinehart & Winston, 1971)

K GRAY & SF GRAY, 'The Idea of Property in Land' in S Bright & J Dewar eds. *Land Law: Themes and Perspectives* (Oxford, Oxford University Press, 1998)

K GRAY, 'The Ambivalence of Property' in G. Prins, ed. *Threats Without Enemies: Facing Environmental Insecurity* (London, Earthscan, 1993)

K HAAKONSSEN, 'Natural Law and the Scottish Enlightenment' in DH Jory and CS Robinson, *Man and Nature* (Edmonton, Academic Printing and Publishing, 1985)

JW HARRIS, 'Ownership of Land in English Law' in N MacCormick and P Birks eds. *The Legal Mind: Essays for Tony Honore* (Oxford, Clarendon Press, 1986)

P HARRISON, 'Reading the Passions: the Fall, the Passions and Dominion over Nature' in S Gaukroger ed. *The Soft Underbelly of Reason: the Passions in the Seventeenth Century* (London, Routledge 1998)

G KAVKA & V WARREN, 'Political Representation for Future Generations' in R Elliot & A Gare eds. *Environmental Philosophy: A Collection of Readings* (Milton Keynes, Open University Press, 1983)

MH KRAMER, 'In Praise of the Critique of the Public/Private Distinction' in MH Kramer, *In the Realm of Legal and Moral Philosophy* (London, Macmillan, 1999)

T MAUTNER, 'Pufendorf and the Correlativity Theory of Rights' in S Lindstrom & W Rabinowicz eds. *In So Many Words: Essays for Sven Danielson* (Dept of Philosophy, Uppsala, 1989)

K MORROW, 'Nuisance and Environmental Protection' in J Lowry and R Edmunds eds. *Environmental Protection and the Common Law* (Oxford, Hart 2000)

R MULLENDER, 'Prima Facie Rights, Rationality and the Law of Negligence' in MH Kramer ed. *Rights, Wrongs and Responsibilities* (London, Palgrave, 2001)

A OGUS, 'The Regulation of Pollution' in G Richardson with A Ogus and P Burrows, *Policing Pollution: A Study of Regulation and Enforcement* (Oxford, Clarendon Press, 1982)

JE PENNER, 'Nuisance, Neighbourliness, and Environmental Protection' in J Lowry & R Edmunds eds. *Environmental Protection and the Common Law* (Oxford, Hart, 2000)

R SCHOCK, 'Lawyers and Rhetoric in Sixteenth Century England' in J Murphy ed. *Renaissance Eloquence: Studies in the Theory and Practice of Renaissance Rhetoric* (Berkeley, University of California Press, 1983)

J SIMMONS, 'Original Acquisition Justifications of Private Property' in EF Paul, FD Miller & J Paul (eds.), *Property Rights* (Cambridge, Cambridge University Press, 1994).

NE SIMMONDS, 'Rights at the Cutting Edge' in MH Kramer, NE Simmonds & H Steiner, *A Debate Over Rights* (Oxford, Oxford University Press?, 1998).

M WARREN, 'The Rights of the Nonhuman World' in R Elliot & A Gare eds. *Environmental Philosophy: A Collection of Readings* (Milton Keynes, Open University Press, 1983)

FG WHELAN, 'Property as Artifice: Hume and Blackstone' in *Nomos XX: Property* ed. JR Pennock & J Chapman, (New York, New York University Press, 1980)

Articles

AGORA, 'What Obligation Does Our Generation Owe to the Next? An Approach to Global Environmental Resonsibility' 84 *Am. J. Int'l L.* 190

T BALDWIN, 'Tully, Locke and Land' 13 *Locke Newsletter* 21–33

J BRENNER, 'Nuisance Law and the Industrial Revolution' 3 *Journal of Legal Studies* 403.

E BROWN WEISS, 'The Planetary Trust: Conservation and Intergenerational Equity' 11 *Ecology L. Q.* 495

J CAIRNS, 'Blackstone, the Ancient Constitution and the Feudal Law', 28 *Historical Journal* 711.

P CANE, 'What a Nuisance' 113 *LQR* 515.

R COCKS, 'Enforced Creativity: Noel Hutton and the New Law for Development Control, 1945–47' *Legal History* Vol. 22, 2001 21.

R COSGROVE, 'The Reception of Analytic Jurisprudence: the Victorian Debate on the Separation of Law and Morality 1860–1900', 74 *Durham U J* 47.

J CRIMMINS, 'Bentham's Political Radicalism Re-examined' *Journal of the History of Ideas* 259–81

JP DAY, 'Locke on Property' 16 *Philosophical Quarterly* 207–21

SB DRURY, 'Locke and Nozic on Property' 30 *Political Studies* 28–41

A D'AMATO, 'Do We Owe a Duty to Future Generations to Preserve the Global Environment?' 84 *Am. J. Int'l L.* 190–193

N DUXBURY, 'When We Were Young: Notes in the *Law Quarterly Review* 1885–1925', 116 *LQR* 474.

RA EPSTEIN, 'Justice across the Generations', 67 *Tex L.Rev.* 1465

DA FARBER & PP FRICKEY, 'In the Shadow of the Legislature: The Common Law in the Age of the New Public Law' *Michigan Law Review Symposium: The New Public Law* [1991] 875 at 888 *et seq.*

D FRENCH, '1997 Kyoto Protocol to the 1992 Framework Convention on Climate Change' 10 *BJEL* 2

J GALBRAITH, 'Economics and the Quality of Life' 45 *Science* 117.

C GEARTY, 'The Place of Private Nuisance in the Modern Law of Torts' 48 *CLJ* 214.

K HAAKONSSEN, 'Hugo Grotius and the History of Political Thought' 13 *Political Theory* 239–65

T JEWELL & J STEELE, 'UK regulatory reform and the pursuit of "sustainable development": the Environment Act 1995' 8 *JEL* 283.

D LIEBERMAN, 'From Bentham to Benthamism' *Historical Journal* 199–224

T MAUTNER, 'Natural Rights in Locke' 12 *Philosophical Topics* 73–77

—— 'Locke on Original Appropriation' 19 *American Philosophical Quarterly* 259–70

JPS MCLAREN, 'Nuisance Law and the Industrial Revolution—Some Lessons from Social History', 3 *OJLS* 155

SFC MILSOM, 'The Nature of Blackstone's Achievement', 1 *OJLS* 1.

J MOORE, 'Hume's Theory of Justice and Property' 24 *Political Studies* 107–19

K MORROW & S TURNER 'The More Things Change, The More They Stay The Same?— Environmental Law, Policy and Funding in Northern Ireland', 10 *JEL* 41.

A OGUS & G RICHARDSON, 'Economics and the Environment: A Study of Private Nuisance' 36 *CLJ* 284.

K OLIVECRONA, 'Appropriation in the State of Nature' 35 *Journal of the History of Ideas* 221–30

AWB SIMPSON, 'The Rise and Fall of the Legal Treatise: Legal Principles and the Forms of Legal Literature', XLVII *University of Chicago LR* 632.

C STONE, 'Beyond Rio: Insuring Against Global Warming' *AJIL.* 455

S TROMANS, 'Nuisance—Prevention or Payment?' 41 *CLJ* 87.

J WALDRON, 'Enough and as Good Left for Others' 29 *Philosophical Quarterly* 319–28

Index